PETER CUFFLEY

Australian Houses
of the
Forties & Fifties

The Five Mile Press

For my mother,
Catherine Cuffley.

The Five Mile Press Pty Ltd
67 Rushdale Street
Knoxfield Victoria 3180 Australia

First published 1993
Text copyright © Peter Cuffley
Design: Geoff Hocking
Editor: Maggie Pinkney
Production: Emma Borghesi

All rights reserved. No part of this publication may be
reproduced, stored in a retrieval system, or transmitted in
any form or by any means, electronic, mechanical,
photocopying, recording or otherwise without the prior
written permission of the Publishers.

Typeset by DigiType, Bendigo, Victoria
Printed and bound in Singapore

National Library of Australia Cataloguing-in-Publications
data

Cuffley, Peter.
Australian houses of the forties and fifties.

Bibliography.
Includes index.
ISBN 0 86788 578 5

1. Architecture, Domestic — Australia — History —
20th century. 2. Dwellings — Australia — History —
20th century. 3. Interior decoration — Australia —
History — 20th century. I. Title.

728.0994

Contents

ACKNOWLEDGEMENTS	●	*Page 7*
INTRODUCTION	●	*Page 9*
CHAPTER ONE	●	AUSTRALIA IN THE '40S AND '50S *Page 14*
CHAPTER TWO	●	IDEAS AND OPPORTUNITIES *Page 32*
CHAPTER THREE	●	FROM WARTIME TO PEACETIME *Page 55*
CHAPTER FOUR	●	THE POST-WAR HOUSING BOOM *Page 73*
CHAPTER FIVE	●	ARCHITECTS AND THEIR WORK *Page 91*
CHAPTER SIX	●	DEFINING THE STYLES *Page 112*
CHAPTER SEVEN	●	ENVIRONMENTAL INFLUENCES *Page 127*
CHAPTER EIGHT	●	GARDENS FOR EVERYONE *Page 138*
CHAPTER NINE	●	INTERIOR DESIGN *Page 152*
CHAPTER TEN	●	FURNITURE, FURNISHINGS AND FITTINGS *Page 174*
CHAPTER ELEVEN	●	RENOVATIONS AND COLOUR SCHEMES *Page 187*
CHAPTER TWELVE	●	COLLECTING THE MEMORIES *Page 193*
BIBLIOGRAPHY	●	*Page 195*
INDEX	●	*Page 197*

• Banyan, formerly Bon Haven, Eaglehawk Road, Bendigo, Victoria, built for well-known Bendigo butcher Clark Jeffery in 1953. Its 'ship style' carries over the fashionable Art Moderne of the interwar years.

PHOTOGRAPH: THE AUTHOR

Acknowledgements

In the creation of this book, thanks are due to many people who have helped in a variety of ways. My wife Barbara provided practical expertise through her skill with the word processor — she also offered unfailing support. Important memories and encouragement were once again offered by my mother Catherine Cuffley and by longtime friend Vivienne 'Babs' Mair.

My friend Fran Townsing of Perth was vitally involved, searching out information and photographs as well as providing clear recollections. Peta Townsing took a series of important photographs. Architects John and Phyllis Murphy were essential to the project, lending material from their collection, sharing professional insights and suggesting valuable leads. Queensland architects Peter Newell and John Dalton gave generous support as did Victorians Dione McIntyre, Professor Peter McIntyre, John Mockridge, L. Hume Sherrard, Ted Ashton, Keith Streames, Douglas Alexandra and the late Professor Frederick Romberg. Geoffrey Summerhayes, Raymond Jones and W.M. 'Bill' Barton, all of Perth, contributed, as did Gavin Walkley of Adelaide. Peter Muller, Harry Seidler and Dr Miles Lewis were also helpful.

Charles Pickett of the Powerhouse Museum exchanged insights into housing of the 1950s and Tracy Watt lent magazines. *Australian Home Beautiful*, through its editor-in-chief Tony Fawcett, once again offered enthusiastic support. Dennis Russell patiently copied illustrations and photographs, while Geoff Hocking brought to the design his usual dedication and flair. Editor Maggie Pinkney provided both her expertise and a personal interest in the era.

Thanks are also due to Barbara Barnes, Peter Glass, Ernest Rodeck, Judy Jensen, Philip Ward-Dickson, Tony Pisano, Margaret Mellor, Jacqueline Urford, John and Mandy Gullen, Guy Vowles, Tony and Sue Toleman, Mary Patrick, Joan Dorney, Beryl Johns, Fiona Whittle, Ken Charlton, Don Garden, Mr and Mrs R.C. Dixon, Mrs N.J. Stewart, Mr and Mrs. L.R. Taylor and Pat Lakey and Sue Mooney, of the Castlemaine Library.

I'd also like to thank the following companies and institutions: Dulux Australia; Laminex Industries; Clark Rubber Ltd; Feltex Carpets Ltd; Tennyson Textiles; South Australian Housing Trust; State Offices Library, Hobart; Northern Territory Department of Lands and Housing; ICI Australia; Email Limited; John Oxley Library, Brisbane; State Library of Tasmania; Historic Houses Trust of New South Wales; State Library of Victoria; Archives Office of Tasmania; Fryer Library, University of Queensland; Australian Heritage Commission; State Housing Commission of Western Australia; Mitchell Library, State Library of New South Wales; Judith O'Callaghan and the Powerhouse Museum; The Royal Australian Institute of Architects; Warburton Franki; Crown Glassware Ltd and the Herald and Weekly Times Ltd.

— Photographs —

Special thanks are due to Wolfgang Sievers, Mark Strizic, Fritz Kos and Eric Sierins of Max Dupain and Associates Pty Ltd. Also to *Australian Home Beautiful*, State Offices Library, Hobart, Peta Townsing, Bruce Anderson, Ivie Hocking, May Vernon, Adrienne Dansie, Jennings Industries Ltd, Commonwealth Bank Archives, Victoria, South Australian Housing Trust, Keith Streames, John Dalton, Rolf and Lorraine Zegelin, Gavin Walkley, Archives Office of Tasmania, State Library of Tasmania, Beryl Johns, Geoffrey Summerhayes, Robert Hadden, *The West Australian*, The Launceston *Examiner*, and National Library of Australia. Finally, Johanna Murray of Canberra and Christine Finnimore of South Australia both helped as professional researchers.

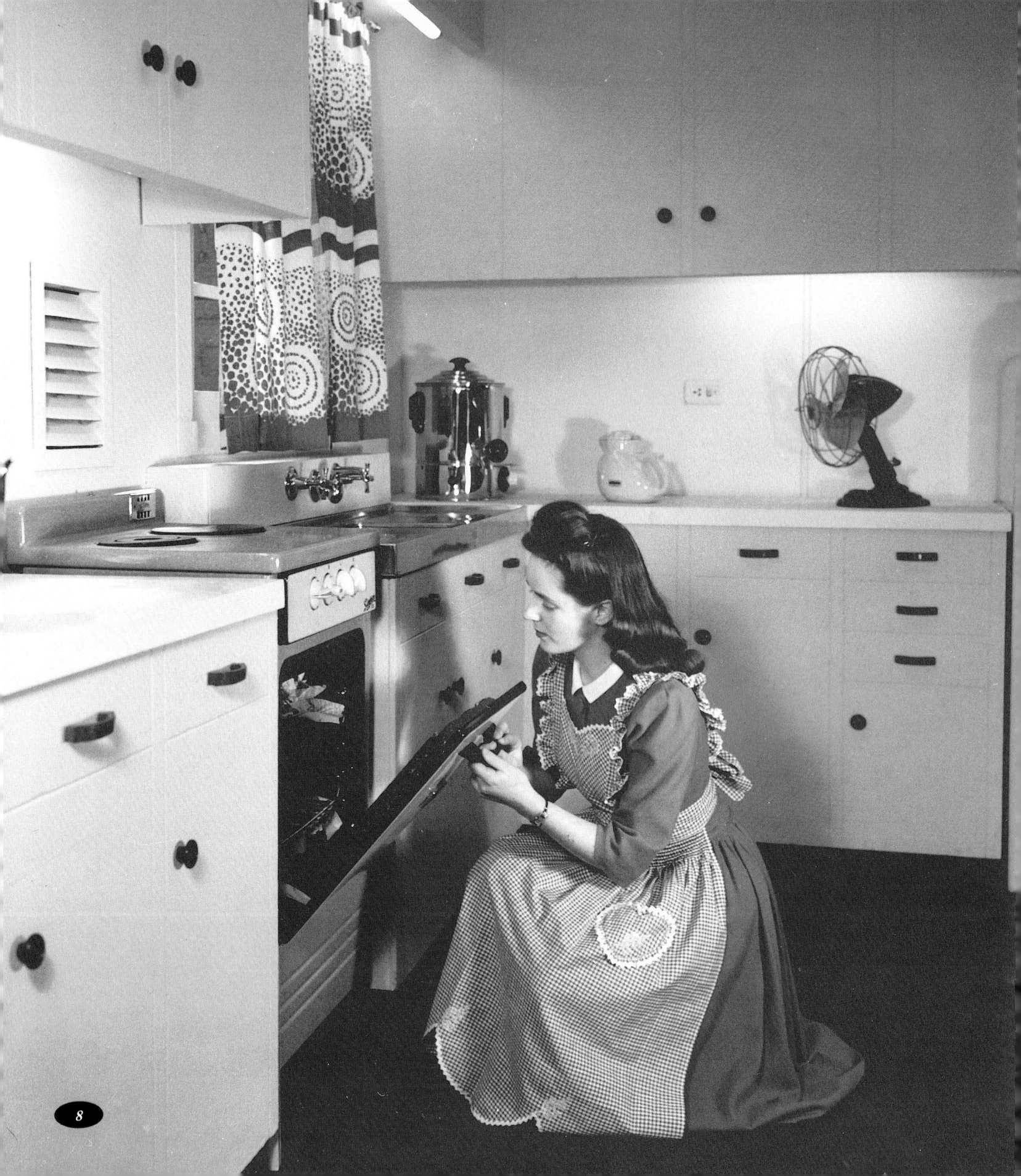

Introduction

AUSTERITY AND PROSPERITY are words which sum up the two fundamental influences on the Australian house in the period between 1940 and 1960. Wartime conditions brought construction to a virtual standstill, and when the war was over continuing restrictions and shortages of materials were a clear recipe for austerity. When conditions relaxed and the economy gathered momentum a new era of prosperity began. Many readers will recall those two decades, others will have gathered a mixed bag of impressions based on the facts and fictions of the spoken word, printed works, or film, television and the stage. History is constantly being presented in every form, from documented 'reality' to pure mythology.

When we see the '40s and '50s recreated as part of popular culture, there is a tendency to gloss over the less desirable aspects and even to alter the images to fit current expectations. For example, some productions depict Australian teenagers of the '50s as looking just like their American counterparts when in fact they were subtly different. Cars and juke boxes might have been important symbols, but they were usually less glamorous or up-to-the-minute than those we see in Hollywood films or television shows.

During the Second World War, music and civilian fashions reflected a growing American influence. However, we also continued to be different, an important fact not lost on Australians in the services.

During recent decades, young Australians have taken to collecting 1940s and '50s memorabilia, much to the surprise of older generations who are puzzled or amused to see respectable price-tags on all sorts of familiar artefacts — from plastic and chrome light-fittings to sets of multicoloured ceramic ramekins. Music from the '40s and '50s has long been a subject of great interest, with numerous revivals and an ever-growing catalogue of collectors' albums finding ready markets. Clothing fashions have also made cyclical journeys back to the '40s and '50s. The ubiquitous 'blue jeans', as a teenage fashion, came to stay, simply adapting to passing fads.

Interior designers and architects looking to make bold statements have revitalised the popular abstractions of the post-war era. Vibrant colours, startling geometry, metal and plastic are once more in vogue. In the field of mass consumerism, graphic artists have created an

• *Opposite page:* The idealised role of housewife and mother was given new emphasis in the post-war years.

COLLECTION: NATIONAL LIBRARY OF AUSTRALIA, CANBERRA

• AUSTRALIAN HOUSES OF THE FORTIES & FIFTIES

• Waterfall-style house of 1954, Wesley Hill, Victoria.
PHOTOGRAPH: THE AUTHOR

INTRODUCTION

• Grant Featherston's R152 Contour chair of 1951.
Australian Home Beautiful, May 1956

• *Below:* Sketch of the River House, Dione McIntyre, Melbourne 1955.
COURTESY: PETER AND DIONE MCINTYRE

explosion of dots, triangles and squiggles in a cacophany of 'pop' colours. All this could be perceived as nostalgia for an age of innocent exuberance. Indeed, this may be part of the story, but there is also the natural process of reappraising past eras, searching for inspiration, tracing social patterns and making sense of our origins.

Architectural historians, along with preservation organisations and educational institutions, have important roles to play in raising public awareness of the need to identify the significant architecture of a given period. Robin Boyd may have reviled many aspects of ordinary suburban housing in the '40s and '50s, but his great contribution was in opening our eyes to it all. In the preface to his 1952 book, *Australia's Home*, he begins, 'This book, a study of the vernacular in domestic building in Australia, is concerned for the most part with the small houses which have taken up some two thirds of the building capacity of the nation'. Since that time there has been an ever-increasing interest in our domestic architecture, with many publications to satisfy a wide range of demands.

Professor J. M. Freeland's comprehensive *Architecture in Australia: A History*, first published in 1968, includes houses of the '40s and '50s, placing them in a broad perspective. It soon became an essential handbook for anyone interested in the development of our architecture up to that time. Younger readers were offered a clear and concise insight into the same subject by Robin Boyd's, *The Walls Around Us* (1962). Another important work of a similar character which used photographs as well as drawings was *Homes in Australia* by Unstead and Henderson (1969).

Two important works published in the 1980s have become essential references. *The History and Design of the Australian House* (1985) is a sumptuous compilation dealing with every aspect of our domestic architecture. It was followed in 1989 by *A Pictorial Guide to Identifying Australian Architecture* (Apperly, Irving and Reynolds), dedicated by its authors to the memory of Emeritus Professor J. M. Freeland.

Articles in magazines are usually a reflection of popular trends, and in some cases they are early indicators of things to come. Fiona Whittle captures the 1950s

INTRODUCTION

• *Opposite page*: Seen from below, this 1959 house at Northbridge, NSW, by Harry Seidler presents a striking contrast between sparse geometry and the natural setting.

PHOTOGRAPH: MAX DUPAIN
COURTESY: MAX DUPAIN AND ASSOCIATES PTY LTD

era and its influences in two articles published in the *Period Home Renovator* in 1990.[1] An important observation made is that one clear reason for the popularity of '50s decor and memorabilia is linked to the punk movement, with its penchant for vibrant colours and striking abstract shapes. Affordability has been an additional impetus, although prices have risen, with 'op shop' bargains harder to find.

This book is written for those who seek an introduction to the subject of Australian houses built between 1940 and 1960. It provides a broad overview, as it would take many volumes to define and analyse such an extensive subject.

Houses designed by architects make up only a small proportion of all those built in the period in question, and so to tell the whole story a wide selection of owner- or builder-designed houses is included, along with the kinds of furniture, furnishings, appliances and bric-a-brac likely to be found in them. In my book, *Australian Houses of the '20s & '30s*, I sought to provide a reference for those who are refurbishing or restoring a house of that era. Houses of the following two decades are now gaining wider acceptance as being worthy of particular attention. If many were austere and some badly built, many others continued the old tradition of pride in a comfortable and well-built dwelling.

To contrast the ponderous solidity of a featuristic, triple-fronted suburban brick house with the bold, imaginative designs of the young architects of the period is to sense the challenge we have in evaluating our built heritage. The National Trust of Australia continues to raise public awareness of the need to retain important examples of domestic architecture from each era. Harry Seidler's historic 1948 design, now called the Rose Seidler house, at Wahroonga, New South Wales, has been restored and is open to the public.

Houses of the '40s and '50s are worthy of our attention because they represent — across the whole spectrum — a fascinating diversity, from the mundane to the extraordinary. Although austerity, both bland and imaginative, was the dominant theme, environmental building was finding a new beginning, Edna Walling's cottages captured many hearts and the creations of the avant-garde shocked conservative souls while assuring many others that this was the beginning of an exciting new age.

Introduction Endnotes

[1] Fiona Whittle, 'The Fabulous '50s — a '50s Fanatic,' *Period Home Renovator*, vol. 5, No. 1, 1990, pp. 32-40.

CHAPTER ONE
Australia in the '40s and '50s

FOR MOST AUSTRALIANS the 1940s began with an ever-darkening cloud of ominous uncertainty. In the mid-1930s there had been a gradual easing of the Great Depression, but nobody watching the world could fail to be disturbed by events in Europe and Africa. Italy had invaded Abyssinia in 1935. Germany marched into Austria early in 1938 and, with the invasion of Poland in August 1939, Britain and France were left with no alternative but to declare a state of war. Australians heard the news on the Sunday evening of 3 September 1939.

Loyalty to Britain and the Empire ensured an immediate declaration by Prime Minister Robert Menzies that 'in consequence of a persistence by Germany in her invasion of Poland, Great Britain has declared war upon her, and, as a result, Australia is at war'.

After the initial feeling of shock and the fear of immediate catastrophe a strange lull developed. For most Australians it was 'business as usual', although recruitment for a Second Australian Imperial Force was soon under way. For the following ten months the lack of dramatic action caused the conflict to be called a 'phoney war'. The latter half of 1940 saw the end of any complacency. Mussolini had joined with Hitler, Paris had fallen and the British forces had made a miraculous retreat from Dunkirk.

For Australians serving in Northern Africa and the Mediterranean there were heroic battles, celebrated victories and tragic losses. In April and May 1941, 6000 Australians were killed, wounded or captured on Crete or in Greece. This calamity and other losses began to touch the whole community as families and friends received the grim news.

Germany invaded Russia in June 1941, and the Japanese, not yet officially at war, were moving into Indo-China. Their attack on the American Naval Base at Pearl Harbor in December 1941 brought the United States into the war. Japan swiftly moved through South-East Asia and in February 1942 began its bombing raids on Darwin. Australia's new Prime Minister John Curtin had already declared that we depended on America rather than Britain for our survival. Japanese raids on Darwin, Broome, Wyndham and Townsville early in 1942 brought the prospect of invasion one step closer. While government censorship restricted news of this gathering threat, the civilian population was nevertheless preparing for the worst. By March 1942 General Douglas MacArthur had arrived with an initial American force of about 30 000 troops.[1] Australian troops were arriving home from the Middle East and were

• Family group, Bendigo, Victoria, 1941.
COURTESY: IVIE HOCKING

• *Opposite page:* All the comforts of home. Mrs Varadi proudly sits by the book and record cabinet she has made from two fruit cases and other odds and ends.
Australian Home Beautiful, September 1953

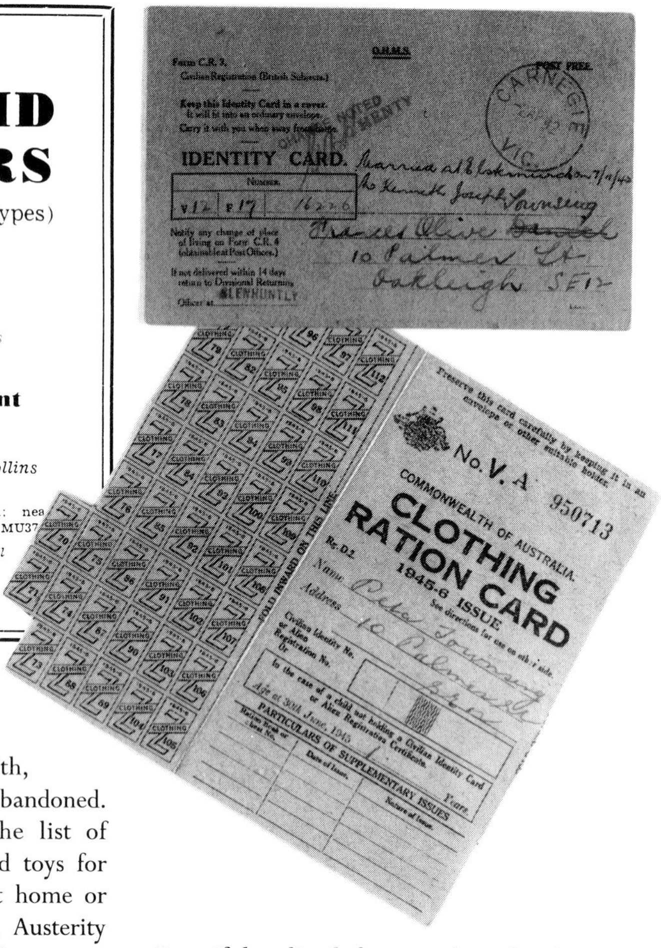

• Identity and ration cards were a part of life from the early 1940s.

COURTESY: FRAN TOWNSING

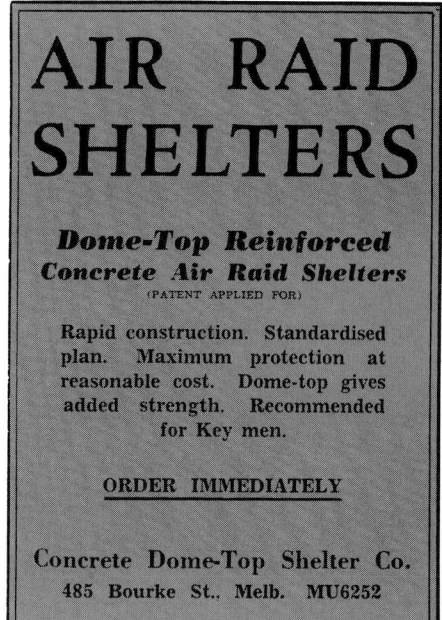

joined by freshly trained enlisted men. An additional 90 000 American soldiers also arrived; the struggle to turn the tide had begun.

Restrictions affecting the civilian population included rationing of food, clothing, footwear, liquor and the various liquid fuels. Petrol rationing had been introduced as early as October 1940, with an allowance limiting private travel to about 16 miles (26 km) per week.[2] Many people fitted charcoal-burning gas producers to their cars, keeping their mobility and, in the long term, saving money as well. Rationing of footwear and clothing began in June 1942, while tea was limited from July of that year to eight ounces (250 grams) per person every five weeks.[3] In August 1942 sugar rationing began, and there was a drastic reduction in the range of confectionery on the market. All kinds of substitutes for tea, coffee and tobacco were experimented with, some acceptable, others soon abandoned. Even bath-heaters were on the list of non-essential manufactures, and toys for Christmas were either made at home or old ones were given new life. Austerity clothes and austerity meals became a challenge for traditional Australian ingenuity. In spite of the shortening of hotel hours and limits on the production of beer and other alcoholic beverages, people somehow managed to maintain their drinking habits. Black markets in liquor and other sought-after products ensured a steady supply for those who were willing to pay inflated prices.

Restrictions on building were detailed in government pamphlets distributed in September 1941. The *Australian Home Beautiful* outlined them in their October issue of that year under the heading, 'A Summary of Wartime Restrictions'. Houses not exceeding a total cost of £3000 ($6000) could gain a permit. Others already begun were also subject to controls (see Chapter 3).

Air-raids were seen as a grim possibility from early in the war and by mid-1941 Australian cities had begun to practise 'blacking out'. In its September 1941 issue, *Home Beautiful* reports: 'Sydney has had a more or less successful rehearsal and

• Captain and pilot, Flight Sergeant John Ryan (centre, back row) with his crew, RAF Squadron 576, Fiskerton, 1945.

COLLECTION: THE AUTHOR

Melbourne is due to render itself invisible on September 23'. The article then discusses various methods of covering windows. Blackout curtains, blinds and panels of plywood or wallboard are all suggested as suitable. 'One thing to remember — take the globes out of entrance hall and front door lights so that no light will show when the front door is opened, if only for a moment.' Air-raid wardens patrolling the back lanes were often heard calling out, 'Pull those blinds down'.[4]

Air-raid shelters became an important issue in newspapers and magazines. Under the heading, 'Family Air-raid Shelters', the *Home Beautiful* of January 1942 published suggestions from Victoria's State Emergency Council. 'Recent dramatic developments in the national situation have revived public interest in the question of air-raid shelters which, at the present moment, is a topic of absorbing interest to most Australian householders.' Such shelters varied from simple open trenches to comfortable underground quarters. Most were partly submerged or fully underground shelters with roofs of corrugated iron over which the excavated earth was banked. The entrance ramp was dug at right angles to the main trench or excavation. *Home Beautiful* included in its article an illustration from the English magazine, *The Studio* of comparatively luxurious 'underground sleeping quarters'.

Support for the war effort resulted in many household gardens and even public parks being given over to growing food. In the June 1943 *Home Beautiful* we read:

Gardening is still a vital interest with householders. It is therefore very pleasing to note that, whilst there is no slackening of enthusiasm about the growing of vegetables, the flower garden, which had fallen into second place owing to the crying need of vegetable growing, is coming into its own again.

With the war turning against the Japanese and victories such as the Battle of the Coral Sea giving a boost to morale there was some easing of the fear of invasion.

Wartime food production on a national scale was given great impetus by the formation in July 1942 of the Australian Women's Land Army.[5] More than 3000 volunteers made an important contribution to the war effort, undertaking a range of tasks in the production of fruit, vegetables and cotton, as well as in dairying, poultry farming and sheep farming. Women were also playing a much greater role in industry, commerce, retailing and administration — in many cases in jobs previously seen as the province of men.

If life on the homefront for most people was to a greater or lesser degree different from that during peacetime, it is interesting to note that couples managed to get married with traditional weddings, even if every aspect of the event was affected by conditions and restrictions. Bridal costumes were somehow created, wedding breakfasts arranged, using every saved ration coupon, and, for those in the services, enough leave was found for a short honeymoon. However, even this precious time could often be suddenly curtailed by the demands of war. Wedding rings were the only jewellery allowed to

• Wartime wedding — Catherine Ryan marries William Cuffley, 23 January 1943.
COLLECTION: THE AUTHOR

be manufactured throughout the war, an indication that while it was a time of great austerity such symbols remained sacrosanct.

Hollywood films provided an escape from the war as well as stirring propaganda. Newsreels placed strong emphasis on the victories of the Allies and Australians appreciated seeing their own men and women battling against all sorts of odds in unfamiliar places far from the comforts of home. Dreams of how life might be when the war was over helped to keep many people going, both in war zones and at home. One of my uncles who was serving in the Islands carefully planned a garden with lots of stonework; others dreamed of houses they might build. Even at the front line, architects found themselves providing a free advisory service for their mates who would seek tips on their dream plans, created on scraps of paper or any other suitable surface. The favourite subject in home magazines was 'ideas for post-war homes'.

As building had virtually ceased by 1942, housing was in short supply and there was little chance for newlyweds or young families to find places of their own. It was suggested that the best foundation for a post-war home was to invest savings in War Bonds.[6]

My parents were married in January 1943 and lived with my paternal grandparents, who thankfully had a house large enough to accommodate them. Grandfather's photographic studio became a bedroom and living area for my aunt and two cousins, and by early 1944 there were five adults and three children living in the house. Letters arrived from loved ones in the services, and we sent off many letters and parcels to England or the Pacific Islands. One of my uncles was a prisoner of war in Central Europe, having been captured on Crete in 1941.

My mother's brother Johnny was flying Lancaster bombers with the Royal Air Force and managed to get a letter off to her about every two months. On Saturday 6 January 1945 he wrote a three-page airletter telling of Christmas with a family in a village near Birmingham, of trying to dry washing in the hut and recalling that, exactly a year before, they had arrived in New York after a journey across America. He and his wireless operator had decided to stay in for the weekend.

I'm glad in a way I'm not out, for with each hour that passes it seems to get colder; all the water is frozen solid, the ground is hard and crunchy and a searing, cutting wind tops it off. This weather is not for me and I'd give a month's pay for just one nice hot Sunday down at the one and only Quiet Corner.

Wistful visions of a favourite beach on Port Phillip Bay, and then:

As I sit here now, behind that sound of Glenn Miller's Moonlight Serenade is the deep-throated roar of countless bombers heading for Germany; their sound becomes so common these days it is like living beside a railway track and never hearing the trains till they stop. All night and all day you hear the throb of motors. Well, with that dramatic end I'll sign off hoping Bill, Pete and you are all tip-top. Johnny.

Some months later a parcel arrived with my first birthday present — a brightly-coloured ABC of aircraft, all drawn in caricature. The accompanying note promised all the 'gen' on the 'kites' at some future date. It wasn't to be, for Flight Sergeant John Ryan was lost in action just a few weeks later. The war in Europe was over by May 1945, while the fighting in the Pacific continued until August, when atomic bombs dropped on Hiroshima and Nagasaki brought about the formal surrender of the Japanese.

Total losses for Australia's armed forces during six years of war were 33 826.[7]

Almost five-and-a-half times that number were wounded or injured and more than 23 000 taken prisoner.

Rehabilitation became an immediate and ongoing task, with many important schemes introduced to offer those who had served, some opportunity to return to a normal civilian life. Many were able through commonwealth government retraining schemes to undertake tertiary studies, including architecture, building practice, engineering and town planning.

War Service housing loans enabled many thousands to realise their hopes of owning a new house. When added to a general demand for housing in the wider community there developed a new boom, but one beset with problems such as rising costs and severe shortages of building materials.

By 1946 my father, no longer on defence work at Fisherman's Bend, was back in the building industry. Suburbs were springing up in nearby areas and even golf courses were being subdivided. Grandfather, having spent his entire working life as a professional photographer, agreed to operate a small-scale cement-tile factory in the backyard of the family home. As a small child I was fascinated. The moulds were based on the traditional Marseilles pattern and, with terracotta tiles in short supply, builders were pleased to have as many as could be made. Not that cement-tiles were new — they had been popular throughout the 1920s and '30s, having been found to be free of the slight distortions of

• Christmas 1945 was a celebration of peace and new hopes. Even if people had to wait for years, that dream house was now a possibility.

Australian Home Beautiful, December 1945

• *Left*: Meeting the *Shropshire* at Station Pier, Port Melbourne, L—R: Stewart Goodwin, Patricia Johnson, Geoffrey Johnson.

COLLECTION: THE AUTHOR

terracotta tiles they also fitted better, thus allowing lower pitched roofs.[8]

When 'set' but not dry the tiles were turned out of the moulds and given a coating of powdered colour on one side, then put aside on racks to dry. Grandfather fussed over them as if he were baking cakes. At odd times he would dash out the back to see how the latest batch was going. Grandmother was not very impressed with having the curved gravel driveway churned up by trucks.

• *Below*: Construction of state housing, Ridley Grove, Woodville Gardens, South Australia, c.1945.

COURTESY: SOUTH AUSTRALIAN HOUSING TRUST

Change is often well advanced before it comes to the notice of ordinary people going about their daily lives. Few realised in those immediate post-war years that Australia was moving toward a new kind of society, one that in future decades would be multicultural to a degree never previously experienced. In the Old World, millions of people had been displaced by the war and were living in camps or amidst the ruins of their former homes. Others simply felt that new opportunities in a young country offered a brighter future when compared to the bleak conditions of war-scarred Europe. Agreements on migration signed by Australia and the United Kingdom in March 1946 came into operation exactly a year later. There were both free and assisted passages for British residents who wanted to settle in Australia, and by 1956 more than a quarter-of-a-million had arrived.[9] Included in this group were well over 4000 unaccompanied children and youths. The implications and experiences of this child migration scheme have since become a controversial issue, with many sad and bitter memories brought to light.

Australia's need for a larger population was widely accepted in a country having just escaped invasion. Arthur Calwell, the Minister for Immigration, summed up the situation in stating that, '. . . without immigration, the future of the Australia we know will be both uneasy and brief. As a nation we shall not survive'.[10] He was able to convince the unions that an influx of workers would be of great benefit in building national security, including a larger, healthier economy. When availability of migrants from northern Europe, including the British Isles, was not meeting the demand it became clear that southern Europe could be an important source. The agreement on Maltese migration was ratified in May 1948, beginning the flow of people from the Mediterranean region. March 1951 saw the agreement which began large-scale migration from Italy, and late in 1952 an arrangement was made enabling migration from Greece. Hungarian refugees from Russian military action arrived from the end of 1956. By December 1956, 1 671 704 assisted migrants had landed in Australia.[11]

The TRITON Prefabricated HOUSE
Type 832
(832 sq. ft.)

Unlined and Unfitted—delivered in pre-built sections ready for assembly.

Sectionised constructions delivered by road anywhere in Victoria. Terms. For full particulars, illustrations, specifications and prices, write:

TRITON CONSTRUCTIONS (AUST.) PTY. LTD.
Prefabrication Specialists
Registered Head Office: 35-39 Little Latrobe Street, Melbourne
THE WELL-KNOWN TRITON HUTS FOR COUNTRY USE ARE STILL AVAILABLE

• Typical sectionised construction is seen in this compact design of a mere 832 square feet.

COLLECTION: THE AUTHOR

Each wave of immigrants has faced numerous difficulties, many of a similar nature at any given period. In more than 200 years, the difficulty of finding housing or even basic shelter has remained a formidable obstacle in settling in Australia. The majority of post-war immigrants began as had so many before them, at the lower end of the scale, and patiently battled their way up. To own a house was the ideal shared by both 'new' Australians and 'old' Australians. The original inhabitants, Australia's Aboriginal population, were hardly noticed at this stage. For a few Aborigines there were housing schemes, but most lived in poverty on the fringes of European society.

Rationing of clothes and meat continued until 1948, with many other items in scarce supply. Restrictions on housing also remained in place until the early 1950s. One of the most positive forces which was working to improve life in Australia was the increased demand for primary products. Wool prices rose in the late 1940s to record levels and, along with improving sales of wheat, helped bring a new prosperity to farmers who had struggled through the Depression, the war and then the severe drought of 1944-45. In November 1948 the Holden, 'Australia's own car' was launched. In the following year the Snowy Mountains Hydro-Electric Authority began the huge construction scheme which was to employ a workforce of some 5000 people. Cheaper electricity and water for irrigation were the primary benefits, but Australians also gained new levels of expertise and saw the largely immigrant workforce employed on the scheme working hard to give Australia a growing pride in national achievement.

• AUSTRALIAN HOUSES OF THE FORTIES & FIFTIES

• Sunny skies, warm sand and a sparkling new 1956 FJ Holden. 'Australia's Own Car' became a symbol of post-war prosperity.
COURTESY: GENERAL MOTORS HOLDEN'S AUTOMOTIVE LTD

AUSTRALIA IN THE '40S AND '50S

• *Left*: Tricycles and pedal cars were favourite backyard toys.

COURTESY: DOWDELL FAMILY

• *Below:* Backyard cowboy John Scarrott, Lawton, Queensland, 1955.

COLLECTION: THE AUTHOR

• *Below left.* The motor car was increasingly seen as essential for every household. Mid-1940s, Balwyn, Victoria.

COURTESY: MAY VERNON

Children born in the two decades following the war are popularly referred to as 'Baby Boomers'. The term has widened to include those of us born during the war who grew up in the 1940s and '50s. Australian servicemen returning home from the war began to settle down and have families. Couples married before or during the war also contributed to the boom, as did new settlers who were starting families in a new land.

Increasing economic growth resulted in almost full employment and a secure lifestyle for most Australians. Having carried the nation through wartime and the early years of peacetime recovery, the Australian Labor Party lost office at the end of 1949. Robert Menzies, leading the coalition parties, had won on a promise of 'putting back value into the pound', and a strong stance against socialism. If later evaluation has brought to light many issues which could have raised wider concern, for most Australians the '50s were a period of contentment, a happy preoccupation with family and community life. For those who grew up in that era it has now taken on a strange dreamlike quality, mostly representing good times, with a few disturbing elements and only the occasional nightmare.

We know that our memories are often selective but from the perspective of the troubled 1990s it is interesting to search back through the recollections and images. I'll never forget being five years old. I clearly remember playing in a sandheap, gathering up offcut blocks of wood for make-believe cars, trucks, houses and bridges; and in the background were the sights and sounds of our first house being built. For a long time it seemed only yesterday — now half a lifetime away it has become part of history. In 1949 we were just one of many thousands of hopeful young families struggling to make a reality of that Australian ideal, our own house on our own land — in our case in the foothills of Victoria's Dandenong Ranges.

As an owner-builder, my father put in a superhuman effort, digging all the stump-holes through rock and shale, tamping round the base of every redgum stump with the head of a heavy iron crowbar. To raise the frame he needed another pair of hands, and set off down the unmade road to find a helpful neighbour. With the frame up, he could call in a bricklayer to build the two chimneys. Twenty years as a carpenter had taught him that this was a job for a specialist.

It was a time when building materials were still in short supply so that, while a gabled roof of corrugated iron had been planned, it was found that there was no iron to be had. Ironically, tiles seem to have been out of the question. Dad scratched his head and came up with an idea — he would change the roof from gabled to a low skillion, lay down floorboards and sheet it with Malthoid. It wasn't the ideal compromise, because the house was clad in weatherboard with traditional colonial-style sash windows and was going to have real shutters painted Wedgwood blue. Somehow the skillion roof gave it a surprised look and it was

23

AUSTRALIAN HOUSES OF THE FORTIES & FIFTIES

• Sunport, Ferntree Gully, Victoria, built by the author's parents in 1949. The pictures were taken in the early 1950s and late 1960s.
COLLECTION: THE AUTHOR

years before 'Sunport' settled comfortably into its garden.

We moved in as soon as the house was weathertight. Only a couple of the internal walls were lined; the rest were draped with curtains. In those days our house was set in a corner of the bush, with only one neighbour to be seen further up the hill. For a while Dad trundled our water from the neighbouring property in a brand-new galvanised rubbish bin, carried in a wheelbarrow. The day we finally got the tank up on its stand word arrived that we could have a private extension from the nearest water main.

Kerosene lamps were familiar from another family house in the hills, but we children still counted them as an exciting novelty. The quiet of lamplit evenings, with no wireless to break the spell, focused our thoughts or encouraged a reverie certain to ensure a peaceful sleep. For me the tranquility was shattered by the hard knocks of a rough-and-tumble country school. Left to himself, my brother who was only a toddler would sometimes wander off into the bush. To find him, my mother would whistle for the dog and set off in the direction from which it appeared. Down the hill through the trees was an old quarry, but somehow we survived that potential danger. And my brother later developed into a first-class bushman.

Cooking was generally done on a small cast iron wood stove although in the warmer months, or for quick meals, the single-burner 'Primus' was used. Our mother performed almost magical feats

24

AUSTRALIA IN THE '40S AND '50S

• Kitchen of the first Soldier Settler's house completed at Mingbool, South Australia, in May 1947.

COURTESY: SOUTH AUSTRALIAN HOUSING TRUST

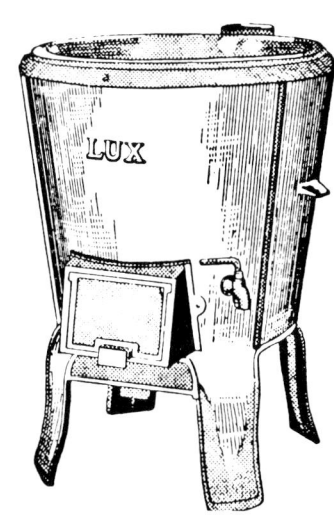

with that little kerosene stove, producing complete meals in a juggling act of pots and pans. Collecting 'mornings wood' was a ritual we could join in from an early age. Light wood in the form of fallen branches was plentiful and was needed for the kitchen stove and, on Mondays, for the copper in the washhouse. Much of the leftover scraps of timber from the construction of the house became 'chips' for the bathroom hot-water heater which was perched on a shelf at the end of the bath. The fire in the lounge/dining room also demanded a good share of the available wood.

In the 1950s refrigerators were becoming more familiar even in average households. We kept our ice-chest for a few years after electricity was connected, and a short distance away in the hills Grandmother continued to use a Coolgardie safe. It was a very proud day when our Lindberg-Foster refrigerator arrived from the big store in the city. By this time the house had received most of its finishing touches, including striped exterior blinds and a permanent letterbox on a post. This post also had a special stand for the billy in which we received our milk. Horse-drawn deliveries were still commonplace and the milk was measured directly from a can into each household billy. Our cousins in the suburbs got their milk in bottles. By the mid-1950s we too had progressed to this more hygienic convenience.

Our first real neighbours occupied an asbestos-cement and weatherboard-clad house built by a local 'spec' builder. It was a basic austerity cottage with a recessed

• Newly-planted lawns, Townsing house, Mount Lawley, Western Australia, 1953.

COURTESY: FRAN TOWNSING

front porch, one of many to be seen in various parts of our area. A large, brick-veneer perched on the top of the hill echoed more affluent Melbourne suburbs, such as Burwood or Balwyn.

On the fringes of Australian cities bushland and open paddocks were being devoured by the post-war housing boom; these areas are now considered 'inner' suburbs as the sprawl continues unabated. Having left local employment for work in the city, my father became a commuter, spending two hours each day on the train. Life, for much of the time, was as regular as a railway timetable. He arrived home for tea at six, while the end of each day for us children meant our favourite serials on the wireless and the comfortable anticipation of the evening meal. We usually had the same meals on particular nights, so we generally knew what we'd be having by the day of the week.

Our imaginations saved us from finding life too humdrum, as did the wild freedom of being able to roam far and wide in different kinds of bushland. We could choose from swamp with dense thickets of tea-tree, the willow-lined creek, paddocks hedged in hawthorn, quarry cliffs, ponds and dams. Children in the suburbs found space in backyards, streets and lanes, playgrounds and reserves, building sites, the boundaries of golf courses and, in some cases, the beach. Saturday afternoon matinees were a kind of refuelling of the imagination. For weeks we might be followers of Rob Roy Macgregor. Then, in a leap from the Old World to the New, we would join Davy Crockett and his frontier world. Hopalong Cassidy was a supreme hero, and to own a full outfit, complete with pearl-handled revolvers, was to ride tall, even if only on a broom handle — with or without a wooden horse's head attached.

Each new house in our area was greeted by us with mixed feelings. It could mean new playmates, but it also meant yet another part of our wild domain lost forever. In the district there continued to be a wide cross-section of living standards and dwellings. Old holiday cottages and Depression shacks were a refuge for those at the lower end of the socio-economic scale. But these were not the minimum standard; there were many people living in caravans, sheds and garages and a few in tents or humpies. In the bush opposite our house a couple lived in a tent. We knew the pattern of their existence and would sometimes creep about their camp to satisfy our curiosity.

Log cabins were not unfamiliar in and around the Dandenong Ranges. They continued to be a practical low-cost construction where timber was plentiful, and detailed articles on building them were published in such magazines as the *Australian Home Beautiful*, even as late as the 1940s. Post-war settlers, with little or no capital, were forced to join the ranks of battlers and lived in all sorts of dwellings. Imported goods such as cars

- Housing Estate Tasmania, early 1950s.
COLLECTION: STATE OFFICES LIBRARY, HOBART, TASMANIA

ROY
It's the whole Story of Rock and Roll!
ROCK AROUND THE CLOCK
FURY AT GUNSIGHT
AMBASSADORS
65A

• *Opposite page:* A matinee screening of *Rock Around the Clock* in Perth, 1956. The same excitement was seen at theatres throughout Australia.

COURTESY: THE WEST AUSTRALIAN

• Brick veneer of the late 1950s, State Savings Bank of Victoria design.

COLLECTION: COMMONWEALTH BANK ARCHIVES, VICTORIA

came in large wooden crates and quite a few families began their rise to prosperity in humble cottages made from these low-cost 'modules'.

Comparatively affluent households were usually the first to have the latest gadgets, gleaming appliances, bright new furniture and modern kitchens, with every drawer and cupboard door painted in different colours. Those less well-off were beginning to trust the employment opportunities and were risking 'hire-purchase' to acquire the new status symbols. When television finally arrived in 1956 many previously cautious people took the plunge and joined the ranks of households which could proudly say, 'Yes, we've got television'. Our grandmother had one in her cottage in the hills, its blue light strangely out of key with the golden hues of a cosy, basically Edwardian interior. We sat spellbound in front of her television whenever we visited her. Little did we realise that TV would profoundly change our lives, shrinking the world and making us part of the 'global village'. The 1956 Olympic Games held in Melbourne provided the first great televised event for Australian audiences. Excited crowds gathered in front of shop windows and yelled, 'Shirley, Shirley, come on Shirley', as Shirley Strickland made her dash, winning a gold medal in the 80-metre hurdles. Betty Cuthbert won both the 100- and 200-metre sprints, while Dawn Fraser swam for gold in the 100-metre freestyle. Australians won thirteen gold medals and began to feel more than ever a nation of great sporting prowess.

From 1955 we were overtaken by an invasion which profoundly changed popular music and added further distinction to the growing cult of the teenager. Rock and roll hit the world like a series of earthquakes. Someone in my class brought a portable record-player to school, vibrating the old sixth-grade room with sounds that seem tame in retrospect but were revolutionary to a generation brought up on Nat King Cole and Rosemary Clooney.

The Saturday matinee screening of *Rock Around the Clock* ensured the final conversion. Oh, the excitement of it all! People danced in the aisles and that was really something, even for the usually boisterous 'Saturday arvo' crowd. My young brother was staying with Grandmother up in the hills and somehow managed to convince her to bring him down on the bus. What she made of it all I can only guess. Our very own breed of Australian rockers, the 'bodgies' and 'widgies', hung about the local milk bar or 'lairised' about on motor bikes and in hotted up 'bombs'.

Following the pervasive American model was the inevitable result of being a small nation still somewhat confused about its identity. The school system continued to chant the praises of the old British Empire, but thankfully a few teachers in both primary and secondary school were prepared to offer some insight into Australia's own history and unique character.

Films about Australia were a rare treat at those Saturday matinees. Who could forget *Smiley* (1956), or *The Shiralee* (1957)? *Jedda*, released in 1955, was something else again. Here was our own outback in blazing colour — for most of us a revelation. Interest in Aboriginal culture was gathering strength, leading to the use of traditional designs as inspiration for murals, carpets, fabrics, floor tile patterns and other goods. Cross-cultural paintings by Albert Namatjira and his compatriots began to appear as prints in

● *Opposite page:* The kitchen was a key area for modernisation.
Australian Home Beautiful, February 1941

● *Right:* 'Contemporary' style, late 1950s. James Hardie & Co., 1958.
COLLECTION: THE AUTHOR

schools, offices and living rooms. More people were visiting the outback on family trips or with tours.

As living standards improved and cars became more reliable people ventured further afield on weekend trips and annual holidays. 'Going overseas' usually meant travelling by ship to England or the Continent, but an increasing number began to travel by air. Steam locomotives remained a familiar sight throughout Australia in the 1940s and '50s, but from around 1950 the diesel began to replace steam on the main lines. Suburban lines had been electrified since the 1920s in Victoria and New South Wales and motor-rails worked many country passenger services.

Looking back from the late 20th century confirms the feeling that Australia in the 1940s and '50s was an extraordinary mixture of new and old, of simple crafts and expanding technology. Ordinary clothes still recalled 19th-century styles, and horses continued to haul delivery vehicles. On most house building sites the methods and the tools used were timeless. In contrast, gleaming new cars proudly arrived at drive-in picture theatres to pay homage to an idealised America. On the big screen, the small screen and in glossy magazines there were glamorous American houses, colonial or contemporary, with ultra-modern kitchens and all the latest appliances. Quiz shows, first on radio and then television, had an American twang to them, preaching the gospel of mass consumerism. For Baby Boomers, the late '50s began the voyage into higher education. Schools were springing up or expanding, with a growing percentage of students reaching levels well beyond the opportunities offered to their parents. New schools and colleges were, for many, a first taste of functionalist architecture, including modern furniture, well-lit rooms and central heating. By contrast, many older primary schools were basically 19th century, even to the furniture and fittings.

Education brought a new awareness of Australian society and its origins, including the sophistication of being able to satirise our own suburbia. Barry Humphries began his stage career in 1955 and by the end of that decade Edna Everage and Sandy Stone were well on the way to becoming household names. We were losing that innocence which is remembered as an essential element of life in the 1950s.

Chapter 1 Endnotes

1. John Molony, *The Penguin Bicentennial History of Australia*, Viking, Ringwood, Victoria, 1987, p. 287.
2. *Australia's Yesterdays, A Look at Our Recent Past*, Reader's Digest Services Pty Ltd, Sydney, 1974, p. 316.
3. ibid.
4. Recollections of Mrs Vivienne 'Babs' Mair, 1992.
5. Molony, p. 288.
6. *Australian Home Beautiful*, May 1944, p. 40.
7. Molony, p. 290.
8. J.M. Freeland, *Architecture in Australia: A History*, Penguin Books, Ringwood, Victoria, 1972, p. 267.
9. *Yearbook of the Commonwealth of Australia*, no. 43, 1957, p. 577.
10. Public statement recorded by a newsreel camera in 1946.
11. *Yearbook of the Commonwealth of Australia*, no. 43, 1957, p. 580.

CHAPTER TWO
Ideas and Opportunities

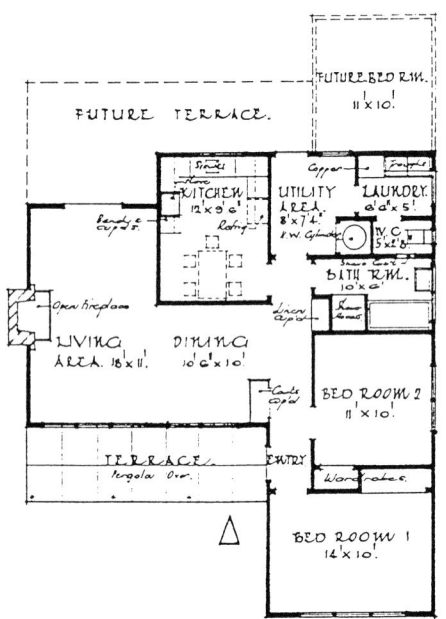

• 'Contemporary' design offered by the State Savings Bank of Victoria in 1957.

COLLECTION: COMMONWEALTH BANK ARCHIVES, VICTORIA

MANY SUBTLE FORCES have acted upon the Australian ideal of the detached house in its own ground. In essence, the typical suburban house is the ultimate diminution of the family estate. Settlers in Australia have tended to seek dignity through the independence of home ownership, as if in a democracy each household were a separate state. The tradition of separate houses for each family unit can be found in various parts of the world. Here in Australia, individual house ownership is the product of an evolutionary process which can be traced back to the cottages and smallholdings of the British Isles and of Europe generally.

It is ironic but to be expected that the idea of individual freedom and identity in house ownership for a whole population can lead to some stunning conformity and a seemingly endless sprawl of suburbs. The inter-war period and particularly the 1920s had brought the suburban house to a compact form which was to become a standard for decades to come. Home ownership reached new levels in that era, and suburbs, moving ever further from the city centres, took on their familiar character.

Once firmly established in the national psyche the house and land ideal was nurtured by all those who benefited either directly or indirectly. Land speculators had reached dizzy heights in the boom period of the 1880s and, while many were wiped out in the inevitable crash leading to the 1890s depression, the whole cycle eventually began again, as the economy picked up. The depression of the 1930s was the next crunch, with housing just recovering when the Second World War began. The building industry was vitally interested in promoting housebuilding, as were many sections of commerce and industry. Moralists preached the gospel of model households in which thrift and hard work were synonymous with well-kept houses. Here active hands could find fulfilment in gardening, keeping poultry, various hobbies and other wholesome pursuits far removed from the temptations of the hotels, racetracks and two-up schools.

IDEAS AND OPPORTUNITIES •

• House design of 1948 offers a view of a typical interior layout. The plan was by L. Hume Sherrard and features in *Home Beautiful*'s issue for December of that year.

A peep inside our architect's Christmas house which can be adapted to blocks of land facing many different ways.

- Catalogue and guide 1958.
  COURTESY: JAMES HARDIE INDUSTRIES LIMITED
  COLLECTION: THE AUTHOR

IDEAS AND OPPORTUNITIES

Books, magazines and newspapers further contributed to the idealisation of household life. Romantic songs, first circulated as sheet music, then on records or broadcast through radio, often promised undying love in a cottage or a bungalow — usually with roses around the door. With the growth of advertising and advances in printing processes, words and images were ever more pervasive. Catalogues of house designs conjured up dreams for young couples. These continue to be a powerful medium. Magazines such as the *Australian Home Beautiful*, the *Home*, *Australian House and Garden* and *Australian Homemaker* have all had a powerful influence in maintaining popular ideals as well as in identifying or directing trends. Films have also exerted a strong influence on public taste throughout this century — beginning as silent, flickering visions, but eventually adding sound and then colour to their impact. Hollywood grew to dominate the field, bringing to cinema screens an idealised American picture of the house and garden. An extension of that influence was the publication of photographs and articles on the homes of the stars. Australian magazines were happy to offer readers a glimpse of these dream places, as were imported magazines such as *American Home* and *American House and Garden*.

Affluent families recognised the ownership of property as the very foundation of society. Through land holdings and the building of substantial houses various degrees of social status were clearly defined. Australia's upper classes generally saw themselves as thoroughly British, so it was not surprising that magazines such as *English Country Life* should be influential in matters of domestic architecture and interior decoration. In the 1930s society architects continued to offer wealthy clients the choice between Georgian Revival and Old English styles or, very rarely, a dignified example of modern functionalism. These styles remained in favour from the 1930s to the '50s, with smaller versions appearing in respectable middle-class suburbs.

Having celebrated the English Vernacular Revival style and other period styles early in the century, the famed British magazine *The Studio* was, by the 1940s and '50s, a champion of modernism. Through its annuals it had always promoted fine design, with a strong emphasis on furniture, furnishings and associated 'applied arts'. Australia's quality magazine the *Home*, beginning in

• AUSTRALIAN HOUSES OF THE FORTIES & FIFTIES

• Corrugated sheet steel was advertised in 1957 as ideal for contemporary low-angle roofs.
Australian Homemaker, May 1957

1919, unfortunately ceased publication in 1942. *Decoration and Glass*, also emanating from Sydney, continued to provide through to 1949 a variety of articles for a discerning but restricted readership.

Architects and builders were offered a basic range of local and overseas journals in the period under review. *Architecture*, the journal of the Royal Australian Institute of Architects, changed its name to *Architecture in Australia* in 1955. As the national journal it offered a general coverage of local news along with reports of overseas developments. There were also state-based publications such as the *Journal of the Royal Victorian Institute of Architects*, the *Architect* (Western Australia) and the *Tasmanian Architect* (from 1957). The *Australian Journal of Architecture and Arts*, launched in 1952, was welcomed as a new forum and as an indicator of improving faith in the standing of Australia's architectural profession.

Overseas journals continued to be an essential resource for most Australian architects. Few offices would be without copies of the *Architectural Review* from Britain, or the *Architectural Forum* and *Architectural Record* from the United States. Other publications in the field were *Architect and Engineer* (USA), the *Architects' Journal* (UK), and *Arts and Architecture* (USA).

Isolation continued to affect Australia to a degree not easily understood in these times of satellite communications and jet travel. When overseas journals published

• State Saving Bank of Victoria design of 1941.
COLLECTION: COMMONWEALTH BANK ARCHIVES, VICTORIA

articles on architecture in Australia there was naturally a feeling of pride in being recognised in the wider world. Houses were well represented in a special number of the *Architectural Review* published in London in July 1948, under the title 'The Architecture of Australia'. Prime Minister J.B. Chifley comments in the foreword: 'We need houses in Australia, but we shall not be satisfied with just building houses ... we intend that our public buildings and private homes shall be worthy of our future'.

In this special issue, Vance Palmer writes on the land itself, Walter Bunning on historical and socio-economic influences on Australian architecture, Raymond McGrath on 'Australian Early Colonial', and John Moore on the recent past and the contemporary scene. A.G. Stephenson gives a historical review of Australian hospitals, linked to a pictorial review covering hospitals, commercial buildings, hotels, public buildings, churches and houses. The latter includes eleven houses in New South Wales, one at Surfers Paradise, two blocks of Melbourne flats by Roy Grounds and a house on the Yarra.

English architect Bryan Westwood sums up with impressions gathered during a wartime visit to Australia:

The clear sunny climate has not, so far as I can see, had as much effect on architectural character as one would expect. From the time of the earliest settlers up to the present day, Australian architectural inspiration has evidently sprung from Europe, with latterly a crop of plagiarisms from California via the housekeeping magazines.

While he looked in vain for a distinctively Australian form of architecture he was at least an early observer of the special place of corrugated iron buildings, '... widespread in the countryside and still lingering extensively in the towns, which has an attraction of its own with its great variety of uses of the material'. While noting 'the great handicap of isolation' affecting Australian architects he places stronger emphasis on the lack of background in good design in a new country. With only the oldest settlements offering examples of 'sincere craftsmanship' in such buildings as churches or traditional houses or cottages, he suggests there is little to inspire clients toward a high standard of design.

Books on Australia's domestic architecture published from the 1940s to '50s might seem scarce by current standards, but perhaps when viewed in the light of the limited range of Australian books offering in those years the situation was reasonable. John D. Moore's *Home Again! Domestic Architecture for the Normal Australian* was published in Sydney in 1944. *Homes in the Sun: The Past Present and Future of Australian Housing*, by Walter Bunning (Sydney, 1945), was a well-presented work by contemporary standards, with a potted history of architecture, discussion of the need for urban planning and a cross-section of better-quality houses. *Houses of Australia* by George Beiers (Sydney, 1948), was again a large-format illustrated work offering a broad perspective of the house through 150 years of European settlement, albeit with some gaps in the story. A few notable contemporary houses were included and, despite the lack of text, it is considered to be the first history of the house in Australia published in book form.

Robin Boyd's *Victorian Modern* (Melbourne, 1947), written in his typically lively style, is a well-illustrated, analytical work which presents an account of the progress of architecture in Victoria from first settlement up to the mid-1940s. An important aspect of this study is Boyd's identification of the approach to house design which he terms the 'Victorian Type'. He describes the 1946 J.F. Spears house in the Melbourne suburb of Beaumaris as, 'the basic Victorian Type: One long simple stretch of low roofed

• AUSTRALIAN HOUSES OF THE FORTIES & FIFTIES

• One of the most important symbols of post-war affluence was the holiday house. They were usually plain and functional, following contemporary ideals.

COURTESY: JAMES HARDIE INDUSTRIES LIMITED
COLLECTION: THE AUTHOR

HARDIE'S "FIBROLITE"

the only logical building material for your holiday home!

Escape from the realities of everyday life to a holiday home of Hardie's "Fibrolite." You'll build it for less and spend next to nothing on maintenance. "Fibrolite" is white ant and borer proof, unaffected by sea air, will not rust and provides complete protection from all weathers. It's cooler in summer, too! Another point—"Fibrolite" is fire retardant. Use the money you save for extra "home comforts."

PLAN HF13: "Fibrolite" holiday home of only 660 square feet featuring one bedroom.

PLAN HF13: Revised holiday home plan featuring two bedrooms. Area: 732 square feet.

You build more for less more easily with "Fibrolite"

Use Hardie's "Fibrolite" for exterior and interior walls and ceilings. Corrugated "Fibrolite" for roof and "Tilux" for kitchen and bathroom. Supplies are available from hardware and timber merchants everywhere. "Fibrolite" is easy to handle and erect; it's the ideal material for week-end builders!

38

• Scrolls and stonework, Banyan, Bendigo, Victoria, 1953.

PHOTOGRAPH: THE AUTHOR

house, taking its orders only from the Victorian trees, the Victorian sun, the Victorian hardwood of which it is built'.[1] Kenneth McDonald's 1954 book, *The New Australian Home* was a slim volume, but was significant in its summary of recent designs in the modern style:

This year, and possibly this book, will mark a new era in the development of the Australian house. The experimental period is finished, and little excuse remains for "half-baked modern" houses.[2]

Imported books on architecture, townplanning and design in general were a continuing influence for practising architects, designers, builders, students and clients. Typical of the available works were *Marcel Breuer* by Peter Blake, published in New York in 1949; *The Book of Small Houses* from the Architectural Forum (New York, 1940); *The Modern House in America* by James and Catherine Fold (New York, 1940); and *The Daily Mail Ideal Home Book*, an annual published in London, which sometimes included Australian houses.

Exhibitions could be a vehicle for the presentation of the work of innovative young architects and a general force in public education. Melbourne's Centenary Homes Exhibition in 1934 included an architectural competition, with three of the five sections for complete houses. Donald C. Ward won all three, with plain, flat-roofed cube forms indicating a clear acceptance that 'modern' domestic architecture had truly arrived. Homes exhibitions were held in cities throughout Australia in the latter half of the 1930s, but from 1940 to 1945 wartime restrictions made such events a luxury. An important exception, seen as a valuable insight for the whole population, was the Exhibition of American Housing and Planning which travelled in Australia in 1944. Dr H. C. Coombs of the Ministry of Post-War Reconstruction had seen the exhibition at the Museum of Modern Art in New York. Some 200 000 people are said to have visited the exhibition in Sydney. It later opened in Melbourne where it drew a similar crowd.

Designed as a pictorial narrative it was presented as 'a series of first-class photographs linked by explanatory comment supported by facts and figures'.[3] America's experiences in tackling its housing schemes were seen as important lessons for Australia. The exhibition included striking photographs of houses by such noted architects as Walter Gropius and Marcel Breuer.

At the end of the war, the James Hardie and Wunderlich companies sponsored a travelling exhibition of asbestos-cement houses. It ran in Melbourne for three weeks from 22 January 1946, having already been viewed in other state capitals.[4]

Included in the exhibition were twenty-one scale-models of houses, plans for more than 100 houses, numerous photographs and a full-size section of an asbestos-cement house. A free booklet was available containing illustrations and plans for twenty-two houses. At this same time, businesses such as the Modern Home Building Advisory Bureau offered a free booklet of architect-drawn plans. Clients made a choice from the booklet and then bought a full-scale plan.[5]

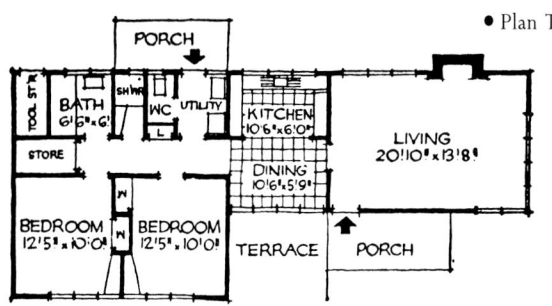

• Plan T297 of the *Age* Small Homes Service of the Royal Australian Institute of Architects.
Australian Home Beautiful, November 1952

• *Opposite page:* View of the living room from the upstairs studio landing in the 1955 Saphin house, Alton Avenue, Brighton, Victoria. Architects John and Phyllis Murphy created this house for an artist and his family in part of a very old garden.
PHOTOGRAPH: WOLFGANG SIEVERS
COURTESY: JOHN AND PHYLLIS MURPHY

The many low-cost design books or catalogues which became available in the immediate post-war era are an indication of the demand for housing. *The Sun's Book of Post-War Homes*, published by Melbourne's *Sun News-Pictorial* in 1946, was the product of an architectural competition. *The Australian House*, by Norman Jenkins, contained fifty house plans along with hints on buildings. *Your Post War Home* by Watson Sharp offered 'Home plans of distinction for Australians who are planning to build'. Florence M. Taylor's *The Book of 150 Low-Cost Houses* was a substantial work published in Sydney in 1945.

Post-war austerity is also evident in the range of books offered on low-cost furniture, furnishings and general interior decoration. *Furnishing on a Budget* by Edna Horton Lewis, published in Melbourne in 1948, is a small but tasteful work which avoids rampant 'featurism', an increasingly popular theme in magazines and books of that time. The interiors shown are restrained, often eclectic and perfectly liveable. Some of the furniture is new, but much of it is old or antique. Edna Walling also suggested simple, homely interiors in her 1947 book, *Cottage and Garden in Australia*. These books serve as a reminder that houses and interior decoration in the 1940s and '50s cannot be readily lumped into a single, easily-defined category. Modern functionalism may have been a dominant philosophy but it was certainly not the only influence. In fact, stylism and eclecticism were quietly regenerating and were to emerge as powerful elements of the 'post-modern' era of the 1970s and '80s.

Antique Georgian furniture had been popular for refined interiors in the 1920s and '30s and continued to be fashionable. By the 1940s and '50s better-quality Early Victorian was also regaining its old status in conservative schemes. Magazine articles and imported books on interior decoration did much to promote the various permutations of 'American Colonial' style. Publishing in the United States was in a strong position, with a high level of technical expertise and a large home market. *The American Woman's New Encyclopedia of Home Decorating* by Helen Koues, published in the early 1950s, offered 976 pages, with hundreds of illustrations, many in colour. While most interiors shown were functional and many were 'contemporary', a large percentage were in a period style or included antiques or reproductions. This encyclopedia contained material seen in earlier home-decorating booklets. In fact, nine of the photographs had appeared in the *Australian Home Beautiful* of November 1944 in a feature entitled 'A Home Favoured by Americans'. Strangely, the photographs and notes were supplied by the US Office of War Information, so it seems that 'Early American' style was considered a comforting inspiration for war-weary Australians.

In April 1953, well-known Sydney interior designer Margaret Lord wrote:

When it comes to the planning of a colour scheme, the combining of colours in effective and interesting ways, the average Australian is not so well informed, not so knowing as the average American. We haven't the same scope for visual experience which most American stores provide and therefore tend to follow safe but rather dull colour recipes.

IDEAS AND OPPORTUNITIES •

• AUSTRALIAN HOUSES OF THE FORTIES & FIFTIES

JOSIAH WEDGWOOD CHINA
COPELAND SPODE CHINA
GOR-RAY SKIRTS
HORROCKSES' SHEETS

42

IDEAS AND OPPORTUNITIES

• *Opposite page*: Sitting room at the Burkitt residence, Palm Beach, New South Wales, by noted interior designer Marion Best.

Published in *Art and Design 1*, Sydney 1949
PHOTOGRAPH: MAX DUPAIN

Her recent travels had also included England, France, Switzerland, Italy, Denmark and Sweden. In summing up trends in Australia she noted signs of Australians becoming more colour conscious.

This is most apparent in exterior painting, but in this field particularly, it is important to remember that it is often better to have no applied colour at all than to have the wrong colours. An indiscriminate use of bright crude colours can have a disastrous effect on the appearance of any city or suburb.

Margaret Lord's words alert us to two important sources of images or ideas: the retail stores and the companies promoting products such as paints and fabrics. Through their advertising and promotions in newspapers and magazines well-known stores such as the Myer Emporium, Patersons, Anthony Horderns, Maples and Grace Brothers were able to shape popular ideals. Grace Brothers published house designs in the *Sunday Telegraph*, while standard plans seen in the *Australian Women's Weekly* from 1957 were available at the Home Plans Service Bureau at the Myer Emporium in Melbourne. Plans could also be ordered by mail and cost £7 7s ($14.70), complete with specifications.[6] The *Women's Weekly* also established a home-planning centre at Sydney's Anthony Horderns.

Increased awareness of the good sense in having architects prepare standard plans for low-cost houses resulted in the Small Homes Service of the Royal Victorian Institute of Architects in conjunction with Melbourne's *Age* newspaper.

From July 1947, the *Age* published a plan and perspective drawing each week along with a detailed description. Popularly known as the *Age* Small Homes Service, this scheme was responsible for many hundreds of well-designed houses which in themselves became models to influence the builders and owner-builders who designed their own constructions.

In 1953 the Small Homes Service (NSW) was established by the New South Wales Chapter of the Royal Australian Institute of Architects in conjunction with the *Australian Home Beautiful*. Plans were submitted by members of the Institute and approved for publication by an expert committee. The stated criteria were 'appearance, sound design and economy in

• *Above:* Contemporary dining room designed by Anthony Hordern's furniture designer Miss Joyce Brown.

Published in *Art and Design 1*, Sydney, 1949.

43

• Devised in 1952 to illustrate 'good taste' and 'bad taste', these settings were arranged by Robin Boyd and Melbourne furniture retailer Bruce Anderson. In the photograph at right is Grant Featherston's R152 Contour chair, a cabinet by Douglas Snelling, lamp by Clement Meadmore and a Frances Burke oak leaf pattern cotton print.

COURTESY: BRUCE ANDERSON

construction'. Readers of the Sydney *Sun-Herald* were also offered this service either by mail or by visiting the Small Homes Service Bureau at the David Jones store on the corner of George and Barrack Streets, Sydney.

Robin Boyd, who was the primary force in the establishment of the service based in Victoria, noted that there was a section of the architectural profession who resisted the idea.[7] They felt it was unable to provide the individual attention needed for each site and each client, and that it reduced the architect's work to something of a production-line role. Boyd continued to support the notion that it was not only a positive influence toward 'simpler and more efficient plan shapes', but also extended the boundaries of ordinary domestic architecture by including, 'a sprinkling of more advanced, imaginative designs'.[8] His final point was that it gave

IDEAS AND OPPORTUNITIES •

• Design no. 328 offered by the *Australian Women's Weekly* and Myer Emporium Home Plans Service Bureau in 1957.

COURTESY: AUSTRALIAN CONSOLIDATED PRESS AND MYER STORES LTD

less affluent people the chance to live in architect-designed houses, traditionally the privilege of the well-to-do.

Plans offered by the Small Homes Service (NSW) could be modified to suit individual requirements by special arrangement. A standard set of plans, including blueprints, additional drawings and necessary documents for the erection of the house, cost £10 10s or 'ten guineas' ($21) in 1957. In 1949, the *Age* Small Homes Service of the RVIA was offering working drawings and specifications for £5 ($10), post free.

The substantial house seen above is plan no. 328, offered by the *Australian Women's Weekly* and Myer Emporium Home Plans Service Bureau in May 1957. Hundreds of other plans were said to be available from stock, and plans prepared to any individual design were offered at £1 1s or 'one guinea' per square (10 ft × 10 ft), based on total area.

Wunderlich Limited, a major supplier of asbestos-cement building sheets for both interior and exterior use, added further to the influence of the small homes services by including perspectives and plans from both the New South Wales and Victorian schemes in their advertising in such magazines as *Home Beautiful*. This ensured that these designs were seen throughout Australia. At the same time, Wunderlich offered their own free book of house plans. Such books had been available since the 1920s and it is suggested that the producers of timber and asbestos-cement had to some extent prepared the way for the later services through their promotion of standard plans for low-cost houses in the inter-war period.[9]

It would require a wide-ranging and highly complex study to measure the impact and continuing influence of house

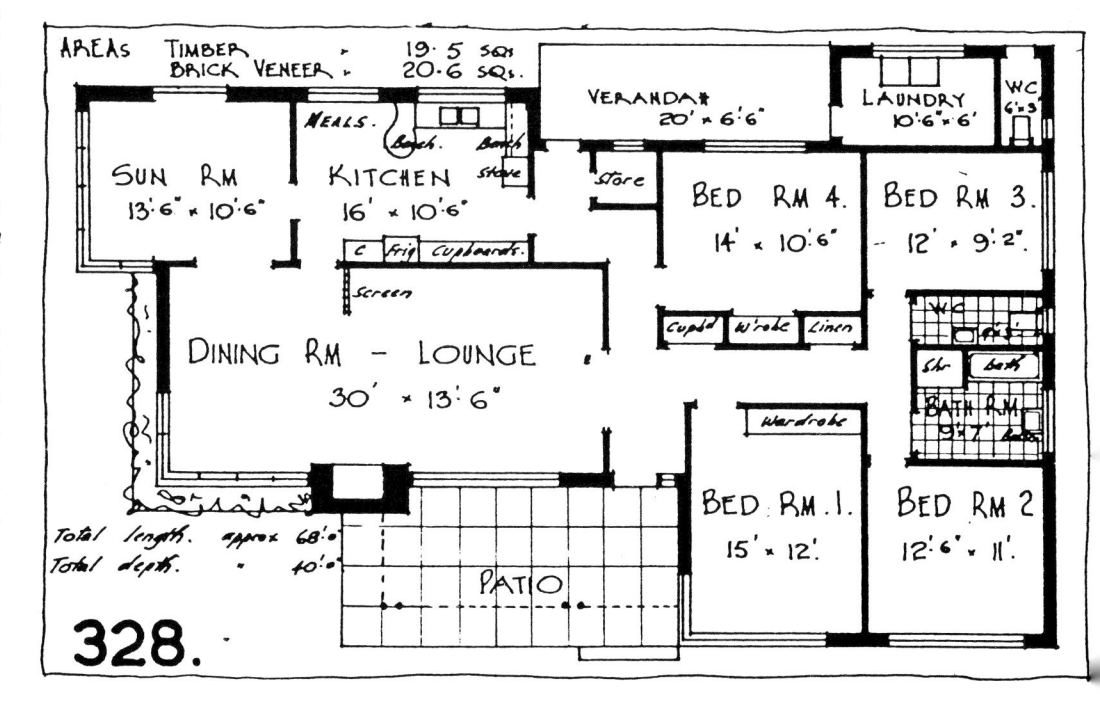

45

• AUSTRALIAN HOUSES OF THE FORTIES & FIFTIES

• Designs from a 1958 guide to building homes using Hardie's 'Fibrolite' asbestos-cement sheets.
COURTESY: JAMES HARDIE INDUSTRIES LIMITED

designs offered through the small homes services of architects' institutes. Many other companies and individuals offered similar services, with designs varying from uninspired suburban boxes to thoughtful examples of modern functionalism. Builders, 'designers' and 'planning consultants' happily borrowed ideas which they felt had appeal to the public. Aspects which seemed too avant garde were rejected or modified. In 1949 Robin Boyd wrote of the forces acting against the architects who designed for advisory services. He felt that about half the houses had lost the integrity of the original design having been 'Dolled up and fussed by the owner, sabotaged by the builder...'[10] This was Boyd in a pessimistic mood.

IDEAS AND OPPORTUNITIES •

• Standard mass-produced blueprints satisfied the needs of many homebuilders in the post-war era.
COLLECTION: THE AUTHOR

More typically, he was one of many who believed that the modest suburban house was worthy of any practical effort which might promote good design. Younger architects of the post-war years were often influenced by the left-leaning idealism which was found in universities and intellectual circles, generally. This was manifested in a concern for the welfare of the general population, for better living conditions and for setting aside the old order where architects were mostly concerned with the needs of affluent clients or large companies and institutions controlled by the establishment.

An even clearer concern for ordinary people was expressed in two slim but powerful books published in the 1940s. The first was *Housing the Australian Nation* by F. Oswald Barnett and W. O. Burt, published by the Research Group of the Left Book Club of Victoria in 1942. The second was *We Must Go On: A Study in Planned Reconstruction and Housing* by Barnett, Burt and Heath, published in Melbourne in 1944. In the foreword of the latter work, Dr H.C. Coombs, Director-General, Ministry of Post-War Reconstruction, writes:

Housing is more than the designing and building of houses, for the house is the smallest unit in the complex of capital equipment, which is necessary if men, women and children are to carry out easily and efficiently the great variety of activities which make up human life. The house, therefore, must be seen, not as an isolated unit, but as an integral part of a much greater whole, a part of a neighbourhood, of a town,

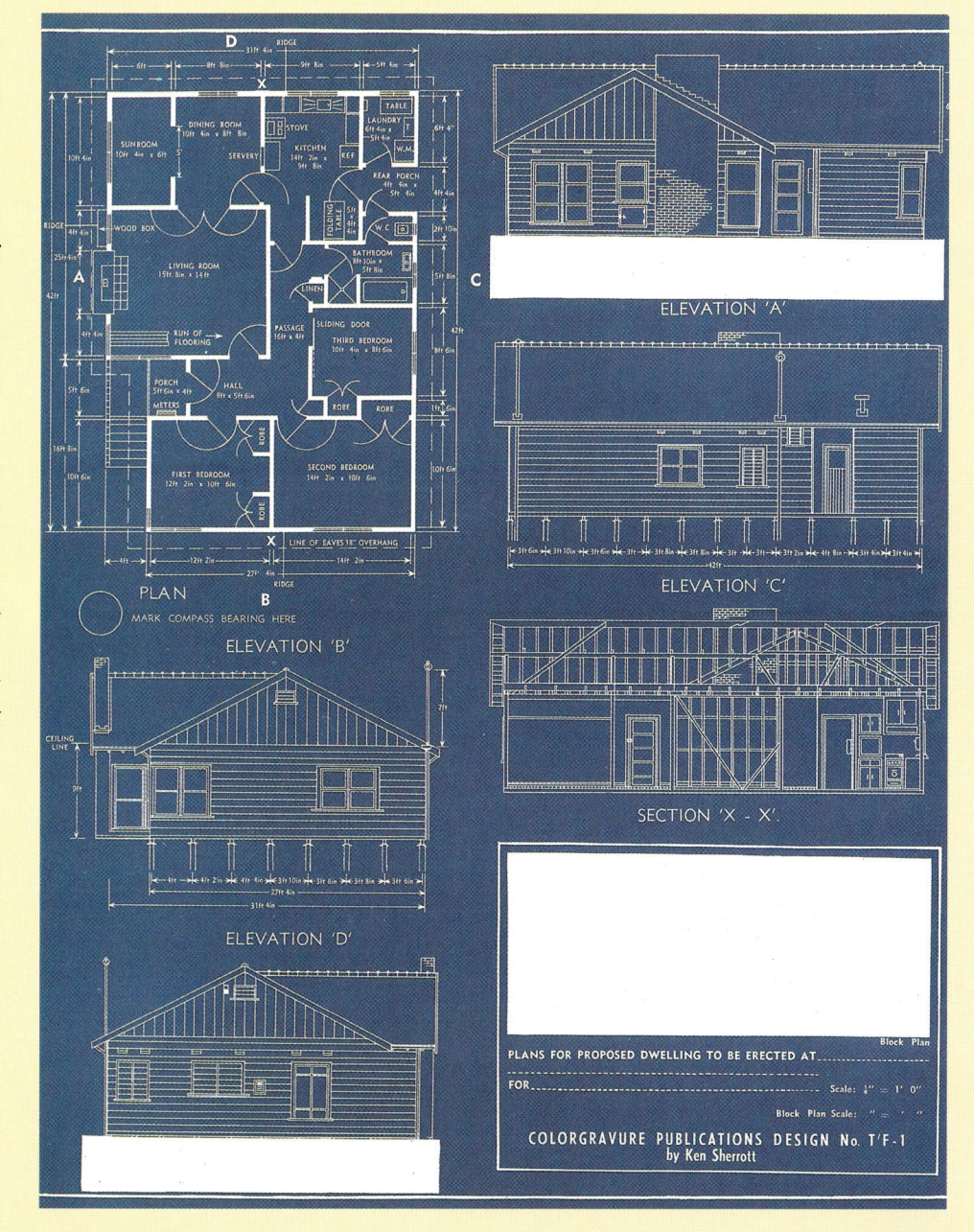

47

• Weatherboard house with brick porch.
State Savings Bank of Victoria 1946.
COURTESY: COMMONWEALTH BANK ARCHIVES, VICTORIA

of a region, each of which possesses some sense of unity and common life.

The authors of *We Must Go On* were putting a case for planned development from a nationwide point of view. Using Victoria as a model, they covered a wide range of concerns, from the planning of towns and garden cities, decentralisation, transport systems, slum reclamation, land conservation to low-cost housing — including prefabrication. Using post-war reconstruction as an opportunity to create a better society was the central theme. 'An essential part of winning the peace is the formulation of a clear conception of post-war plans for producing better environments and higher standards of living.'[11] It was felt that a national housing scheme would 'provide every good Australian with adequate shelter at a cost within his capacity to pay', and that it was 'fortunate that as a by-product it will provide a tremendous amount of employment'. Figures given in this important work indicate the desperate state of housing at that time. It is stated that by the end of 1944 Australia would require a further 365 000 houses.

This pathetic need calls for a building programme throughout Australia of at least 1000 houses a week, and in Victoria at least 300 homes a week, for the next ten years. Therein lies a grand opportunity to provide in abundance two of the greater human needs — full employment as well as housing.

At the rate suggested by the authors, approximately 520 000 houses would be constructed in a decade. In reality, the number of houses completed in Australia between July 1945 and June 1955 was 576 440.[12] In 1944, the authors would not have imagined that, aside from the expected increase in population, the decade 1946–1956 would see more than 860 000 migrants arrive to dramatically increase the demand for housing.[13]

The Commonwealth Housing Commission, appointed in 1943, undertook a nationwide inquiry which resulted in an extensive report on Australia's housing and on the likely requirements in the post-war years.[14] One recommendation of the Commission was that the commonwealth and state governments, along with private enterprise, would share the building program. With large-scale government financing and construction, the need for low-income housing could be addressed. It was also recommended that half the houses would be available for purchase and half for rental. In a modified form, the Commission's recommendations were introduced in the Commonwealth–State Housing Agreement of 1945, which provided low-interest loans to state governments for the construction of rental housing. Tasmania withdrew from the agreement in 1950, and South Australia did not begin to operate under it until 1953. The first Agreement expired on 30 June 1956, the second in 1961.

Funds provided under the Commonwealth-State Housing Agreements operating in the 1940s and '50s were applied not only to rental housing but also to dwellings built for sale to eligible

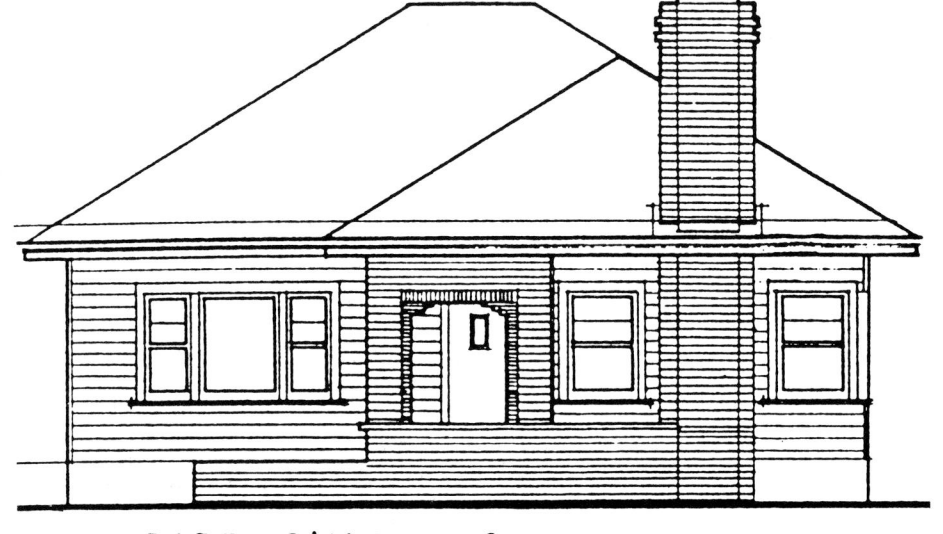

THE STATE SAVINGS BANK OF VICTORIA
o TWO BEDROOM UNIT o

IDEAS AND OPPORTUNITIES

• Elevated Queensland version of the standard 'triple-fronted' design seen in many parts of Australia in the 1940s and '50s. This one was offered in the 1950 book of designs.
COLLECTION: QUEENSLAND DEPARTMENT OF HOUSING, LOCAL GOVERNMENT AND PLANNING.

applicants. Advances were also made to enable occupants to purchase their rental homes. Between 1945 and 1956, about 96 000 dwellings were completed.[15] Under the 1956 Agreement added emphasis was placed on the construction of homes for private ownership. This included having 20 per cent of the money allocated to each state made available to building societies and other approved institutions for lending to private house-builders.[16]

War Service Homes were another area of commonwealth funding. Since 1918, the nation had taken on the responsibility of helping to provide housing for ex-servicemen. In the 1940s and '50s the concern was mostly directed toward those who had served in the Second World War and, subject to the statutory provisions of the Act, to persons selected for service in Korea or Malaya.[17] This was a scheme based on loans or advances and was directed toward the purchase or construction of houses.

Banks, both government and private, played an important role in housing and in some cases were directly involved in design and construction. From 1920 the State Savings Bank of Victoria operated a housing scheme through its Credit Foncier Department and was responsible for the building of thousands of houses in the inter-war years. In the '40s and '50s the bank's books of house designs continued to capture many who hoped to make the Australian dream a reality.

Designs in these books ranged from compact, four-roomed houses to larger styles with attic rooms. Thirty different

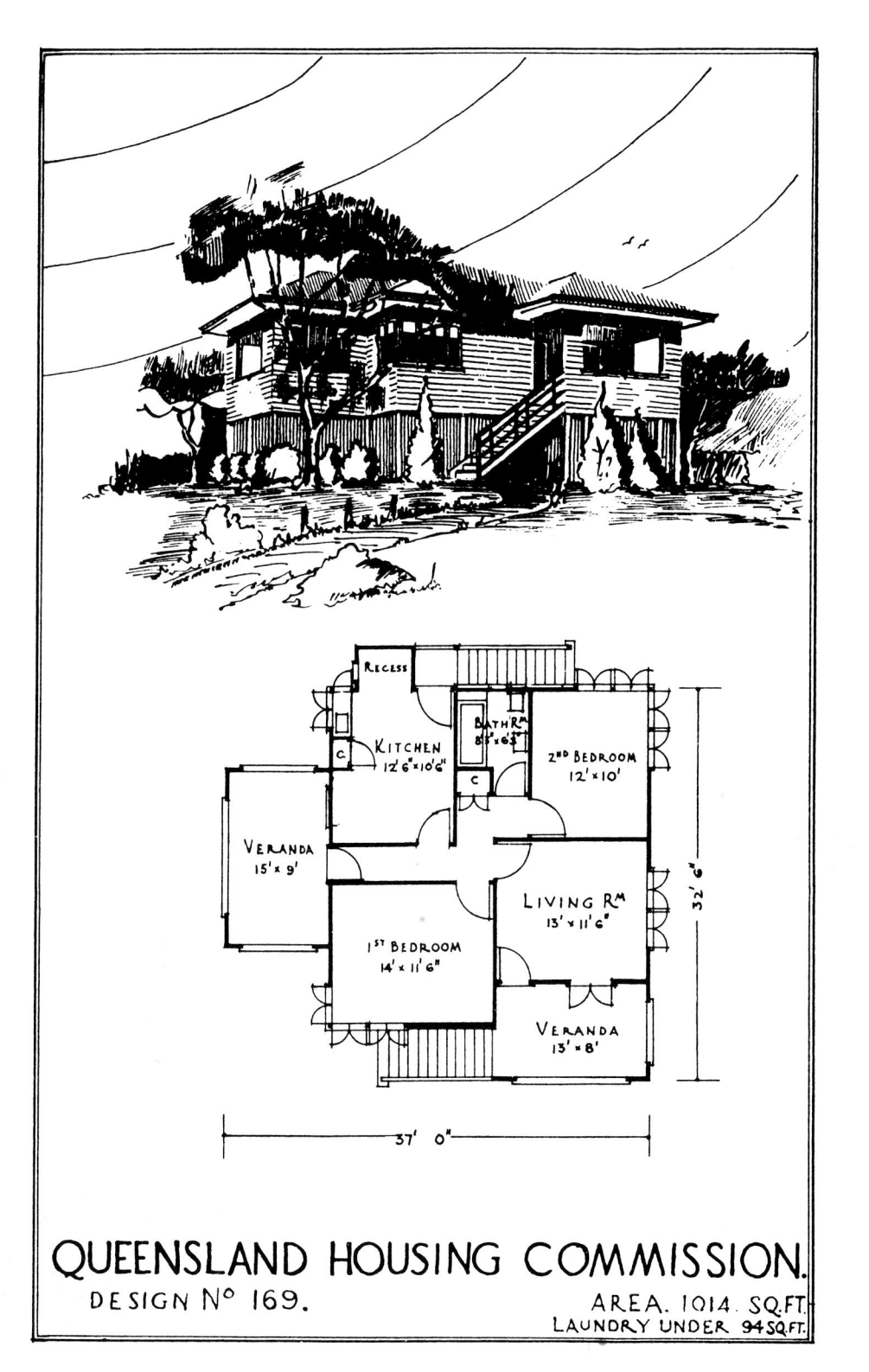

49

• AUSTRALIAN HOUSES OF THE FORTIES & FIFTIES

• Gardens in the 1940s and '50s typically concentrated on bold floral effects. This well-kept scheme perfectly compliments a 1951 house in Hill Street, Daylesford, Victoria.
PHOTOGRAPH: THE AUTHOR

IDEAS AND OPPORTUNITIES

• *Right:* Sober brick piers flank a frivolous gate of wrought steel.
PHOTOGRAPH: THE AUTHOR

• *Below right:* An important first impression was offered by good quality suburban houses.
PHOTOGRAPH: THE AUTHOR

designs were offered in the book released in February 1941, although these included many simple variations, such as a reversed plan or change of details and trimmings.

Books or catalogues of designs were also available from state governments. The plan on the previous page shows standard design no. 169 in the range offered by the Queensland Housing Commission in 1947. Conservative design was the keynote of housing offered through state governments, as was it in design services operated by banks and private companies offering finance and construction. By the mid-1950s, the State Housing Commission of Western Australia had begun to break the mould and was offering new designs 'incorporating contemporary planning and many modern features normally only encountered in more costly contemporary homes.'[18] The example seen on page 116 included floor-to-ceiling glazing following the slope of a low-pitched roof. It also boasted open planning throughout the spacious living areas, with a typical peninsula bench dividing the kitchen and living room.

South Australia's Housing Trust also began to introduce some modern designs in the 1950s. One example included an upper storey of a quick-cooling framed construction for the bedrooms and play area. The ground level which included the kitchen, dining and living rooms, bathroom, toilet, and laundry was of solid masonry. It was an innovative design but was condemned by one suburban council as a 'rabbit-hutch'.[19]

Identifying the many ways in which popular ideals are reflected and to a great degree shaped by books, magazines, newspapers, catalogues, brochures, films, television, exhibitions and even popular songs leaves out one area of influence which cannot be overlooked. Actually seeing houses in the neighbourhood, in other suburbs, regions, states, or even other countries can also be a powerful means of spreading ideas, fashions and attitudes.

When garages were finally integrated with the house itself and gained large lift-up or fold-away doors the decoration of these doors in brightly coloured patterns was one of suburbia's essential status symbols. A double garage offered greater impact and proudly announced a two-car family now that ownership of one car was becoming *passe*. Other elements that could be seen from the street, and would be bound to impress, were the quantity and decorative character of the so-called 'wrought' iron, the house name, the plant tubs and statuary, a fancy letterbox, an unusual front fence, outdoor lighting, window awnings, and last but not least, the front garden.

Visitors were likely to be further impressed when they got to see the interior of the house, then the even more important backyard, now beginning to be regarded as an outdoor living space rather than a rustic or utilitarian area.

In the *Australian Home Beautiful* for May 1943 we find a detailed article on the 'barbecue deluxe'. An 'out-of-doors fireplace' or 'barbecue fireplace' had been pictured in an article on a house in the Dandenong Ranges in the January issue.[20]

This inspired a reader to write asking just how such a structure could be built. The editor noted, 'The type of barbecue just described is the kind that Californians build in the garden where they entertain their friends at informal parties.'

Home Beautiful's next feature on the barbecue was in the February 1948 issue. The main illustration (see opposite) is described as an American barbecue layout which would suit our gardens. By the 1960s, Australians had taken to the barbecue with such enthusiasm that it came to symbolise an important part of the Australian identity. By the 1980s many were convinced that it was our very own invention, with advertisements cajoling Americans into journeying across the Pacific for a real Aussie treat.

Increasing affluence, bringing new mobility, greatly increased the opportunities for travelling about. Train, tram and bus journeys were all interesting for those who watched housing developments. Driving around in the family car offered everchanging panoramas of open spaces turning block by block into suburbs. When fully serviced, with all the vacant sites developed, they became complete neighbourhoods, mellowed by time and the softening effect of maturing street trees and household gardens.

Many more substantial houses of the 1950s were grand symbols of renewed optimism. Restrictions had been lifted, material shortages were easing. Here was a chance to show the world that the dream was bigger and better than ever.

IDEAS AND OPPORTUNITIES

• *Opposite page*: A classic 'triple fronted' brick veneer of the 1950s. String courses of dark manganese bricks give horizontal emphasis. Note painted garage door and 1954 Holden.
COLLECTION: COMMONWEALTH BANK ARCHIVES, VICTORIA

• *Below*: American barbecue layout featured in the *Australian Home Beautiful*, February 1948 issue.

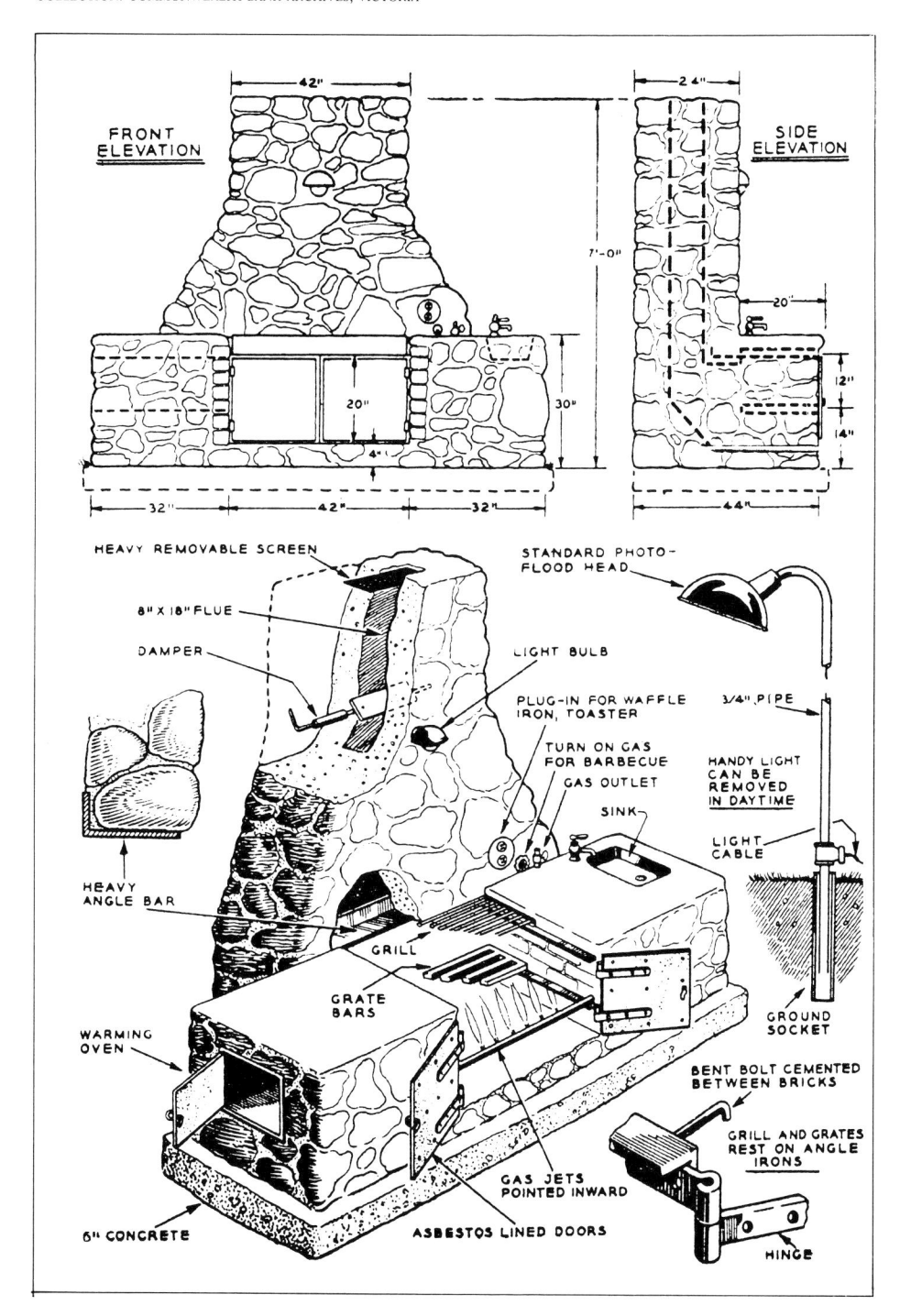

Chapter 2 Endnotes

[1] Robin Boyd, *Victorian Modern*, Architectural Students' Society of the Royal Victorian Institute of Architects, Melbourne, 1947, p. 63.
[2] Kenneth McDonald, *The New Australian Home*, published by Kenneth McDonald, Melbourne, 1954.
[3] 'An Exhibition of U.S. Architecture, Its Lessons for Australians', 'N.C.', *Australian Home Beautiful*, November 1944, p. 18.
[4] *Australian Home Beautiful*, January 1946, vol. 25, no. 1, p. 5.
[5] ibid., p. 37.
[6] *Australian Women's Weekly*, May 22, 1957.
[7] Robin Boyd, *Australia's Home*, Melbourne University Press, 1952, p. 259.
[8] ibid., p.289.
[9] Charles Pickett, 'Modernism and Austerity: the 1950s House', Ch. 5, *The Australian Dream – Design of the Fifties*, Powerhouse Publishing, 1993.
[10] Robin Boyd, 'Reach-Me-Down-Architecture', *Architecture*, July 1949, p. 84.
[11] F.O. Barnett, W.O. Burt, & F. Heath, *We Must Go On – A Study of Planned Reconstruction and Housing*. The Book Depot, Melbourne, 1944, p. 12.
[12] *Yearbook of the Commonwealth of Australia*, no. 40, 1954 and no. 43, 1957.
[13] *Yearbook of the Commonwealth of Australia*, no. 43, 1957.
[14] Susan E. Marsden, *Business, Charity and Sentiment*, Wakefield Press, Netley, South Australia, 1986, p. 14.
[15] *Yearbook of the Commonwealth of Australia*, no. 43, 1957 p. 628.
[16] ibid., p. 629.
[17] ibid., p. 635.
[18] State Housing Commission of Western Australia, Annual Report, 1956/57, p. 12.
[19] Marsden, op. cit., p. 173.
[20] 'California in Kalorama, An Interesting Home in the Ranges', *Australian Home Beautiful*, January 1943, pp. 24-25.

53

Home Beautiful

JUNE, 1942

Price 1/-

Registered at the General Post Office, Melbourne, for transmission by post as a periodical.

How This House Was Built

Pise Building Explained

CHAPTER THREE
From Wartime to Peacetime

AFTER THE DECLARATION of war in September 1939 house construction went through a period of decreasing activity. But it did not drop to its minimal level until February 1942 when National Security Regulations imposed severe restrictions. Private building ceased in many areas and was limited in others. However, under the War Housing Program, state and commonwealth authorities did continue with essential housing, such as that needed for munitions workers and their families. Clear indication of the degree of change is seen in the official statistics. More than 40 000 new homes were built throughout Australia in the financial year 1938–39, but in 1942–1943 there were fewer than 4000.[1]

In the editorial of the *Australian Home Beautiful* for January 1942, we read of conditions up to that time.

Building restrictions, at the moment of writing, limit expenditure on new domestic buildings to £3000 and on renovations to £250; but conditions grow harder week by week. In spite of this, a great deal of new and interesting building is being carried on over a widespread area and this will continue so long as materials are available.

War in Europe and North Africa was distant enough for Australia to seem relatively secure. With the Japanese bombing of Pearl Harbor on 7 December 1941, and their inexorable advance in our direction, any remaining complacency evaporated.

A. V. Jennings, the well-known construction company founded in 1932, continued building houses on its

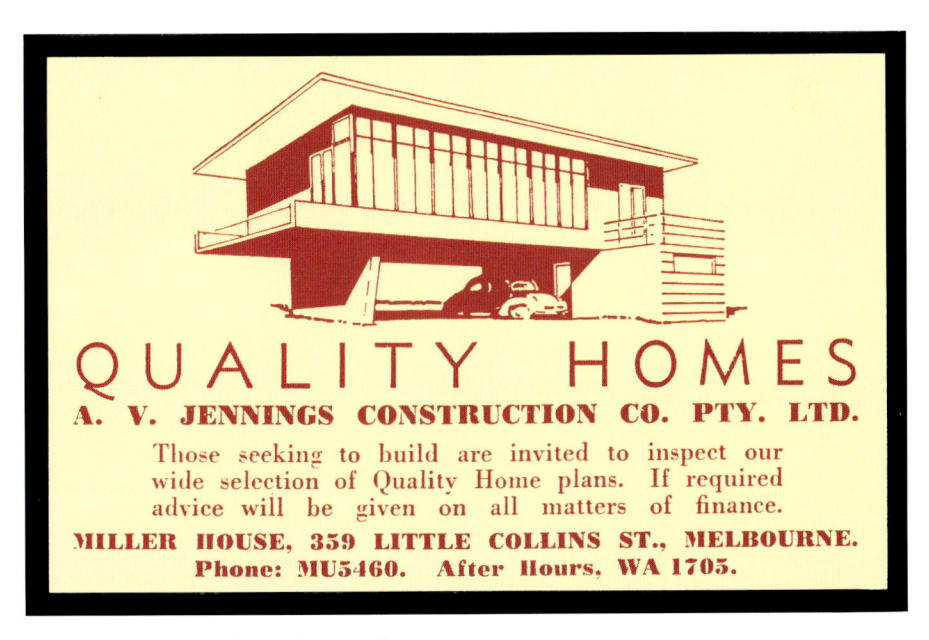

QUALITY HOMES
A. V. JENNINGS CONSTRUCTION CO. PTY. LTD.
Those seeking to build are invited to inspect our wide selection of Quality Home plans. If required advice will be given on all matters of finance.
MILLER HOUSE, 359 LITTLE COLLINS ST., MELBOURNE.
Phone: MU5460.   After Hours, WA 1705.

'Beauview Estate' in the Melbourne suburb of East Ivanhoe throughout 1941, but in early 1942 the ban on new house

• Various forms of 'Colonial', 'Cape Cod' and 'Old English' were popular in the 1940s and '50s. This design for a timber house described as 'English treatment' was offered by The State Savings Bank of Victoria in 1941.
COLLECTION: COMMONWEALTH BANK ARCHIVES, VICTORIA

TREATMENT OF ELEVATION
TIMBER CONSTRUCTION

construction within 25 miles (40 km) of the Melbourne GPO as well as restrictions on the transfer of land brought development of the estate to a halt.² As early as May 1941 wartime conditions had begun to cause shortages of building materials and dwindling sales. In that month A.V. Jennings advertised seventeen villa sites and seven business sites, all lots to include, electricity, gas, sewerage, roads, paths and crossings.³

Of the 121 residential blocks, fifty-nine houses had been completed by the beginning of 1942. They were typical of the well-built, double-brick houses constructed by Jennings over the previous decade. Beauview Estate was in a very attractive elevated area with panoramic views and a mere six-and-a-half miles (10.50 km) from the city. In 1942, with home building now at a standstill, A.V. Jennings averted complete disaster with the sale of all unsold blocks on the estate to the large Melbourne estate agency T.M. Burke.⁴ As a company Jennings actually gathered strength through the challenges offered by wartime government construction contracts, so that when it returned to housing on a large scale in the mid-1950s it was able to regain and extend its early reputation in the domestic field.

Brick houses of the type built by A.V. Jennings between 1932 and 1942 were basically conservative in their design when compared with the few examples of International Modern built at the same time. Some of the forms or details suggested the continuing popularity of 'Spanish Mission' or 'Old English', but generally, there was a tendency toward a commonsense functionalism with easily maintained surfaces, modern kitchens, hot-water services reticulated to five or six points, internal toilets and many other features taken for granted by later generations. The forty-first brick house erected on the Beauview Estate was completed in mid-1941. Beauview homes were proudly advertised as having the finest hot-water service, the latest sinks, French polished joinery, built-in wirelesses, refrigerators and brick garages. Prices varied from £1500 to £2500 ($3000 to $5000) and included the land and all services.

An example of the well-designed, solidly-built house typical of the early 1940s was featured in *Home Beautiful*'s August 1944 issue. Situated near the highest point of Balwyn Road in the Melbourne suburb of Balwyn, it was a T-shaped plan with the main bedroom projecting toward the street. Designed by Marcus Barlow, it was described by *Home Beautiful*'s Nora Cooper as follows:

... a forecast of post-war design, the house is of special interest. With its sloping tiled roof, simple whitewashed brick walls and blue-painted front door, it is a direct descendant, without being unduly stylised, of our early colonial tradition, so that this suggestion of a link with the past, and the feeling of warmth and friendliness it imports, may come as a welcome reassurance to those who fear that, after the war, we will enter on a period of bleak, mechanised mass production, unrelieved by any human charm.

Marcus Barlow, noted for his thoughtful interpretations of California Bungalow and Georgian Revival styles in the 1920s and '30s, continued to draw upon historical precedence in the 1940s.

• This 1940s interpretation of the Georgian tradition satisfied the contemporary demand for simple forms while maintaining an old world dignity. Lindsay house, Boxhall Street, Brighton, Victoria; architects, Yuncken Freeman Brothers, Griffiths & Simpson, 1946.

PHOTOGRAPH: WOLFGANG SIEVERS

His designs for low-cost housing for the Sol Green housing scheme in the Melbourne suburb of Sandringham were closely related to the Balwyn house. Officially opened in July 1945, the estate, funded by the Sol Green Trust, was created to offer returned servicemen a chance to buy modern homes at reasonable prices without interest charges.[5] Houses in this development were all given simple gable roofs with windows and other details displaying the influence of American Colonial style which had been gathering popularity for more than two decades. It is interesting to note that in the houses which were constructed between 1940 and 1945 there is clear evidence of equal popularity of the two main roof styles, that is, hipped or gabled. In addition there was a small percentage of mixed hip and gable (see opposite) and a few with flat or skillion roofs.

'Chicago-style' modern steel windows, with horizontal proportions or similar shapes in timber, were combined not only with flat roofs but also with hip or gable styles. Georgian or Old Colonial windows, usually associated with hipped roofs in earlier decades, were now more likely to be part of a New England or true Cape Cod Cottage style with plain gables. The *Australian Home Beautiful* published many photographs and drawings of new American houses in the Early American or American Colonial style, whereas Old English was now rarely seen.

In February 1941 the *Australian Home Beautiful* gave a glowing account of the recently-completed Davey house in Haverbrack Avenue in the Melbourne suburb of Malvern. It is described as being, 'somewhat reminiscent of early New England architecture in its simplicity and fineness of line, but it has none the less achieved a refreshing originality not through any attempt at innovation, but by the exercise of sound judgement in its arrangement, and intelligent appreciation of the possibilities of the site.' Two storeys and in off-white painted brick, with grey shutters and a slate roof, its first floor was given a cantilevered verandah more typical of colonial houses in Florida or Louisiana.

Many architects were committed to keeping alive the dignity and uncluttered good taste of houses which drew upon the broad tradition of Georgian architecture. Others who aspired to less conservative functionalist designs found the need to compromise when clients wanted Georgian or Colonial styles. Simplicity and quietly liveable design were already a part of the thoughtful architect's interpretations. Leslie Wilkinson and others had, by 1940, provided many fine examples which captured the essence of Georgian and Mediterranean traditions while considering modern needs and the drive to reject useless ornamentation.

An example of the Georgian sense of balance and proportion was seen in a two-storey house built circa 1941 for Mr and Mrs E. Hausa at East Malvern. Architect

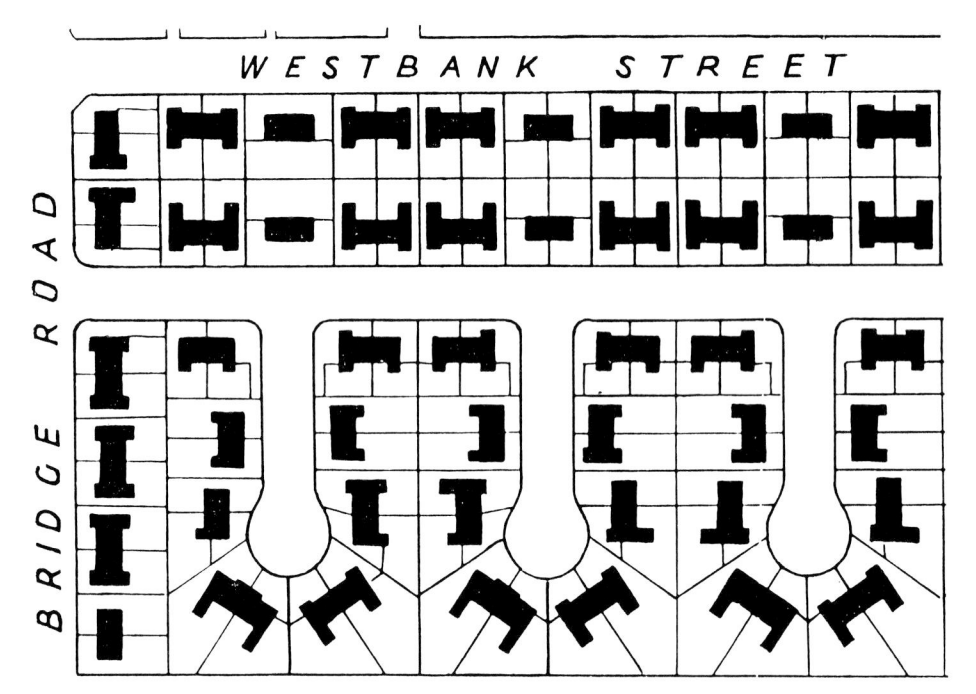

• Plan by Frank Heath for the Housing Commission Estate developed at Richmond, Victoria, from 1941. Children's playgrounds were not included; however, it was felt that ample garden space and quiet cul-de-sacs would make up for this deficiency.
Australian Home Beautiful, December 1941

• *Opposite page*: Designed by its owners Dick and Peggie Macfarlane in 1946, Loch Sloigh was built on the Golf Course Estate at Croydon, Victoria. Featured in *Australian Home Beautiful's* issue for June 1947, it was described as an ex-servicemen's 'dream' house. Dick Macfarlane was broke when he joined the army as a private, but at the end of the war he had accumulated savings and deferred pay and his wife was working. This simple Colonial-style house was home to a collection of antique furniture including Australian cedar pieces.
PHOTOGRAPH: THE AUTHOR
COURTESY: TONY AND SUE TOLEMAN

• *Opposite page, below left*: Hobart architect Esmond Dorney built this unusual steel-framed house in Churchill Avenue, Sandy Bay, in 1956.
PHOTOGRAPH: KEITH STREAMES

A. J. Ralton of Bates, Smart & McCutcheon, Melbourne, used cream-washed walls of brick, raked along every third row, a low-pitched, tiled hip roof and plain single-pane windows:

The essential simplicity of style and the arrangement of the plan made it possible to build the main portion of the house first. The very real advantage of this will be realised by homebuilders after the war, when materials will be in tremendous demand, as it means that the essentials of a high-class home can be obtained far more quickly without having to put up with eyesores or makeshifts in the meantime, and without spoiling the charm and unity of the ultimate design.[5]

Houses of this quality, a subtle blend of tasteful conservatism and modern ideals, were to be found in each state in the late 1930s and early 1940s. In scale they ranged from compact five-roomed designs constructed by private builders and housing authorities to large residences in wealthy suburbs. Traditional materials and conservative design were chosen for most low-income housing built during the war. From 1945 onwards various forces acted upon housing to cause notable changes. A panel of architects appointed by the Housing Commission of Victoria were responsible for the design and layout of 136 units on an old racecourse at Richmond, Victoria, in 1941. These houses were given external walls of brick with tiled roofs and were built in semi-detached pairs, each with their own 'block' of land.[7] Frank Heath, designer of the subdivision, chose a 'keyhole' plan with a wide road through the middle.

The Richmond group of Commission houses were designed to suit a variety of needs, from those of childless or aged couples to large families. To accommodate the latter, provision was made for weatherboard sleepouts with 'properly constructed windows'. Monotony was avoided by varying the designs of each type of house and front doors were painted in pastel colours, 'apple green, pale blue, primrose and ivory, varied by an occasional orange yellow'.[8]

South Australia's Housing Trust, founded in 1936, was at the same period committed to building low-cost housing in pairs, claiming that 'in this State the semi-detached cottage can provide the maximum reasonable standard of convenience and comfort with the minimum expenditure of materials and labour'.[9]

For three to four years, from the beginning of 1942, house building throughout Australia was limited to completing work started, the construction

FROM WARTIME TO PEACETIME •

• *Below*: This collection of Art Deco pieces is at home in a 1950s house.

PHOTOGRAPH: THE AUTHOR

59

• House designed by Hume Sherrard as 'a cottage planned for extension'.
Australian Home Beautiful, March 1944.

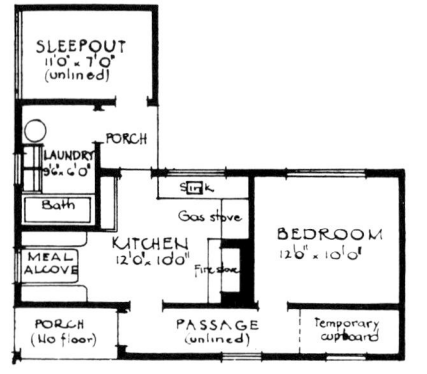

Plan and sketch of the first stage.

Plan and sketch of the cottage after extensions.

• *Opposite page*: Newly completed rental houses built at Woodville West in 1945–46 by the South Australian Housing Trust. These substantial five-roomed dwellings in pairs were described as 'an improved double unit type'.
COURTESY: SOUTH AUSTRALIAN HOUSING TRUST

of government housing and a few individual projects where permits and available materials allowed work to be done. *Home Beautiful*'s issue for March 1944 included a cottage designed to be extended at a later date. Architect Hume Sherrard had been providing readers of the magazine with plans and ideas since the 1930s. In the illustrations on this page we see his design for stages one and two of a house estimated to cost £400 ($800). It was specially designed for a young war widow whose husband had been killed while on service as a flying officer in the RAAF. She had two small children and a limited amount of capital. Materials selected were timber frame with weatherboard and galvanised iron or tiles for the roof. 'If asbestos-cement were used for walling, corrugated cement sheets might be suggested for the roof, but for the sake of appearance if nothing else tiles would be a better proposition.'[10]

Most ordinary houses built between 1940 and 1945 were of materials from the standard range which had been in use for anything from a few decades to hundreds of years. Bricks as an easily handled 'modular' building material date back thousands of years. By the late 19th century they were usually machine made. In the 1940s each region had its standard bricks for general work; the pressed imperial-size red brick made by brickworks in Victoria was typical of these. Then there were the fancy types of various colours and textures, including the popular machine-textured or 'tapestry' bricks. Overfired bricks known as 'clinkers', originally discarded, had found favour in the inter-war years and continued to be used in the '40s and '50s.

It has been noted that painted or rendered brick was widely used in the era around 1940, but there were also many houses where the brickwork is an important feature. Colours and textures were employed to give a desired effect, such as the use of string courses to enhance the modern horizontal emphasis or as trims and textures to evoke a rustic or 'olde worlde' effect. Raking each horizontal joint, or at certain intervals, was another way of achieving the fashionable horizontality. An unusual effect was created in a large brick house in Victoria where specially selected glazed bricks were used. At the base of the walls the bricks were chocolate brown and gradually shaded to a deep cream at the upper levels of the walls and the imposing entrance tower.[11]

Houses in Georgian Revival style might use bricks of a creamy-rose colour in an effort to capture something of the look of handmade bricks, although it was not until recent decades that reasonable copies of handmade bricks were mass-produced by machines. Brick houses have generally been considered desirable, with local authorities often specifying 'all brick' areas where less prestigious timber houses are not allowed. In Victoria the use of brick-veneer gave the ordinary timber-framed house an air of solid respectability. Gathering popularity through the 1930s, the brick-veneer was finally accepted by lending institutions as a legitimate system. Some local municipalities, even in the late 1930s, were holding out against allowing the brick-veneer into designated brick areas. In post-war Victoria, the triple-fronted brick veneer house was a standard symbol of comfortable suburbia.

American influence seems to have helped raise the status of weatherboard from its humble vernacular image to one of acceptable refinement. From the 1920s, Early American- or Colonial-style houses began to appear. Clad in white painted weatherboard, their 'Georgian' windows were suitably dressed with shutters painted green or blue. In February 1942, at a time when Australia's security was looking grimmer by the day, the *Home Beautiful* published photographs of three variations on a white weatherboard attic house in New York State. With elevations and plans for other variations also included, these fresh, sunny images must have provided dreamers with some respite from the darker preoccupations of war.

In the decades after the war the weatherboard suburban house continued to be a standard type and variations were seen in each state, with the exception of South Australia where a scarcity of timber

• Riley Newsum prefabricated homes being erected on the Canberra plain in the early 1950s by A.V. Jennings Construction Company (Canberra) Pty Ltd. Designed by Australian architect A.B. Armstrong, they were developed by James Riley who was on the staff at H. Newsum, Sons and Co. of Lincoln, England.
COURTESY: JENNINGS INDUSTRIES

resources had led to a tradition of building in brick and stone. Shortages of bricks caused South Australian builders to gradually adopt brick-veneer, but many low-cost timber-framed houses were given asbestos-cement cladding. For interior lining, the now universal plasterboard was established in South Australia when fibrous plaster was still a common material in other states. In the mid-1950s, fibrous plaster manufacturers were widely advertising the merits of their sheeting against other linings such as Gyprock or Victorboard, but in time they would lose that area of the market.

Stained weatherboards or vertical boards were used on a variety of houses designed by architects in the post-war era. Even if they were looking at cost-savings, there was also an appreciation of the character of the timber itself as well as the overall texture and shadow effects. On the opposite page we see a prefabricated house built by the Tasmanian Housing Department in around 1950. Its walls are vertical timbers given a creosote stain, while the gable ends are in painted weatherboard. Constructed as panels, the walls are set on concrete foundations.

Asbestos-cement (fibrous-cement) sheeting was heavily promoted from early in the century and was the only cladding material advertised in the *Australian Home Beautiful* during the years of maximum wartime restrictions. Few other building products were advertised. Australian Cement Limited suggested that readers use 'ARC' brand Geelong cement for 'essential' home repairs and small jobs. Drastic paper rationing had forced the *Australian Home Beautiful*'s print-run down to 9000 maximum for each edition and the quality of the paper down to newsprint.[12] By 1946 circulation had rapidly shot to 40 000, said to be in part due to 'the demands of house-hungry soldiers — returned, returning or still in the field'. At the peak of the housing shortage and do-it-yourself books, the magazine reached a record circulation with sales for December 1955 exceeding 100 000 copies.[13]

Mt Gambier stone was one naturally-occurring material used extensively for house construction. In Mt Gambier itself there are many examples of typical suburban house designs which use the local stone (see page 66). This light-weight, easily-worked, limestone was used in many areas of South Australia and to some extent in Victoria.

The simulation of stone was attempted in large concrete building blocks cast in moulds. In the Tasmanian example illustrated on page 64 it is interesting to observe that traditional quoins (corners) of dressed stone have been imitated, while the main surfaces suggest rusticated ashlar. Concrete building blocks of this type had been used in the United States since the late 19th century. To create a lightweight concrete block or brick, a type known as cindcrete or breeze block was developed. Crushed cinders were mixed with cement and compressed in a mould

FROM WARTIME TO PEACETIME

• Three-bedroom prefabricated house manufactured by the Agricultural Bank of Tasmania's factory in the early 1950s. Foundations for the walls were precast concrete panels fitted into precast piers.

COLLECTION: STATE OFFICES LIBRARY, HOBART, TASMANIA

• House, fence and garage all of concrete bricks, Tasmania. Traditional stone construction is imitated in the use of 'dressed quoins' to contrast with the 'rusticated blocks'.
COLLECTION: ARCHIVES OFFICE OF TASMANIA

to form these bricks. A plain concrete block with two core spaces and closed top or 'full bed' was the standard type in the 1940s and '50s. These were used for houses, sheds, garages, farm buildings, fences and retaining walls. When rendered and painted, any suggestion of cheap construction could be avoided. Sometimes they provided the base for a veneer of stone or perhaps of a better-quality brick.

Houses of concrete formed *in situ* were another important attempt to reduce costs and to develop efficient modern building techniques. In Victoria, as early as 1912, there had been an all-concrete house. This important example was built by engineer and contractor George Higgins for John Monash at Beaumaris, now one of Melbourne's bayside suburbs. Monash, a pioneer in the use of reinforced concrete in Australia, had designed the house to have foundations, floors, walls and roof in that material.[14] It was unique in its time in having the low-pitched roof of the upper storey constructed of shallowly dished slabs four feet (1200 mm) wide.

Victorian architect Leslie M. Perrot was responsible for a number of houses in reinforced concrete built in the 1920s. By the 1930s, concrete was widely accepted, particularly for designs influenced by European functionalist models. A technique called the Rose system, for casting cavity walls of reinforced concrete, was used to build houses in Victoria and New South Wales. Using a patented system of removeable and re-useable formwork, the technique was in time extended to include a suspended concrete floor slab, using modular formwork that could be extracted and re-used.[15]

Architect L. Hume Sherrard chose the Rose system for a number of houses built before the restrictions of 1942 and for others in the post-war era. An interesting example (illustrated opposite) is the Zegelin house built on a farm near Rochester, Victoria, and completed early in 1941. It is described in the *Australian Home Beautiful* issue for March 1941 as being planned 'more or less on the lines of the California farm house, adapted, of course, to local conditions'.[16] Given small-paned windows, some with shutters and a conventional tiled roof, the Zegelin house was typical of the tasteful interpretations of traditional American architecture of that period. Expectations of a fine garden to complement this country house are noted in the article and were realised in the ensuing decades.

Mr E. W. Rose believed that his patented system was especially suitable for rural homes in that it offered protection from the ravages of white ants. For the suburban house of normal dimensions, the whole of the exterior and interior walls could be poured in a single operation. In a large construction such as the Zegelin house, the walling was poured in three sections. At Goulburn, New South Wales,

FROM WARTIME TO PEACETIME •

• Two sketches of suggested designs by L. Hume Sherrard published in *Australian Home Beautiful*, September 1944.

• *Below right*: Concrete house cast *in situ* using the Rose System, Nanneella, Victoria. It was designed for K.F. Zegelin by L. Hume Sherrard in 1940 and completed early in 1941.

COURTESY: ROLF AND LORRAINE ZEGELIN

a building society sponsored the Rose system as being of benefit to their members.[17] There was some economy in its application, but it has been stated that its success was due to Mr Rose's enthusiasm to build, even on a very small margin, along with the efficiency of his hardworking team.

Among the benefits of redirection of manpower and materials to the war effort were the advances made in further development of building systems and in the greater understanding of the value of efficiency. Architects and builders, working in their areas of expertise, were confronted with the need for no-nonsense functionalism to a degree not usually found in private domestic constructions before the war. Designers of housing estates for munition workers or service personnel were required to eliminate wasteful construction and to see houses erected in as short a time as possible.[18] Such concerns led to government-funded research into improving both the quality and quantity of building materials.

The Commonwealth Experimental Building Station at North Ryde, New South Wales, investigated a whole range of concerns affecting ordinary housing in the immediate post-war years. Possible alternatives to the standard materials of that time included the study of various types of traditional earth walls, for example, mud-brick and *pise de terre*. As early as 1923, Victorian architect Archibald C. MacKnight, was writing in the *Australian Home Builder* of the value of *pise* as a building material.[19] Part of

DESIGNED FOR 50-FEET FRONTAGES

No. 3 of a Series

Architect, L. Hume Sherrard, A.R.I.B.A., Melbourne.   Australian Home Beautiful, Sept., 1944.

• AUSTRALIAN HOUSES OF THE FORTIES & FIFTIES

• *Below*: Local limestone sawn into blocks has been used in this 1950s house in Mt Gambier. The stonework of the terracing is typical of that seen in many parts of Australia.

PHOTOGRAPH: THE AUTHOR

• Post-war austerity is reflected in this version of the Beaufort 'Steel House' photographed in Canberra in 1947.

COLLECTION: NATIONAL LIBRARY OF AUSTRALIA, CANBERRA

G.F. Middleton's research for the Experimental Building Station was to travel around the country finding examples and interviewing anyone who might be able to contribute information. He went to Corowa to interview A.C. MacKnight's son Charles A. MacKnight as well as to Eltham where he discussed techniques with Justus Jorgensen, John Harcourt and Alistair Knox[20] (see Chapter 7). In 1947 G.F. Middleton's E.B.S. Bulletin No.5, *Earth Wall Construction* was published. In 1952 it was enlarged into the influential book *Building Your House of Earth* and has remained an essential reference.

In the decade following the end of the war, the subject of prefabricated housing was high on the agenda. Here, it seemed, was the ideal answer to an overwhelming shortage. Prefabricated houses had been imported since the early years of European settlement, and for many decades small-scale ventures in Australia had been producing designs to suit regional demands. A system developed by Vandyke Brothers of Punchbowl, New South Wales, and known as 'Sectionit', was brought into production during the war and continued into the post-war era. Standard wall panels three feet (914 mm) wide were sheeted both sides with asbestos-cement and could be arranged to incorporate windows and doors as required.[21]

Two prefabricated houses developed in Melbourne were opened to public view in 1946. These were the commonwealth-sponsored Beaufort steel house and the privately developed 'Myer-Ansett' house. The Beaufort house resulted from initiatives to use staff and facilities of the Beaufort Division of the Department of Aircraft Production to develop a metal prefabricated house for the Victorian Housing Commission. In common with the 'Sectionit' system, its panels were three feet wide. Victorians flocked to see the Beaufort house in Melbourne's Treasury Gardens. It was furnished by the Victorian Furnishers Association and for many seemed a satisfactory answer to an ever-increasing demand.[22] Others were critical of certain aspects. *Home Beautiful*'s Nora Cooper commented, 'No fault can be found with its construction or equipment, which are of a high order; the basic question seems to be one of planning and floor space.' It was noted that the Myer–Ansett house, recently on view at Essendon, offered 405 square feet (37.6 square metres) of living space out of a total of 864 square feet (80.2 square metres). The Beaufort's living space was a mere 215 square feet (19.9 square metres) out of a total area of 850 square feet (78.9 square metres). Only 200 houses had been built on the Beaufort system when the project was halted in 1948. A shortage of steel is given as the main reason for its demise, although Robin Boyd suggests in *Australia's Home* that the free enterprise ideals of the new Liberal government in Victoria played a role.[23] Within a short time the Myer–Ansett house project was also cancelled.

Plywood as a major component in prefabricated housing was seen as a possibility following important advances

Build On Your Land

2 BEDROOM HOMES
FROM £1990
DEPOSIT £490

"SKY-LINE"

3 BEDROOMS
FROM £2040
DEPOSIT £540

Weekly Repayments
43'10

"SEAFORTH"

Through many years of experience in the building industry we can offer you many designs at the quoted prices. "Pacemaker" illustrated.

CONTEMPORARY AND LARGER HOMES AVAILABLE AT VARIOUS PRICES.

20 x 12 GARAGES

NO DEPOSIT

EASY TERMS

"PACEMAKER"

"THE COMMONWEALTH'S LARGEST MANUFACTURER OF PREFABRICATED HOMES"

G. E. BROWN & Sons Pty. Ltd.
123 PARRAMATTA ROAD, AUBURN, N.S.W.
Phone: YX 2351

Please mail me your Illustrated Literature.
NAME (block letters)
ADDRESS (block letters)
BUILDING LOCALITY

---

made during the war in plastic bonding glues.[24] A.V. Jennings was commissioned in 1944 by the Melbourne plywood manufacturer Romcke Pty Ltd to design and construct, under a special permit, a prefabricated house which could be mass-produced. Only the prototype was built and still stands in the Melbourne suburb of Balwyn. The firm Veneer and Plywood Pty Ltd established a factory in New South Wales in 1950 to manufacture a house developed with assistance from the Commonwealth Experimental Building Station.[25]

As migration added to the already acute demand for housing in Australia, the late 1940s saw the commonwealth government searching for a means to supplement the number of houses constructed by the Australian building industry. In 1950 it sponsored a plan to import prefabricated houses from Europe. To offset the costs in freight and exchange faced by state housing authorities, the commonwealth agreed to pay a subsidy not exceeding £300 ($600) per house.[26]

More than 14 000 houses were imported under this plan, and of these 7613 units were erected under the 1945 Commonwealth and State Housing Agreement, with the balance going to state authorities concerned with public utilities such as water supply, railways and the generation of electricity. A further 4176 houses were imported by the commonwealth for the Department of Works and the Snowy Mountains Hydro-Electric Authority. Britain supplied more than half of the 18 192 houses imported, with

• *Below*: First Soldier Settler's house at Mingbool in the south-east of South Australia, completed May 1947. These farmhouses were built from recycled materials from a dismantled Royal Australian Air Force training station at Mount Gambier.

COURTESY: SOUTH AUSTRALIAN HOUSING TRUST

France, Austria, Sweden and Germany supplying the remainder.[27]

Between 1950 and 1954, the South Australian Housing Trust imported 3832 timber houses, most of which were erected in Adelaide's metropolitan area.[28] The British houses were known as the 'Cawood-Wharton' and the 'Riley Newsum'. Australian architect A.B. Armstrong designed the latter; it then was developed by James Riley who was on the staff at H. Newsum, Sons and Co. of Lincoln.[29]

Included in the South Australian importation were 500 houses from the German company Wender & Duerholt, who subsequently established an Australian subsidiary and constructed houses locally. A group of 150 German workers arrived to erect the imported houses, having answered advertisements. They paid their own fares and, although were here on temporary work permits, most stayed on as migrants.[30]

In 1950, A. V. Jennings Construction Company won a contract to erect 500 Riley Newsum houses in Canberra. This was followed late in 1951 by a second contract for 600 houses. In an interesting parallel with South Australia, the company recruited 150 German contract workers, who arrived in the first half of 1952 and were immediately sent to Canberra. The commonwealth government had advanced the fares which were to be repaid by deductions from the men's wages.[31]

From 1949, the Victorian government faced the task of housing 1000 British workers recruited for the Victorian Railways. The proposal to import British prefabricated houses for them earned the project the name 'Operation Snail'.[32] Designed by Yuncken, Freeman Brothers, Griffiths & Simpson in association with Baxter Cox & Associates of Melbourne, with contractors being Simms Sons & Cooke of Nottingham, thousands of these houses were imported. Kiln-dried Swedish whitewood was the principal timber used, with early models having asbestos-cement roofing and later models interlocking aluminium sheeting.[33] Local suppliers provided stumps, bearers and joists as well as electrical and plumbing installations, including gas or electric stove and canopy.

If critics questioned the bypassing of Australian-made prefabricated houses which used wood or steel as their primary material, at least the prefabricated concrete house was a local success story. With the establishment of the Victorian

• AUSTRALIAN HOUSES OF THE FORTIES & FIFTIES

On the Job with the Housing Commission
I. The Fowler System of Reinforced Concrete Building

• Victorian Housing Commission construction of concrete houses using the Fowler system.
Australian Home Beautiful, October 1944.

Housing Commission in 1938 an immediate concern was to find ways in which housing could be provided cheaply and efficiently. In 1939 the Commission held a competition and two of the winning entries were designed for the system developed by Thomas Walker Fowler at Werribee South, Victoria, in the 1920s and '30s.[34] Three inch (76 mm) thick concrete walls were cast on horizontal tables, complete with necessary openings. Concrete piers were set out as required and when ready the slabs were tilted up and fixed in position. After the death of T.W. Fowler in 1942 his plant was leased to a firm of builders. From 1944, the Victorian Housing Commission began its development of the Fowler system into a mechanised mass-production of components which were transported to the building site rather than being cast *in situ*.

Concrete house production at the Commission's Holmesglen factory totalled 3000 by May 1951.[35] The Commission also operated a factory at Sandringham, producing prefabricated timber houses which were completed in two sections, with each section then transported to a site on a low-loader to be joined and given finishing touches. Melbourne building contractor G. A. Winwood developed the factory in conjunction with the Housing Commission, having contracted in 1946, to deliver and erect 500 houses over a period of two or three years. Known as the 'Duplex' house, the basic form offered three bedrooms, a kitchen, lounge and bathroom within a total of 900 square feet (83.6 square metres).[36] These were plain weatherboard dwellings with shallow pitched gabled roofs and basic sash windows. Imposed austerity made these simple, functional houses mere cottages in comparison to the larger, showier suburban villas of the 1950s, but in their quiet way, they were closer to Robin Boyd's 'Victorian Type' and were equally honest.

Chapter 3 Endnotes

[1] *Monthly Review of Business Statistics*, 1938–1944. Commonwealth Bureau of Census and Statistics, Canberra.
[2] Don Garden, *Builders to the Nation. The A.V. Jennings Story*, Melbourne University Press, 1992, p. 53.
[3] Garden, p. 46.
[4] Garden, p. 54.
[5] Nora Cooper, 'New Homes for Servicemen', *Australian Home Beautiful*, September 1945, p. 19.
[6] 'Two-storied House in East Malvern', *Australian Home Beautiful*, August 1944, p. 13.
[7] 'New Homes for Old, Work of the Housing Commission (II). The Richmond Group', Nora Cooper, *Australian Home Beautiful*, December 1941, pp. 8-11.
[8] ibid., p. 9.
[9] Susan E. Marsden, *Business, Charity and Sentiment*, Wakefield Press, South Australia, 1986, p. 54.
[10] 'A Cottage Planned for Extension', *Australian Home Beautiful*, March 1944, p. 14.
[11] Nora Cooper, 'Shirwal Court: Werribee — A Very Interesting Piece of Architectural Planning', *Australian Home Beautiful*, March 1941, p. 9.
[12] *Australian Home Beautiful*, October 1962.
[13] *Australian Home Beautiful*, January, 1956, p. 4.
[14] J.M. Freeland, *Architecture in Australia: A History*, Penguin Books, Cheshire, Melbourne, 1968, Ringwood, 1972, p. 267.
[15] Recollections of architect L. Hume Sherrard in correspondence, 1992.
[16] W.A. Somerset, 'A Modern Farm House, Concrete Residence Built on the Rose System', *Australian Home Beautiful*, March 1941, p. 25.
[17] Recollections of L. Hume Sherrard, 1992.
[18] Peter Newell, 'The House in Queensland from First Settlement to 1985', thesis, 1988.
[19] A.C. MacKnight, ' The Australian Country House', *Australian Home Builder*, May 1923, p. 54.
[20] Alistair Knox, *Living in the Environment*, Mullaya Publications, Melbourne 1975, p. 10.
[21] The Portable House, *The History and Design of the Australian House*, Oxford University Press, Sydney, 1985, p. 287.
[22] 'The Steel House Steals the Show', *Australian Home Beautiful*, July 1946, p. 10.
[23] Robin Boyd, *Australia's Home*, Melbourne University Press, 1952, p. 246.
[24] Garden, p. 63.
[25] The Portable House, p. 288.
[26] *Yearbook of the Commonwealth of Australia*, no. 43, 1957, p. 630.
[27] ibid.
[28] Marsden, p. 109.
[29] The Portable House, p. 288.
[30] Marsden, p. 112.
[31] Garden, p. 104.
[32] Boyd, p. 143.
[33] The Portable House, p. 288.
[34] ibid, p. 289
[35] ibid, p. 289.
[36] W.A. Somerset, 'Victorian House Factory', *Australian Home Beautiful*, July 1947, pp. 7,8,9,51.

• AUSTRALIAN HOUSES OF THE FORTIES & FIFTIES

CHAPTER FOUR

The Post-War Housing Boom

OFTEN DESCRIBED in the post-war years as 'the housing shortage', the nationwide effort to address a very serious problem has in time come to be called 'the housing boom'. Undoubtedly it was a boom in demand and activity. There was also a notable increase in home ownership, achieved in many cases through heroic individual effort and years of sacrifice. Changing social conditions offered new opportunities, but also narrowed the options. Emphasis in state housing schemes was at first on rental accommodation; later there was a swing toward the sale of low-cost housing. At a time when various factors had reduced the amount of rental accommodation, government, banks, finance companies, building societies and housing co-operatives were offering greater opportunities for home ownership. Ironically this was paralleled by a rise in building costs.

High on the list of factors linked to rising costs were the introduction in 1948 of the 40-hour week, and steep increases in the cost of building materials. By 1948 an employer had to pay an unskilled building labourer a higher wage than a tradesman had received in early 1946.[1] To keep both labourer and tradesman productively employed the builder needed a continuous flow of materials — a rare occurrence in those times. Lack of skilled workers meant poor quality work and further loss of time. Contract prices were loaded with an increasing profit margin as an insurance against unseen contingencies. Under commonwealth price control builders were entitled to 10 per cent 'profit' on the contract price.[2] Above award payments were not recognised in the price control and yet builders often found a need to pay above award rates to ensure a reasonable output.

Unexpected costs could arise when, for example, hardwood flooring was suddenly unprocurable, and a higher price would then have to be paid for imported baltic flooring. With local cement taking forever to turn up, a batch from interstate was sometimes bought — at nearly three times the price. When compared to 1939 prices hardwood flooring had, by 1948, increased 100 per cent in price. Cement had risen by almost 20 per cent and terracotta roofing tiles by more than 25 per cent. A gallon of first-grade paint costing around 30s ($3) in 1939 had risen some 40 per cent by 1948.[3]

When added to rising costs and shortages of materials the government restrictions, limiting the area of a new house to 1200 square feet (111.48 square metres) for a timber house and 1250 square feet (116.12 square metres) for one in brick, completed the recipe for an imposed austerity. The economical plan was essential; cost-saving and limitations on area made large single-purpose rooms a luxury. Verandahs and spacious porches disappeared, reducing the shelter at the front entrance to a minimum area. Ceiling heights had been gradually reduced from the turn of the century and were now typically nine feet (2745 mm). Until the government restrictions were lifted in 1952 the acceptance of no-nonsense functionalism was as much an imposed state as it was a fashionable philosophy. For less conservative architects it brought a challenge — here was a chance to distil the house to its very essence. Applied

• Demand for housing in the years immediately after the war saw a proliferation of books of plans and 'do-it-yourself' guides.

COLLECTION: THE AUTHOR

• *Below*: Baby Boomer Geoff Hocking on the front porch.

COLLECTION: IVIE HOCKING

ornamentation, romantic stylism and any lack of honesty or logic in the use of materials were all contrary to the principles of the International style.

Two approaches could be taken during the period of post-war restrictions. The first was to build a house in stages and complete stage one within the limit of 1200 or 1250 square feet. The second was to maximise the efficiency of the small house, so that it was complete within the prescribed area. Many interesting smaller houses were built in which intelligent and imaginative design produced pleasing and practical answers to contemporary requirements. Changing notions of quality of life, or indeed families simply outgrowing a small house, have caused many important post-war designs to be altered and in some cases lost within a mass of new building.

In the 1920s typical suburban houses ranged in cost from £500 ($1000) to £1000 ($2000). At the beginning of the Second World War the average five-roomed brick house was about £1200 ($2400). By 1946 this had risen to £1800 ($2600), by 1950 £2500 ($5000) and by 1951 was in excess of £3000 ($6000). In *Australia's Home*, Robin Boyd points out that before the war people in lower income groups expected to pay two or three times their annual income for their house. For an equivalent house in 1945 they would need to pay about four times their annual income and by 1950 up to five times, and then often for an inferior product.[4]

Virtual full employment in the 1940s and '50s brought job security and that in turn engendered confidence in taking on a loan for a greater amount than was expected in earlier times. Such loans were usually on credit foncier terms, which meant they were secured by first mortgage on the house and land, or an interest in land owned by the borrower.

Lending institutions would lend from 60 to 80 per cent of the valuation of a projected house and its land, leaving the owner to find the balance of between 20 and 40 per cent. Some sources such as insurance companies and private banks would only lend 60 per cent of their valuation or twice the annual income of the applicant, if that was the lesser amount.

In reality the valuation was usually well below the real cost of the land and building, and to bridge the gap, the owner needed to raise additional capital. Many would take on a second mortgage at 10 per cent interest with the first mortgage at around 6 per cent.

The period of repayment of loans typically varied from twenty to forty-five years. Government banks in the early 1950s charged interest of 5.25 per cent per annum, with the average loan for a timber-frame house being £1500 ($3000). Loans for houses of solid construction (brick, etc.) were generally between £1750 and £2500 ($3500 and $5000). Maximum periods of repayment ranged from twenty years for a timber-frame house to thirty to forty years for one of solid construction.

• Asbestos cement wall sheeting was an economical and practical material during the period of post-war shortages. In the year 1954–55, more than half the new houses in New South Wales were clad in cement sheet. Although pictured in the 1940s the designs illustrated continued through to the 1950s.

Australian Home Beautiful, August 1941.

Under the *War Service Homes Act*, ex-servicemen could, before 1950, borrow up to 85 per cent of the valuation, with a limit of £1250 ($2500) and a maximum period of repayment of forty-five years. In 1950 the ceiling was raised to 95 per cent of valuation or £1500 ($3000), whichever was less. By the mid-1950s, ex-servicemen could borrow up to 95 per cent of the valuation to a limit of £2750 ($5500).[5]

Co-operative housing societies offered loans of up to 90 per cent of the valuation, with terms up to thirty years.[6] Some state housing schemes applied a maximum level of annual income for loan eligibility. Queensland operated two state housing schemes, one without an income limit and the other under the *Workers Homes Act* for those with a taxable income below a stated amount (£800 in the early 1950s).[7]

Tales of less-than-honest 'builders' taking people's hard-earned deposits and disappearing after making a token effort in starting work worried many prospective clients. So too did the practice of loading a fixed price contract. Even more worrying was the open-ended 'cost-plus' system where the final cost plus a profit could mean a total expenditure far in excess of the original estimate.

In 1948 it was calculated that labour accounted for more than 50 per cent of the cost of building a house.[8] Not surprisingly, people took up the challenge of building their own houses and the owner-builder became a central figure in the housing field.

Clear indication of the situation is given in the figures for houses completed

Three typical outer suburban houses of modern design and planning. In all of them cement sheeting has been used for walling, cement tiling for roof and brick for basework on concrete foundations. The ground plans show variety of arrangement, though there is little difference in the floor area. On the whole they show a vast improvement in style and finish on the average home of this class, say a decade back.

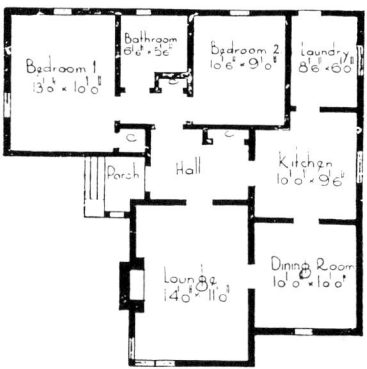

• The manufacturers of asbestos-cement sheeting offered house designs as part of their promotions.
COLLECTION: THE AUTHOR

Plan a DURABESTOS HOME
with WUNDERLICH Terra-Cotta Tile Roof

DURABESTOS (Asbestos-Cement) **External Wall Sheets Offer You:**
SOUND ECONOMY: DURABESTOS ensures Lower Initial Cost, Low Maintenance, Low Insurance.
DURABLE: DURABESTOS does not rot or deteriorate. Painting is unnecessary.
QUICK CONSTRUCTION: Readily nailed to a timber frame. DURABESTOS saves time and cost.
FIRE RETARDANT and Vermin Proof.
ATTRACTIVE Permanent Homes with DURABESTOS.
For Book of Plans write to

WUNDERLICH LIMITED 206 Hanna St., Sth. Melbourne

Compact Plan
of 1100 sq. feet. Note kitchen layout, with living rooms adjacent. Plumbing grouped.
Consult your Architect and Builder

throughout Australia in the financial year 1951–52. Contract-built houses, including the operations of government authorities, totalled 52 125. Owner-built houses totalled 25 988, of which New South Wales accounted for 11 739 and Victoria 8622.⁹ Also noted in figures for the year 1951–52, was that houses with outer walls of wood (weatherboard, etc.) were the most common type, with brick, brick-veneer, concrete or stone only marginally ahead of asbestos-cement. There was a notable decline in the construction of brick houses in New South Wales, the state with the largest percentage of owner-builder's. This would in part indicate the owner builder's preference for lower-cost, easily handled materials such as asbestos-cement.

In the *Australian Home Beautiful*'s January 1956 issue, a Wunderlich advertisement proudly states that more than half the new homes in New South Wales are of asbestos-cement. 'Of 28 176 [houses] erected in 12 months, 14 474 were asbestos-cement'.

These figures are based on the year 1954–55. The 1950–51 statistics for New South Wales show that 16 768 houses were in asbestos-cement sheet as compared to 16 316 of brick, brick-veneer, concrete or stone.

One of the interesting aspects of the boom in owner-built houses was the variety of designs around the standard plans of the era. There were also many individual 'one-off' creations, with examples here and there of rampant individualism. Typical austerity designs shared the common trends such as the combination lounge/dining room where once these were separate. Kitchens were in many examples reduced to the minimum area allowed, (80 square feet or 7.43 square metres), and often included a 'breakfast nook' with built-in table and benches. Architects had gone further, promoting the 'open plan' where the kitchen and general living area were only separated by a low serving bench.

Where husband and wife contributed equally to the planning, or in other cases where the wife had the major input in certain areas, the house was likely to reflect practical experience in daily routines. The *Australian Home Beautiful*'s Nora Cooper interviewed 'Mrs Jim Spears' for the issue of August 1947. The 1946 J. F. Spears house, as previously mentioned, was considered a model of the 'Victorian Type'. When asked if an architect's wife was allowed any say in the planning of her home, Mrs Spears replied: 'Yes — provided she can advance good reasons for her suggestions which will stand the test of criticism'.

While not disclosing the degree to which she had collaborated in their home-building venture she was happy to state that there had never been an easier home to run and that even on the coldest, wettest days every corner was bright and cheerful. Jim Spears had several ideas he sought to develop with the primary aim to see how much flexible planning could be achieved within twelve squares (111.48 square metres) with the lowest cost. The

• *Right*: Design for a house for purchase, South Australian Housing Trust, 1946. Architects James Hall and John Overall prepared several designs for the new building program which was basically aimed at meeting the demand for housing from returned servicemen.

COLLECTION: SOUTH AUSTRALIAN HOUSING TRUST

house faced almost due north and the old central passage was discarded in favour of a gallery walled in glass (see plan below). Some years before popular acceptance, the kitchen, dining and living area flowed from one to the other.

Kitchens in houses built between 1945 and 1960 varied in size from 10 ft × 8 ft (3048 mm × 2438 mm) to 16 ft × 12 ft (4876 mm × 3675 mm). Many remained enclosed as seen in the 1946 South Australian Trust house above and the Blair Smith house, seen on page 79. A folding screen divides the kitchen and dining area from the living room in design S/T 708 of 1957 from the Small Homes Service (NSW) shown on page 81. By tight compression of the space allotted to the eating area and careful planning of the sleeping quarters as a unit, this plan achieved three bedrooms in nine squares (83.6 square metres). Any feeling of being cramped in the dinette was avoided by having only a counter or 'island bench' between it and the kitchen.

Ingenuity in compact planning remained a challenge even after the lifting of the limits of 1200 and 1250 square feet in 1952, because costs remained a major concern for many people and particularly for the owner-builder.

When Blair Smith, a young clerk, set out to build a house for himself and his new bride at Warrandyte, Victoria, in 1954, they managed to fit all they required into a mere 650 square feet (60.38 square metres). Council by-laws set a minimum area, in average suburbs, of around 1200 square feet (111.48 square metres) and so approval was granted only if the planned later additions were agreed to be built as soon as conditions allowed. In this case a 24 ft × 14 ft (7315 mm × 4267 mm) extension of two storeys was included in the plan. The small first stage

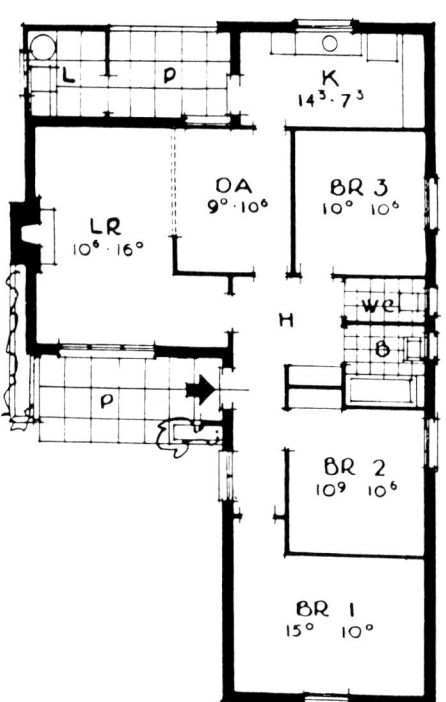

• *Left*: Flexible planning is seen in architect Jim Spears' own house built at Beaumaris, Victoria, in 1946.

Australian Home Beautiful, August 1947

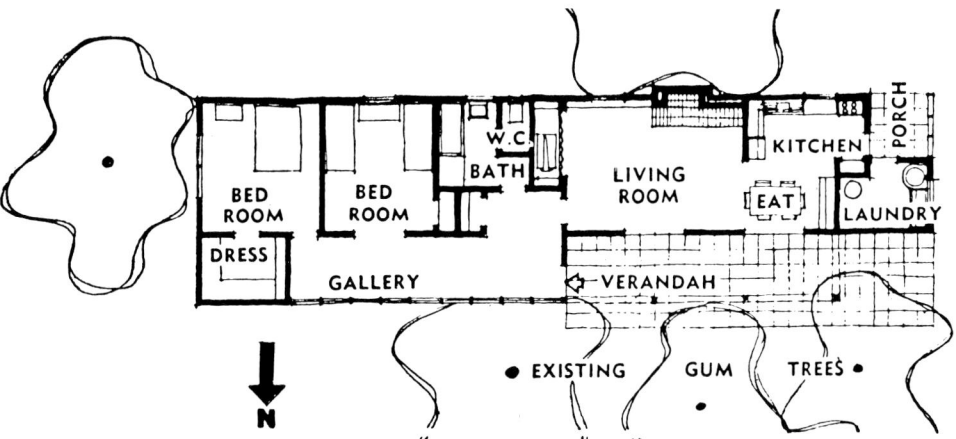

• Pioneer conditions such as seen in this building site in Queensland were familiar in many parts of Australia in the post-war years.

COLLECTION: JOHN OXLEY LIBRARY, BRISBANE

enabled payment for materials over the period of twenty months taken for its completion.[10]

Home magazines had provided the ideas for the Blair Smith House with a how-to-build manual used to calculate the materials needed and appropriate building techniques. Houses being built by professional builders nearby offered answers whenever Mr Smith struck a snag. By the time he got home from work each day the builders had left and he was free to look over their work. By far the hardest job was laying the 2500 bricks which went into the fireplace and large chimney. 'It isn't by any means perfect bricklaying, but it looks quite good and works perfectly'.[11] In all, it was a basically well-constructed and perfectly liveable house.

The *Australian Home Beautiful* certainly agreed that it was a good example of the owner-builder's work; for it was one of two such houses chosen to answer criticisms made by a Western Australian builder's wife who wrote to the magazine complaining that too much encouragement was being given to owner-builders. 'I contend that it is virtually impossible for, say, a shop assistant to expect to build a house of his own that will not have a sagging roof or ceiling, uneven floors, incorrectly hung windows and doors, ragged guttering, and many other faults that a good builder avoids.' She felt that in ten years the 'ever-increasing multitude of "jerry-built" houses, having lost their fresh paint will look cheap and nasty'.

THE POST-WAR HOUSING BOOM

• Plan, 1954, Blair Smith house. *Australian Home Beautiful,* December, 1955

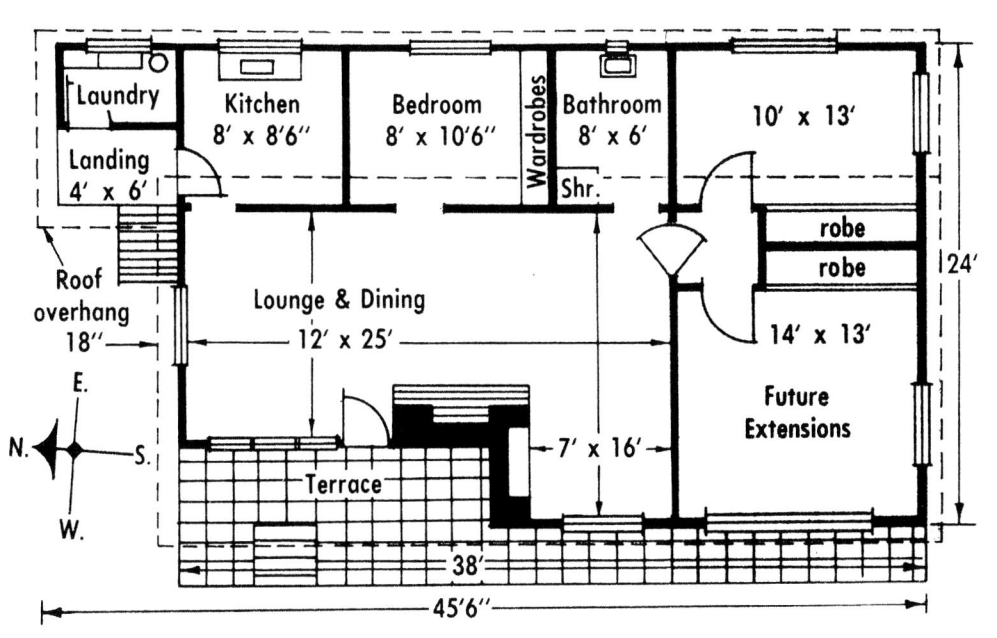

• *Below left*: Fixing the plate to lock prefabricated sections in position, Goodwood subdivision, Tasmania, c. 1947.
COLLECTION: STATE OFFICES LIBRARY, HOBART, TASMANIA

• *Below right*: Erecting prefabricated panel, Tasmanian government housing, c. 1947.
COLLECTION: STATE OFFICES LIBRARY, HOBART, TASMANIA

She ends her letter by saying, 'There *are* still architects and builders who will give an honest price for a good job, and it will be cheaper in the long run, for they will not be facing big repair bills in a short time'. The *Australian Home Beautiful*, confident of their readership, headed their article, '140,000 houses answer this letter!' Offering the two examples, the editorial noted, 'Behind these two are scores of thousands of other Australians with similar achievements. The Commonwealth Statistician reports that, between 1/7/51 and 31/3/55, owner-builders completed 140 000 homes — more than one in three of all homes built in that time.'

Optimism and enterprise were valuable commodities for those who dreamed of their own home but were short of funds. An outstanding and quite successful co-operative building organisation founded in South Australia in 1945 was responsible for the construction of more than 300 houses over a fourteen-year period. As a legally incorporated body, the South Australian Home Builders Club required each member to sign an agreement that he would repay, with his own labour, the number of man-hours put into his own house by other members.[12]

The club began when owner-builder Mr W. Ellenby gained publicity for his low-cost house at Belair in the Adelaide Hills. George Palmer, an Adelaide bread-carter, was one of hundreds who inspected the house. It inspired him to call a meeting of people interested in building their own houses. About 350 attended, mainly ex-servicemen, and by October 1945 a constitution and rules were drawn up.[13] Members came from all walks of life, but there was a special allowance for those skilled in building trades. They received extra time, usually about two hours per day from the other workers.[14] Experienced leaders were in charge of club

79

AUSTRALIAN HOUSES OF THE FORTIES & FIFTIES

• Typical bathroom in the austerity era of the immediate post-war years. The 'chip' heater at the end of the bath was a common feature.
COLLECTION: SOUTH AUSTRALIAN HOUSING TRUST

• *Opposite*: Joiners shop, Agricultural Bank of Tasmania's factory. In 1954 this facility went to the Housing Department as the Prince of Wales Bay factory.
COLLECTION: STATE OFFICES LIBRARY, HOBART, TASMANIA

• *Opposite below*: Plan and perspective for S/T 708, Small Home Service (NSW).
Australian Home Beautiful, July 1957

management and, in turn, controlled their own sections — labour, plans, foundations, bricklaying, carpentry, electrical installations, plastering and plumbing.

Similar clubs were later formed at Loxton, South Australia, Launceston, Tasmania, and in Perth, Western Australia. At Port Pirie, the Broken Hill Associated Smelters sponsored a co-operative home-building club. Its activities were featured in the *Australian Women's Weekly* issue for March 1951.[15] Of particular interest was the contribution of women who, in many cases, worked alongside men making concrete bricks, carting materials and being directly involved with construction.

Houses of all kinds, in all types of materials and built by a variety of means from the efforts of the owner-builder to the various professional contractors, shared basic characteristics due to regulations and current ideals. One clearly definable trend in the period 1945 to 1960 was the combining of the living or lounge room and the dining room. From the 1920s through to the 1940s, a typical suburban house would have a living room of around 16 ft × 12 ft (4876 mm × 3657 mm). If it had a separate dining room that would usually be 12 ft × 10 ft (4876 mm × 3657 mm); if not, the kitchen was usually around that size and accommodated a table and chairs. Houses in the 1950s increasingly offered a living room of from 20 ft × 12 ft (6096 mm × 3657 mm) up to 25 ft × 15 ft (7620 mm × 4572 mm) with a dining area in one portion. Some designs included a dining room which opened directly into a large living area.

Master bedrooms varied in size from 12 ft × 10 ft (3657 mm × 3048 mm) to 16 ft by 12 ft (4876 mm × 3657 mm). Typically they were around 14 ft × 12 ft (4267 mm × 3657 mm). Second and third bedrooms were generally slightly smaller. In the many compact plans the bathroom would have only a handbasin and shower recess. The bath, a hard-won luxury in earlier times, held its place in most schemes, even if the bathroom was as a mere 6 ft × 5 ft (30 square feet or 2.78 square metres). An average bathroom offered 42 square feet (3.9 square metres). Large, well-appointed bathrooms of the pre-war years already included a built-in bath and separate shower as well as a handbasin and matching toilet. Walls and shower partitions were tiled, usually to the height of the top of the door. In the 1940s and '50s, average houses might have a bath and separate shower, although bathroom, shower recess and toilet were given individual access in many designs. If tiles were unprocurable or beyond the budget various pressed sheets in tile patterns were available, some to be painted and others pre-finished in a range of colours. Sheets were also offered in decorative patterns.

• BUILDING MATERIALS •

Often recalled as a time when the range of building and associated materials expanded rapidly, the post-war years without doubt witnessed lively competition in products such as wall cladding, roofing materials, paving, flooring materials, paints, fabrics and plastic laminates. New types of doors and windows, fashionable lighting, more efficient room heaters and a plethora of patent fittings vied for space in newspapers, magazines and journals. Well to the fore were the paint companies, dazzling the public with new colours, new

By tight compression in the sleeping and eating quarters this small home achieves...

3 BEDROOMS in 9 SQUARES

S/T 708

SLEEPING space in this well-thought-out house is sufficient, if not spacious, and the solution of the three bedroom problem in a house of this size makes it an economical home to build.

Sleeping area is a separate unit from the rest of the house, making it a very workable home for a couple with a young family.

Living room is well proportioned, and privacy is planned with a folding screen, which can shut the room off from the rest of the house. Eating space is minimum, but provision of a counter top between the kitchen and dinette does away with any cramped feeling.

The house is suitable for a 50ft. frontage block, on which it would face either the front or the side.

LOW-COST PLAN SERVICE

All the blueprints, other drawings and documents for the erection of any home illustrated each month in this section of Home Beautiful are available for £10/10/- from the Small Homes Service (N.S.W.). Plans may be modified to suit readers' requirements by special arrangement. Readers are invited to discuss their home-planning problems with the Small Homes Service Bureau, on the 5th Floor of David Jones Ltd. store, corner George and Barrack Streets, Sydney, or Box 4360, G.P.O., Sydney.

The service is jointly sponsored by Home Beautiful and the N.S.W. Chapter of the Royal Australian Institute of Architects. From the plans submitted by hundreds of leading architects in N.S.W., an expert committee admits only those approved for appearance, sound design and economy in construction. This is the only plans service backed and conducted by the Institute in N.S.W.

Three folders, each of 28 home plans, are available from the Service for 2/9 each, post free.

• *Right*: Vertical boarding seen in this house which was recently completed when photographed in 1956, plays an important role by adding visual texture to the crisp geometry of the structure. Marshall Gibson house Beaumaris, Victoria; architects, Yuncken Freeman Brothers, Griffiths & Simpson.

PHOTOGRAPH: WOLFGANG SIEVERS

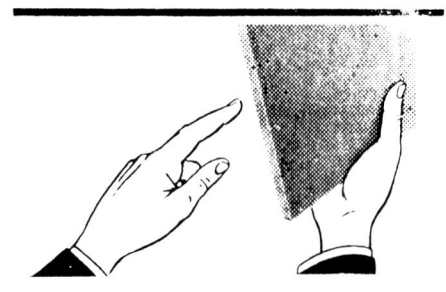

This is the HALF-INCH that keeps Heat OUT in Summer Cold OUT in Winter

CANE-ITE Insulating Board

Manufactured by
THE COLONIAL SUGAR REFINING CO. LTD.
Building Materials Division

Also marketing GYPROCK, ASBESTOS, PLASTER PRODUCTS

• Advertisement 1949.
COLLECTION: THE AUTHOR

formulas and promises of miraculous results.

Asbestos-cement sheeting had been consolidating its place in the market since early in the century. 'Durasbestos' from Wunderlich and 'Fibrolite' from James Hardie dominated the field in the post-war era. Durasbestos and Fibrolite flat sheets were used for exterior and interior walls and ceilings, with corrugated sheets and flat tiles for roofs. Softening the box-like effect of an average-sized house was achieved by using curved sheets on 'waterfall' corners, a favourite device in grander schemes from the 1930s. The fashionable horizontality was enhanced by cover straps of asbestos-cement or painted timber. Painted asbestos-cement sheet was popular in New South Wales and a number of special paints were marketed.

Decorated asbestos-cement wall sheeting such as 'Duradec' by Wunderlich was plastic-surfaced, making it suitable for kitchens and bathrooms and laundries. In April 1957, James Hardie introduced 'Striated' wall panels for interior and exterior use, and in October 1958, its 'Shadowline' for exterior walls. Architects found that wide-gauge corrugated asbestos-cement roofing sheets offered a bold look when compared to the smaller standard gauge which was too close to the humble 'corrugated iron' (galvanised steel). Hardie's 'New Contour' corrugated roofing sheets were advertised in the mid-1950s as suiting both contemporary and traditional styles.

Various forms of compressed fibre boards were found ideal for post-war home building. 'Masonite' and 'Cane-ite' were in use before the war, the latter made from sugar cane fibres and the former from wood fibre. Masonite was developed in the United States in the 1920s and took its name from its inventor, a Mr Mason.[16] In the 1930s, suitable forest timber was found in Queensland and the

THE POST-WAR HOUSING BOOM

• Boards made from compressed fibre were practical and easily worked. Made in various thicknesses as well as a range of textures or patterns, they were widely used in post-war housing.

COLLECTION: THE AUTHOR

manufacture of Masonite in Australia began. Demand by defence industries used up the output during the war and it remained a scarce product even in the late '40s. My father went searching for wall-board in 1949 and managed to locate a crate of European hardboard for which he paid £22 10s, at that time more than two weeks' wages.

'Cane-ite', made by the Colonial Sugar Refining Company, was a softer board with the half-inch thickness as the standard for interior walls and ceilings. In the post-war era it was widely used and particularly suited the owner-builder for its ease of handling. In natural or 'ivory' finish, Cane-ite proved ideal for insulating against both temperature changes and noise. Heavier thicknesses were used for a variety of purposes and there was also the three-quarter-inch 'acousti-tile'. The Colonial Sugar Refining Company also made 'Timbrock' hardboard. The half-inch thick version was used for built-in cupboards and furniture. When supplies of Cane-ite were not able to meet the demand in the 1940s, similar sheets such as 'Finnboard' were imported from Europe.

Plywood had been a favourite lining board in the inter-war years and was promoted by its manufacturers in the late 1950s in an effort to regain areas of the market lost to other boards. The richly grained, highly polished look of the 1930s and early 1940s was changing to a satin or matt finish. 'Graindek' pre-finished plywood panels were advertised in 1960 as ideal for feature walls.[17] Synthetic resin

Children's Room of 1946

While you're on the job, why not modernise that fireplace? Utility, beauty and Masonite are the keynotes of the success of the design shown at right. No more nightly trips between woodshed and fire with the Masonite fuel cupboard. Just open the doors — there's wood on the shelf, coal or coke in the pull-out bins.

By the way: Although Masonite can be effectively worked with ordinary carpenters' tools, a really "super" job is possible if you use the special tools available from your Masonite stockist. Ask about them.

MASONITE CORPORATION (AUST.) LTD.
SALES AND SERVICE DIVISION:
369 Pitt Street, Sydney; 529 Collins Street, Melbourne; 337 Queen Street, Brisbane; 31 Chesser Street, Adelaide.

Beauty and Utility— with MASONITE

Here is a solution to your space problems where two children must share the same room. With Masonite Tempered Presdwood, and the skill of an ordinary handyman, you can construct the attractive, double-decker bunks illustrated at left. The homework desk, with its useful cupboard, is another boon to any space-starved home.

Priority demands are such that Masonite is in very short supply for general needs . . . BUT keep in touch from time to time with your nearest stockist.

MA71-46

Streamlining the Fireside

83

• Perched on a steep bank above the Yarra River in the Melbourne suburb of Kew, Peter McIntyre's River House, (1955), was given wall panels of painted 'Stramit' (see chapter 5).
PHOTOGRAPH: WOLFGANG SIEVERS

glues, in particular those developed during the war, led to plywoods which could be used for exterior walling. When impregnated with oil, compressed hardboards such as Masonite 'Tempered Presdwood' and later tempered Burnie Board were similarly used.

For both interior and exterior walls, solid timber was another material challenged by manufactured surfaces. The traditional interior lining board had continued to be used with the V-jointed 'regency board', stained or clear-finished, having an appeal to those who valued its natural character and hard-wearing solidity. By the late 1950s the timber industry had released a range of moulded lining boards seen as especially suited to feature walls, for room-dividers, or for panels beneath breakfast or cocktail bars. They were available in softwoods and hardwoods and in various patterns. All these boards were applied vertically and when sealed with a clear polyurethane would be less inclined to hold dust.

Insulating materials of all kinds have been used in Australian houses since early settlement, but it was not until the 1940s and '50s that standard types were widely marketed for use in average houses. Rock-fibre under the trade name 'Insulwool' was advertised in the *Australian Home Beautiful* from March 1944. In 1946 it was used in the prefabricated Beaufort house and in the same period architects were finding it ideal for low-pitched roofs where the lining was fixed to the rafters. Cane-ite's insulating qualities were by then widely appreciated.

• Pre-cut houses were very popular in the post-war era. Advertisement of 1957, F.C. Barlow & Co. Auburn, NSW.
COLLECTION: THE AUTHOR

BUILD ON YOUR LAND
YOUR OWN PLAN OR SELECT ONE OF OUR NUMEROUS ATTRACTIVE DESIGNS

ANYWHERE IN N.S.W.

FINANCE AVAILABLE

Completed In **4** Weeks

CARTAGE EXTRA TO COUNTRY AREAS

This Weatherboard Cottage **£2445**
INCLUDING:
P.C. ITEMS,
HOT WATER SERVICE,
FIBROUS PLASTER,
TILED ROOF,
COMPLETE PAINTING.

THIS SPACIOUS, TWO BEDROOM HOME CAN BE COMPLETELY ERECTED ON YOUR LAND FOR A DEPOSIT OF

£200 – REPAYMENTS **75/-** WEEKLY – **5** p.c. INTEREST

GARAGES (ALL SIZES) NO DEPOSIT

F. C. BARLOW & CO.

Building papers such as 'Sisalkraft' and 'Jutex', made from kraft paper bonded to hessian with plastic bitumen, were a form of insulation as well as being ideal as a weatherproof underlay in roofs (sarking) and for walls. Sisalkraft, foil sisalation, introduced in the mid-1950s added the ability to reflect radiant heat and, in time, became a standard material in domestic construction. 'Stramit', a building sheet rigid enough to support its own weight and of high insulating ability, was beginning to attract interest in the early 1950s. Made of compacted straw in two inch (50 mm) thick slabs, it was found to be ideal for ceilings, internal divisions and even as roofing when coated with a bitumenised material.

Competition in the market for hardwearing and yet decorative floor surfaces provided architects, builders and homemakers with an ever-growing catalogue of possibilities. Masonite Tempered Presdwood was promoted as a floor covering in a tile or crazy-paving pattern. Various timbers, stained and sealed, or simply sealed, remained popular as did parquetry for high-quality floors. In 1954, the clear plastic or polyurethane coating, Estapol, an Australian product, was first marketed. British-Bourne entered the field in the same period.

Linoleum had been used for almost a century, with a wide range of patterns available in the pre-war era. Improved forms with fashionable colours and patterns maintained its appeal after the war. From the 1930s Linoleum was increasingly challenged by rubber flooring in both tile and roll form. With a wide range of colours, rubber was ideal for kitchens, bathrooms, laundries and various utility areas. Cork flooring, some colour-impregnated, began its rise to popularity in the 1950s.

Ceramic tiles have been used over thousands of years. The variety of shapes, sizes, colours and decorative patterns available in the post-war years dramatically improved, with tiles for both floors and walls catching the mood of the times. The range of colours in baths, shower bases, handbasins and toilet suites also increased. Kitchen sinks made of acrylic were offered in four colours plus

• *Left*: Neat front fence of pickets with capping. Well-kept paintwork reflects pride and prosperity.

• *Opposite*: The 1954 Brunt House at Kew, Victoria, by Peter McIntyre, was a startling essay in modernist geometry. Triangular sunscreens cast everchanging shadows on walls of white and dark plum. Other colours included golden yellow, Burmese red, rich blue and citron.
PHOTOGRAPH: WOLFGANG SIEVERS

white and cream in the late 1940s, and the range soon increased to seven colours, along with black and white.

Terrazzo flooring was favoured for good-quality bathrooms in the inter-war period and continued to hold a special place in the market. Terrazzo tiles were advertised as a newly-available product in 1959.[18] Vinyl floor tiles became a familiar competitor, with other flooring materials in the latter part of the 1950s. Nylex 'Super-Vinyl' tiles were advertised in 1958 as having 'seventeen glorious colours ranging from pool-cool pastels to vibrant full-strength tones'.[19] As post-war shortages eased and production reached levels where competition in the market was an important concern, the colour range for many products was an essential selling point. Venetian blinds, carpets and rugs, furnishing fabrics, lampshades, tiles, paints, and decorative adhesive plastic sheet, such as 'Con-Tact', were offered in popular colours or patterns.

Plastic laminates under the trade names 'Laminex' and 'Formica' eventually came to symbolise the post-war era — they were bright, 'easy-care' materials, epitomising modernity. In July 1947, Norman Scott wrote in *Home Beautiful*:

One of the most interesting new materials that has made its appearance lately is Laminex, a plastic material that is available in sheets to cover table tops, walls, counters, etc. It is made in a variety of bright colours which are guaranteed fadeless, and also with grain that cannot be distinguished from fine timber.

At that time it had been available in Australia for only a short while, having begun its rise to popularity in the United States from mid-1946.

Linoleum was soon superseded for table and bench tops and ceramic tiles were rivalled in many areas. General advertising of popular new patterns in plastic laminates increased from 1955 when 'two-tone' designs were released.[20] By 1957, both Laminex and Formica were being advertised as available in more than fifty designs and colours. Patterns, weaves and new woodgrains all competed for attention.

Household paints have a long and interesting history, with the pre-mixed commercial brands coming to dominate the domestic market from the inter-war years. The war accelerated technical development in many areas including paints, but also had the immediate effect of limiting supplies of the traditional ingredients, linseed oil and various pigments. In 1947 manufacturers were still restricted to a basic range and stocks were low. The old standby, Kalsomine, a powdered paint mixed with water, was a low-cost substitute for the scarce and expensive oil-based interior paints as well as for the less expensive casein-bound types. The big news was the advent of water-soluble paints, used in the United States. They were able to cover all surfaces, dried to a flat finish and were washable. These new synthetic emulsion or 'plastic' paints reached Australia in various forms from 1948 to 1955. Full gloss exterior paint with a styrene base was released here by Berger in 1952. 'Mural-tone', the matt finish, washable interior paint, was available from the late 1940s and this was joined by 'Kem-tone', again in 1952. Dulux 'Super-Satin' and 'Super Matt' followed in 1953. In 1955, 'Spred Satin' by Glazebrooks entered an increasingly competitive market. It was advertised as having a synthetic rubber

87

• The Melbourne suburb of Balwyn was a favoured area for development in the post-war era. This photograph was taken in 1959.
COLLECTION: NATIONAL LIBRARY OF AUSTRALIA

base and claimed to have been the biggest selling paint in America since 1949.[21]

Synthetic alkyd enamels were the ideal modern paints, fast-drying, washable, and with a consistency which reduced drips and often covered a surface adequately with a single coat. In the mid-1950s the familiar paint roller appeared in Australia. Eventually it rivalled and, in some uses, even eclipsed the traditional paint brush. If average homemakers were attracted to the range of colours and easy application of the new paints, the more adventurous architects used them to great effect. The 1954 Brunt house in Kew, Victoria, by Peter McIntyre, was a striking two-storey geometrical design where the use of colour was essential to the whole scheme.

'Throughout the house the changes are rung on dark plum, Burmese red, a deep, vital green, citron, golden yellow, and rich blue.'[22]

Many people found the new corrugated fibre-glass panels offered interesting possibilities as wall panels, screens and roofing. They were available in a variety of colours in corrugated, crinkle-corrugated and one-inch ripple panels. While natural light was often limited in older houses, modern functionalist ideals saw it as an essential element to be maximised wherever possible. Aluminium, steel and wood-framed windows, in a host of shapes and sizes, were available in the post-war years. Window-walls were the ultimate, with different types of ventilation windows including casements, balanced sashes, horizontal sliding sashes, awnings or hoppers and the ubiquitous louvres. The latter in their common use were seen as the handyman's dream, because they could be fitted so easily.

Roofing materials in the period from 1945 to 1960 were not notably different from those available in the inter-war years. Marseilles-pattern tiles continued to be used for conservative designs, asbestos-cement competed with corrugated galvanised steel sheet and aluminium, while various surfaces were used for flat or low-pitched roofs. Malthoid, Jutex and other pliable bituminous materials were applied to roofs of concrete, timber or Stramit. Mastic asphalt applied hot in two layers was poured onto a base of felt previously laid down over concrete or boarding. To offset the action of the summer sun, light-insulating blocks could be laid on a cement grout over the asphalt.[23] Flat galvanised steel sheet, aluminium and in some cases copper or muntz metal was also used for flat or low-pitched roofs.

Weatherboard and asbestos-cement may have found wide acceptance as exterior wall-cladding in the post-war years, but brick continued to represent, in many people's minds, a respectable solidity not easily set aside. In 1946, brick production was still only 40 525 000 a month for the whole of Australia — in 1939 the rate had been more than 60 million. Slow recovery was claimed to be, in part, due to the reluctance of returned servicemen to work in the brick industry.[24]

• *Right*: Wunderlich Limited had been producing and promoting asbestos cement sheeting since early in the century as well as manufacturing terracotta roof tiles.

Australian Home Beautiful, January 1947

Plan a DURABESTOS Home with Wunderlich Terra Cotta Tile Roof
DURABESTOS (Asbestos Cement) sheets save time and cost during erection. A modern, permanent home of low maintenance cost is assured with DURABESTOS Wunderlich Limited does not erect Homes.

WUNDERLICH LIMITED 206 Hanna St., Sth. Melb.

Coal shortages and limitations on investment also affected production in the immediate post-war years. Shortages of clay bricks encouraged production of cement bricks and calcium silicate or sand-lime bricks. Silicon-cement bricks were not new in Australia, having been produced as early as 1914.[25] From 1946, they were used in increasing numbers and bricklayers were finding they needed to adapt to these accurately-formed, sharp-edged bricks which dried mortar rapidly and clearly showed any irregularity in a wall.[26] When compared with ordinary bricks they seemed sterile. The fashionable cream clay bricks at least offered some subtle variation in colour and texture.

Despite the effects of periods of recession in the 1950s, the years from 1945 to 1960 saw a great upswing in building activity, overall. By 1960 things seemed less frenetic and more ordered. Supplies of materials were abreast of current demand, and enterprising companies expanding their horizons through the development of newer technologies offered exciting materials for the coming decades. As post-war restrictions became a fading memory, domestic architecture could expand and unfold. Conservatism remained entrenched in many places, ostentation was finding new life in fashionable boulevards, and the crop of young post-war architects were well in their stride, creating thoughtful living spaces.

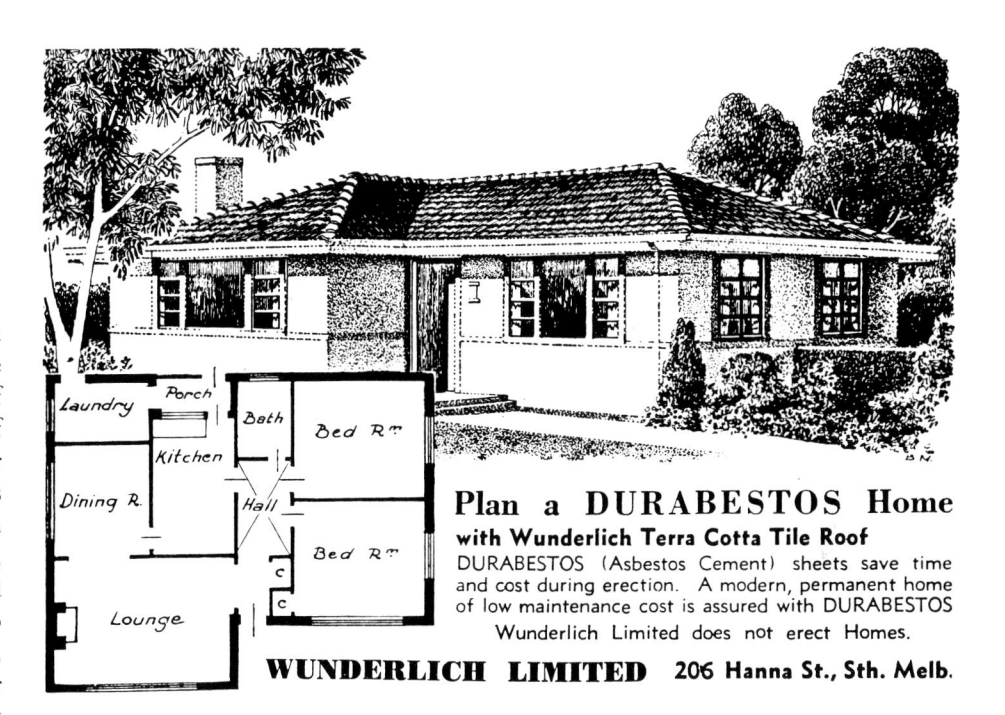

Chapter 4 Endnotes

[1] Laurie Whitehead, 'Why New Houses Cost So Much', *Australian Home Beautiful*,' September 1948, p. 15.
[2] ibid.
[3] ibid.
[4] Robin Boyd, *Australia's Home*, Melbourne University Press, 1952, pp. 102-103.
[5] *Yearbook of the Commonwealth of Australia*, no. 43, 1957, p. 635.
[6] Boyd, p. 262.
[7] *Yearbook of the Commonwealth of Australia*, no. 43, 1957, p. 631.
[8] Whitehead, p. 16.
[9] *Yearbook of the Commonwealth of Australia*, no. 43, 1957, p. 638.
[10] Wynne Scott, 'A Real Home Built Without Debt', *Australian Home Beautiful*, December 1955, pp. 16-19.
[11] Scott, p. 18.
[12] John Sweeny, 'They Build for Each Other', *Australian Home Beautiful*, April 1950, pp. 15, 18, 77.
[13] ibid.
[14] George Palmer, 1983 interview in *Building a Nation*, John Archer, Collins Australia, Sydney, 1987.
[15] *Australian Women's Weekly*, March 1951, p. 27.
[16] Norman J. Scott, 'Home Building Materials', *Australian Home Beautiful*, September 1946, p. 31.
[17] *Australian Home Beautiful*, June 1960, p. 89.
[18] *Australian House and Garden*, July 1959, p. 14.
[19] *Australian Home Beautiful*, November 1958, p. 105.
[20] ibid, August 1955, pp. 3, 7.
[21] ibid, June 1955, p. 59.
[22] Joan Leyser 'Two Unusual Houses', *Australian Home Beautiful*, January 1956, p. 55.
[23] W. Watson Sharp, *Australian Methods of Building Construction*, Angus & Robertson, Sydney, 1946, p. 233.
[24] *Australian Home Beautiful*, December 1946, p. 50.
[25] Bryce Moore, *From the ground up. Bristile, Whittakers and Metro Brick in Western Australian History*, University of Western Australia Press, Perth, 1987, p. 193.
[26] J.M. Freeland, *Architecture in Australia: A History*, Penguin Books, Victoria, 1972, p. 67.

AUSTRALIAN HOUSES OF THE FORTIES & FIFTIES

• One of the important and yet little-known modernist houses of the 1950s was designed for Mr and Mrs Bruce Benjamin of Canberra by Czechoslovakian architect Alex Jelinek. Situated in Gawler Crescent, Deakin, this highly individual work was awarded House of the Year for 1957. Other finalists included Harry Seidler, Robin Boyd, John Dalton, Sydney Ancher, Peter Muller and Stuart McIntosh. Furniture for the house was made by Austrian-trained cabinet-maker Schulim Krimper (see page 183).

PHOTOGRAPH: WOLFGANG SIEVERS

CHAPTER FIVE
Architects and their Work

THOSE FIFTEEN YEARS from the end of the war to 1960 can be seen as an era when many of Australia's architects fervently challenged conventional attitudes. Wars have an awesome power to change ordinary lives as well as national and community directions. They demand rapid development in certain areas, reorganisation of the workforce and a rethinking of ideas and values. Traditionally, the tragic losses and sheer waste of resources brought about by war generate a renewed focus on the values of home, family, friends and community. The clutter of peripheral concerns are stripped away, revealing the fundamental truths of what really matters — being alive in a peaceful, thoughtful community which is at least searching for ways to improve the human condition.

Architects shared with idealists in many other fields the belief in a new order; an opportunity to carry through many of the philosophies which found form in the era of reconstruction in Europe after the First World War. Modern international architecture had begun its journey toward a wider acceptance in Australia in the 1930s, only to be pushed aside by the Second World War. With a flood of aspiring young architects into universities and colleges at the end of the war there was a whole new generation to join those whose work or study had been interrupted. In spite of being hobbled by restrictions, shortages of materials and skilled labour, the architectural profession played a vital role in creating a new Australia.

With hindsight we can see that the period under review was an important time of experimentation when theories were tested, ideas shaped and reshaped, and the essential foundations were created for the mature Australia of the late 20th century. If there was a central question or concern for architects it was one of balancing an acceptance of the international aesthetic with the logic of a regional integrity. This was not a new exploration — earlier in the century other architects in Australia had searched for cultural and environmental relevance while maintaining an awareness of progress in the wider world. A European society, basically on the periphery of a dry continent in the lower reaches of South-east Asia, represents a curious

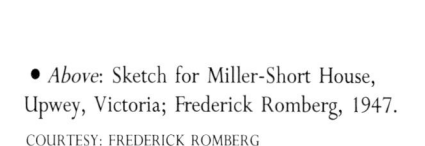

• *Above*: Sketch for Miller-Short House, Upwey, Victoria; Frederick Romberg, 1947.
COURTESY: FREDERICK ROMBERG

• AUSTRALIAN HOUSES OF THE FORTIES & FIFTIES

• *Left*: Givoni House, Wallace Avenue, Toorak, Victoria, architect Roy Grounds 1956.
PHOTOGRAPH: WOLFGANG SIEVERS.

• *Opposite page*: Kotzman house, Alexandra Road, East Ringwood, Victoria. Designed by Melbourne architect Douglas Alexandra in 1951, it was completed in the following year.
PHOTOGRAPH: WOLFGANG SIEVERS

search for identity. This quest continues to engage the nation's thinkers and image-makers.

In an expanded and increasingly competitive profession architects needed a clear focus if they were to avoid being caught up in the confusion of ideologies. Choosing a path less travelled was difficult in an era of vibrant fashions, technological wizardry or the passionate devotion to a particular creed. Houses designed by architects may be only a small proportion of dwellings built in Australia in the 1940s and '50s, but undoubtedly they represent a wide range of ideas, solutions, influences and directions. A summary of the readily identified influences is essential to understand why one house subtly blends with its surroundings while another proclaims itself in shimmering white geometry.

One of the important principles espoused by groups of architects, designers, engineers and craftspeople in the 19th century was the aesthetic and practical good sense in avoiding unnecessary ornamentation. Bridges, buildings, furniture, household utensils and a host of other utilitarian objects were made to simply state their purpose in a manner which was later summarised in the phrase, 'form follows function'. In Europe after the First World War the focus for design reform was on the Bauhaus, an educational institution which existed in Germany from 1919 to 1933. Students received a comprehensive training at the beginning of their studies and then, applying design theories to practical projects, moved toward their chosen field of professional work. An aesthetic of 'design by subtraction' led to the characteristic geometric forms which became so familiar in modern functionalist architecture.

Those associated with the Bauhaus have been revered by generations of architects, and there are interesting links with the profession in Australia. Walter Gropius (1883–1969) visited this country in 1954. He had emigrated to the United States in 1937 to become Professor of Architecture at Harvard University.[1] Harry Seidler attended Harvard's Graduate School of Design from 1945 and came to Australia in 1948. Marcel Breuer (1902–1981), a former student of Walter Gropius at the Bauhaus, was lecturing at the Harvard GSD during Seidler's time there, and later invited him to work in his office in New York.

93

• AUSTRALIAN HOUSES OF THE FORTIES & FIFTIES

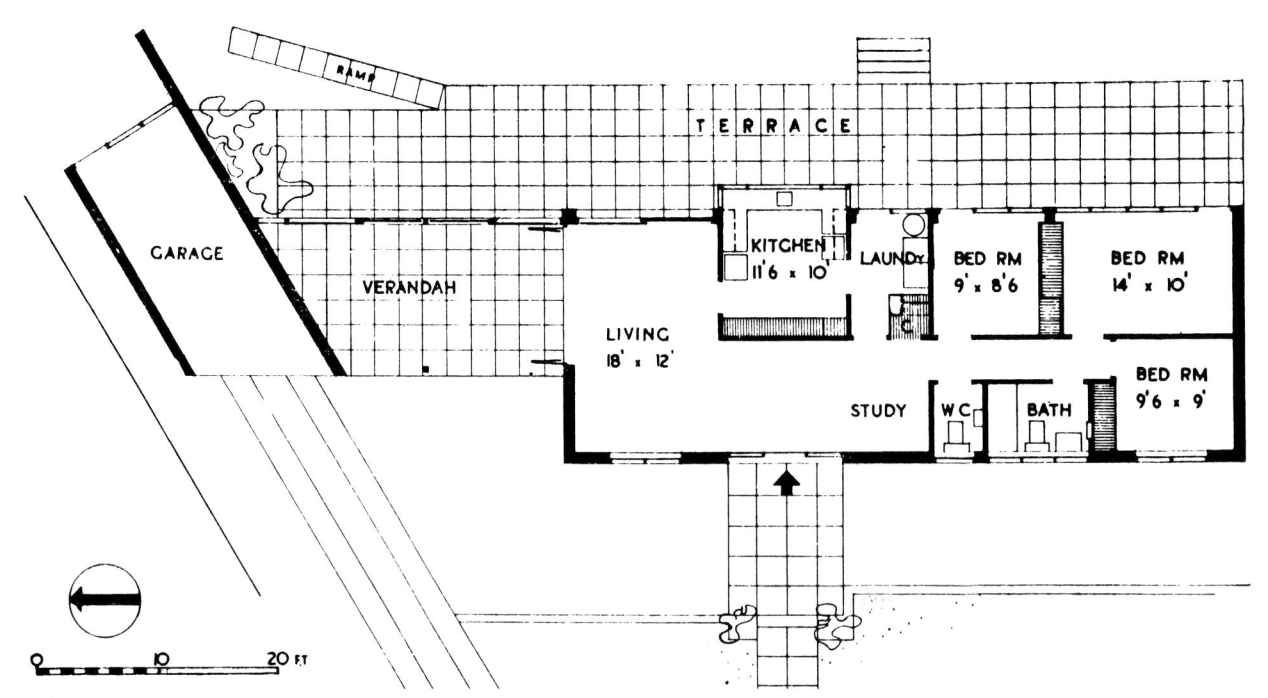

Ludwig Mies van der Rohe (1886–1969), Le Corbusier (1887–1965) and Walter Gropius were profoundly influential in the early decades of this century and, importantly, were still creating great works after the Second World War.

American architect Frank Lloyd Wright (1867–1959), another giant in the field, was influential in many ways. In the 1920s, publications on his work attracted interest with young Dutch architects, inspiring them towards 'greater severity and more geometrical discipline . . .'[2] Architects such as Willem Marinus Dudok (1884–1974) were in turn influential in many countries, including Australia. More directly, Frank Lloyd Wright was known for a great body of work over many decades, including his houses which were described as having an 'organic' relationship with their site. Typically, they emphasised the horizontal dimension with low-overhanging roofs, originally seen as a response to the wide-open prairies of America's mid-West. His integration of outdoor and indoor spaces was particularly relevant for architects designing houses in Australia in the post-war era.

The Californian houses of such architects as Richard J. Neutra and the firm of Wurster, Bernadi & Emmons were another source of ideas and influences. As the nearest parallel in North America to the climatic conditions of Australia's settled coastal regions, California had been providing architectural inspiration since early in the century. Austrian-born Richard J. Neutra (1892–1970) settled in the United States in 1928 and worked briefly with Frank Lloyd Wright. From 1930 he was based in Los Angeles and in time became widely known for his regional interpretation of the International style.[3] His later houses, with walls of glass and widely projecting roofs, are often pictured in a setting of Australian eucalypts. This must surely have made them seem more relevant for Australian architects in search of inspiration.

Travel to Europe and the United States was high on the agenda for the younger architects. Pictures and words were no substitute for first-hand experience. Living in Europe between 1930 and 1936 was a vital period for Sydney Ancher (1904–1979). The works of Walter Gropius and, in particular, Ludwig Mies van der Rohe made a deep impression.[4] Ancher's houses of the 1940s were quietly stated examples of modern functional design created for bushland settings on Sydney's North Shore. One of these, 'Poyntzfield', in Maytone Avenue, Gordon, built in the latter half of 1945, won the Sulman Medal in 1946 as best house of that year. The original design had been for a steel-framed building with walls of plastered expanded metal and a flat roof. Kuringai Shire Council, holding that the design did not meet the requirements laid down for brick areas, would not give their approval. New plans were prepared for brick construction with a pitched roof clad in slate.

Ancher had originally designed Poyntzfield as a home for himself, and had set out to demonstrate that, within the limit of 1250 square feet, modern open-planning could offer a very liveable design. Sliding glass doors opened onto a paved terrace and the kitchen had its own small bay with the upper half fully glazed. *Home Beautiful*'s Nora Cooper noted:

The kitchen is strategically placed between the area designed for dining and the laundry with doors placed opposite one another

ARCHITECTS AND THEIR WORK

• *Opposite page*: Plan of Poyntzfield by Sydney Ancher.

• *Below*: Winner of the Sulman Medal in 1946 as best house of that year, Sydney Ancher's design for Poyntzfield was approved by Kuringai Shire Council only after certain modifications were made, such as substituting a gable roof for proposed flat one.

PHOTOGRAPH: MAX DUPAIN
COURTESY: MAX DUPAIN AND ASSOCIATES PTY LTD

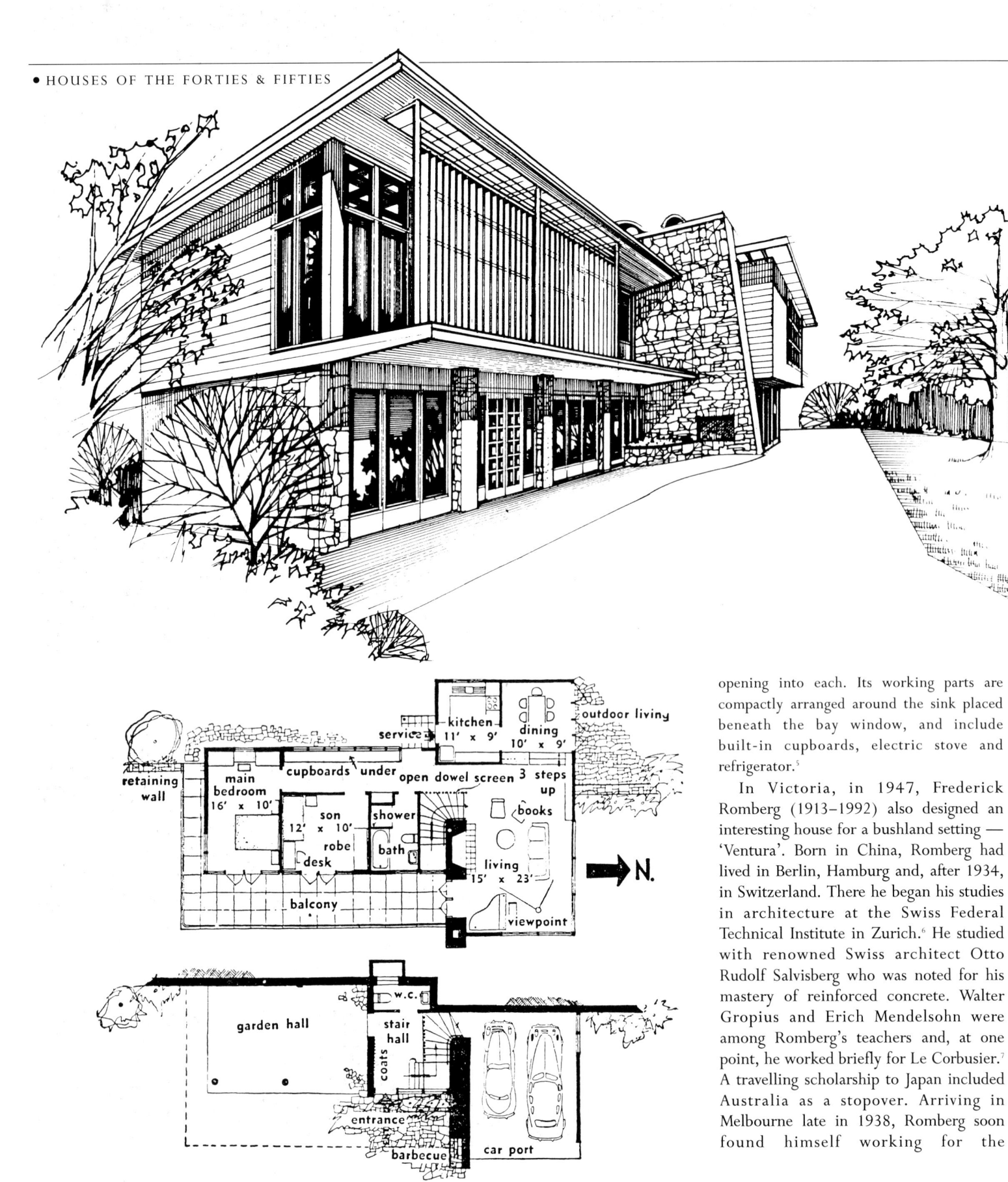

• HOUSES OF THE FORTIES & FIFTIES

opening into each. Its working parts are compactly arranged around the sink placed beneath the bay window, and include built-in cupboards, electric stove and refrigerator.[5]

In Victoria, in 1947, Frederick Romberg (1913–1992) also designed an interesting house for a bushland setting — 'Ventura'. Born in China, Romberg had lived in Berlin, Hamburg and, after 1934, in Switzerland. There he began his studies in architecture at the Swiss Federal Technical Institute in Zurich.[6] He studied with renowned Swiss architect Otto Rudolf Salvisberg who was noted for his mastery of reinforced concrete. Walter Gropius and Erich Mendelsohn were among Romberg's teachers and, at one point, he worked briefly for Le Corbusier.[7] A travelling scholarship to Japan included Australia as a stopover. Arriving in Melbourne late in 1938, Romberg soon found himself working for the

• *Opposite page*: Ventura, now called Berneray, Mast Gully Road, Upwey, Victoria. Designed by Frederick Romberg and built 1948–49, this recent sketch should be compared with that on page 91.

DRAWING: PENNY JACOBSEN
COURTESY: MARY PATRICK

• Plans for Ventura 1947.

COURTESY: PROFESSOR FREDERICK ROMBERG

• *Below*: Unusual barbecue in massive chimney at Ventura (Berneray) Upwey, Victoria.

PHOTOGRAPH: THE AUTHOR

well-known firm of Stephenson & Turner. He set up his own practice at the end of 1939 with a proposal to build twenty-two flats on a site in Queens Road, Melbourne.

Ventura, the Miller–Short house in Mast Gully Road, Upwey, was built in 1948–49. Romberg, by this stage, had designed some notable flats, with an enforced break during the war when he toiled for the Allied Works Council in Central Australia. As can be seen from the drawing opposite, Ventura was given a dynamic quality, with a massive stone chimney wall which incorporated two chimneys, one for the open fire in the living room and the other for the barbecue (see plan opposite). The principles espoused in this house were widely accepted in the following decades. Local natural stone was used for the retaining walls, ground floor walls, and the great chimney, both internally and externally. It was a passive solar house with window walls and projecting eaves wide enough to give shelter from the sun in the hotter months. Ceilings followed the skillion roofs, with exposed rafters in the living room, which was 23 ft × 15 ft (7015 mm × 4575 mm). Timber panelling was used for the interior walls. Ceilings, walls and even the floors were insulated to moderate the extremes of heat and cold which are possible on the slopes of the gullies at the southern end of the Dandenong Ranges.

If Ventura was one of a limited number of houses designed by Frederick Romberg, his main work being on a larger scale, it is important to recognise the individual approach which contrasts with the minimalist severity of the International-style cube or box forms. The influence of the Bauhaus is not denied, but there is also a regional concern and individual complexity, seen by some historians as being derived from Expressionism, a 'second tradition' in European architecture.[8]

A parallel in the blending of internationalism and regionalism is seen in the 1947 project for the William Dobell Studio at Church Point, New South Wales. Architect Arthur Baldwinson created a romantic asymmetrical design, choosing stone from the site as the principal material. The massive chimney wall closely resembles the example designed for Ventura by Frederick Romberg in the same year. The Dobell studio was to be given a long pergola, recalling the English country work of Edwin Lutyens early in the century.

Contrasting with the use of harmonious materials to give an environmental or regional context to the modern functional house was the Rose Seidler house at Turramurra, north of Sydney. Designed by Harry Seidler in 1948, it was a milestone in the acceptance of a sophisticated International-style cubic form.[9] This compact, box-like structure seemed to float above its sloping site. It was actually supported by thin metal columns and sandstone walls (see page 99). The floor was a concrete slab, with the walls of vertical boarding, flush fitted and painted off-white. Accents were painted black or in primary colours. In its bushland setting

AUSTRALIAN HOUSES OF THE FORTIES & FIFTIES

Sussman house, Kurrajong Heights, Harry Seidler, 1950–51.

COURTESY: MAX DUPAIN AND ASSOCIATES PTY LTD

ARCHITECTS AND THEIR WORK

• *Right and below*: Rose Seidler house, Turramurra/Wahroonga, 1948–50. Acquired by the Historic Houses Trust of New South Wales in 1988, and subsequently restored and opened to the public.

COURTESY: MAX DUPAIN AND ASSOCIATES PTY LTD

it created a dramatic interplay between a carefully modulated cubic form and the natural vegetation.

Close study of the plan, seen below right, reveals Seidler's concern for a logical disposition of the living, playing, sleeping and utility areas. Indoor living and playing areas flow from one to the other, with the bedrooms also given access to particular areas; the master bedroom to outdoor living and the children's bedrooms to the playroom.

Harry Seidler was born in Vienna, Austria, in 1923. In 1938, aged fifteen, he moved with his family to England. From 1938 to 1940 he studied building crafts and during this period began to look toward architecture. He was interned in 1940 and subsequently sent to Canada. Late in 1941 he was released to begin a course for the Bachelor of Architecture at the University of Manitoba. From 1945 he studied for his master's degree at Harvard University. Upon completion, he undertook further studies, worked with Marcel Breuer in New York and briefly for Oscar Niemeyer in Rio de Janeiro, before joining his family in Australia in 1948.[10]

In his early years in Australia, Seidler created a number of outstanding and influential houses. The Sussman house at Kurrajong Heights of 1950–51 (see opposite) perfectly illustrates his mastery of rational design. Such buildings did not seek to merge with their surroundings; harmony was achieved through integrity, just as the surrounding natural elements possessed their own beauty. The Rose Seidler house was awarded the Sulman Medal and Diploma in 1952. This was taken by supporters of the International style as important recognition of a new level of maturity in Australian architecture.

Compact planning was naturally the preoccupation of those years of post-war restrictions. In 1944 Dr Karl Langer (1903–1969), a refugee Austrian architect working in Brisbane, published a monograph entitled 'Sub-Tropical Housing' which contained designs for six single-storey houses.[11] His well-conceived plan forms, as can be seen from the example illustrated (page 101), offered an extension of indoor living areas into screened courtyards and terraces which, in turn, flowed out to enclosed areas of lawn and garden.[12]

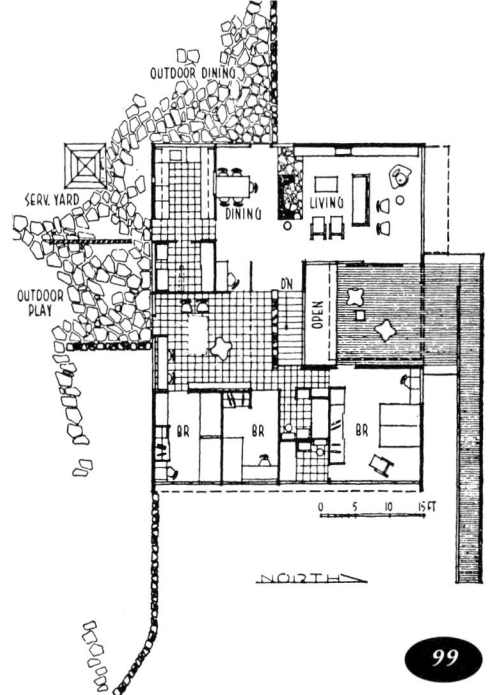

• This small house by John Mockridge in the Melbourne suburb of Alphington was completed in mid-1947. Its large areas of glass in the living/dining room captured the view which was to the rear of the property.

Australian Home Beautiful, May 1947

This theme was taken up in an article in the *Australian Home Beautiful's* December 1947 issue entitled 'Indoors or Out — as You Wish.' Three small houses by Victorian architect John P. Mockridge were illustrated with sketches and plans — a paragraph on each design pointed out the salient features. In the plan illustrated (see page 123) for a brick-veneer house in Point Nepean Road, Mentone, Victoria, 'The paved sun court gives access to the glazed gallery which is wide enough to become an additional sun room. The large living room has a dining alcove off it and an eating bar from the kitchen caters for odd snacks and drinks.'[13]

A very similar design had gained Sergeant John Mockridge third prize in a Sydney-based architectural competition which was conducted by the timber and asbestos-cement industries in December 1944. It had attracted 450 entries from throughout Australasia, claimed at that time as a record. Born in Geelong in 1916, John Mockridge was educated at Geelong College, the Gordon Institute of Technology and the University of Melbourne Atelier of Architectural Design. Before the war, he worked for W.R. & E.R. Butler and Leith & Bartlett and briefly for the Public Works Department before joining the RAAF in 1941. Immediately after the war he worked for the Commonwealth Department of Works and then as a designer with Buchan, Laird & Buchan. In 1948 he was appointed part-time lecturer in the Department of Architecture at the University of Melbourne and began a partnership with Ross Stahle and George Mitchell.[14]

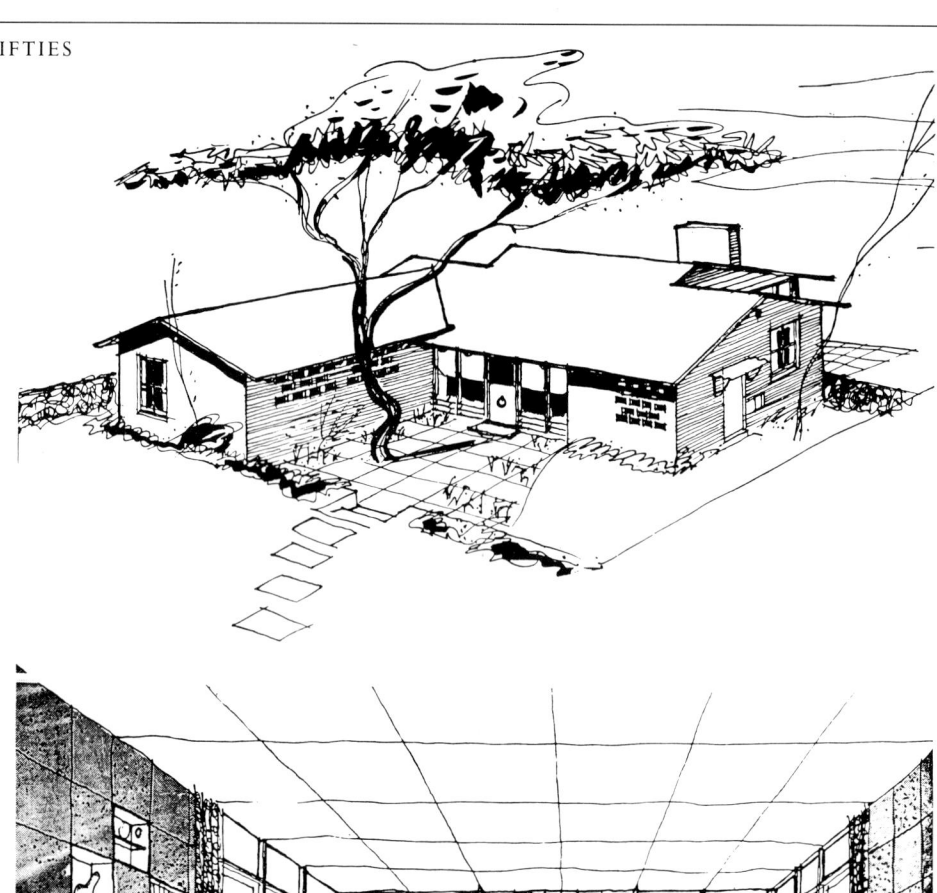

As can be seen from the examples illustrated, John Mockridge's houses were essentially of the Victorian Type, as defined by Robin Boyd. Of sixteen houses built between 1943 and 1960, half were in the region between Beaumaris and Portsea at the end of the Mornington Peninsula. In addition to Mockridge, Stahle & Mitchell, other architects associated with smaller houses in that area during those years were Doug Alexandra, Chancellor & Patrick, Neil Clerehan, James Earle, Roy Grounds, Middleton & Talbot, John and Phyllis Murphy, Petheridge & Bell, Jim Spears and Godfrey Spowers. Boyd noted that the characteristic style was a simple, rational plan with white walls, vertical boards, low roofs and wide eaves. Some were permanent residences, others retreats for weekends and holidays.

Some idea of the typical Mornington Peninsula or Beaumaris setting is offered in the photograph of a Sorrento holiday

ARCHITECTS AND THEIR WORK

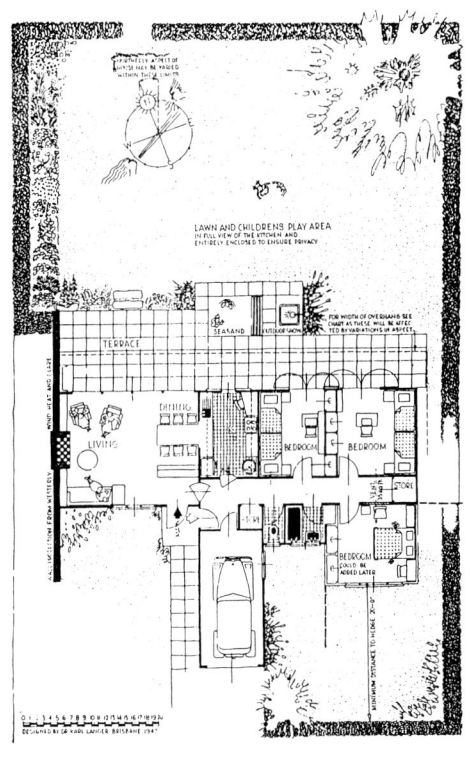

• *Left*: Dr Karl Langer of Brisbane designed this house in 1943.

Sub-Tropical Housing. Faculty of Engineering, Queensland University, Brisbane, 1944.

• *Below*: Holiday house at Sorrento, Victoria; architects, John and Phyllis Murphy, 1955.

COURTESY: JOHN AND PHYLLIS MURPHY

house of 1955 by John and Phyllis Murphy (see below). It illustrates the interplay of contrasting forms, the rustic sinuosity of the coastal tea-tree (*Leptospermum laevigatum*) and the functional geometry of the building.

Roy Grounds (1905–1981) was born at Albert Park in Victoria and went to a number of schools before attending Scotch College for two years. He completed his secondary education at Melbourne Grammar School. After a four-year indentureship with the architectural firm Blackett & Foster, he travelled to Europe and America for further study. From 1929 his American experiences included some years designing film sets in Hollywood. Upon returning to Melbourne in 1932 he went into partnership with Geoffrey Mewton.[15] The progressive work of this firm, over a period of five years, is recognised as a notable advance for modern functionalist architecture in Australia.

In 1937 Grounds retired from practice and lived in France for a period. When war broke out in 1939 he was again practising in Melbourne and, from 1941 to 1945, was a flight-lieutenant in the RAAF, working on airfield construction. At the end of the war he took up farming until he was appointed as a senior lecturer at the University of Melbourne in 1948. He returned to practise in 1954, in partnership with Frederick Romberg and Robin Boyd.[16] One of Australia's most unconventional and flamboyant architects, Roy Grounds was knighted in 1968, and in the same year was awarded the Gold Medal of the Royal Australian Institute of Architects for his contribution to architecture.

Grounds had built innovative houses on the Mornington Peninsula in the 1930s, but his best-known work in that area was the 1952 Henty House, popularly known as the 'Round House' on Oliver's Hill, Frankston. While it retained many characteristics of the regional style, such as widely projecting eaves, exposed rafters and unpainted vertical boarding, it also belongs to a group of houses built in Victoria in the 1950s which were experiments with geometry.

- *Above*: Henty house, Frankston, Victoria; architect, Roy Grounds, 1952.

The New Australian Home, Melbourne, 1954

- The Leyser House, Kew, Victoria; Roy Grounds, 1951.

Australian Home Beautiful, February 1954

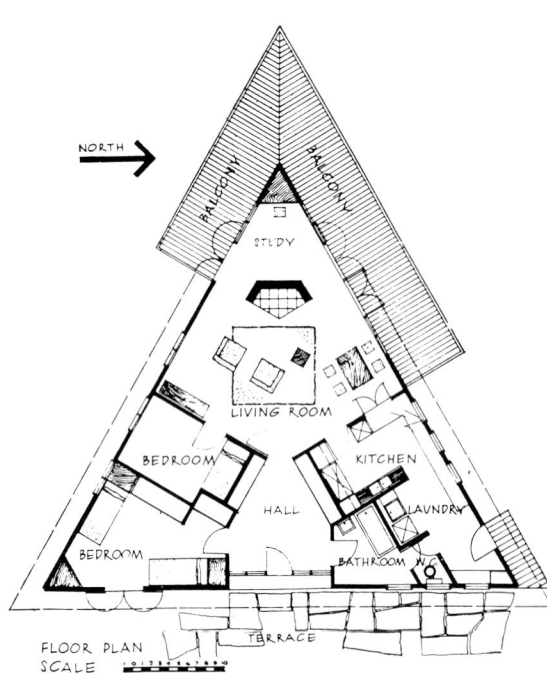

Known as an intensely practical man, with a consummate knowledge of trade skills, Grounds confidently designed houses of various shapes with careful attention to detail. Some were little removed from the mainstream; others such as the triangular Leyser house (of 1951) were quite unorthodox (see plan above right). He had moved away from the rectangle in his 1940 fan-shaped design for 'Quamby', a block of flats in Toorak. In the post-war years, a number of younger Melbourne architects designed houses as triangles, S-shapes, spirals, circles, ovals and combinations of geometric forms. Some explored the possibilities of a boldly structural approach. Two such designs were the 1953–55 house of Peter and Dione McIntyre in the Melbourne suburb of Kew, and a 1956 house by David Chancellor and Rex Patrick overlooking Port Phillip Bay at Dromana.

The Chancellor & Patrick house employed four steel triangles with their points anchored in concrete foundations. These were braced by cross-members of steel channelling at the roof and upper floor level. As can be seen in the plans (see opposite) the balcony, kitchen, passage and bathroom areas were cantilevered, as were portions of a bedroom and the dining room. Apparently the structural concept occurred to David Chancellor while he was doodling in the sand at the beach. The Dromana house had a 'butterfly' roof, but it is interesting to note that Chancellor's favourite was reported to be the low gable which he found restful.[17]

Peter and Dione McIntyre's own house on a steep slope overlooking the Yarra River, just a few kilometres from the centre of Melbourne, was an inspired answer to the challenge of an almost impossible site. Designed and erected between 1952 and 1954, it was a steel A-frame tower supporting a double cantilevered truss structure (see page 104). The wall panels were Stramit compressed straw slabs painted yellow and red to emphasise the geometry of the steel frame. This application was innovative and inexpensive but found to be impractical in the long term due to inaccessibility and the constant maintenance required to keep the walls weatherproof. The bright red and yellow panels which caused the building to be known as the 'Butterfly House' were covered over in about 1957 with hardwood cladding. Treated with Brunswick green tinted creosote, the walls now merged into the tree-clad hillside.[18]

The structural quality of this house evolved during the time that Peter McIntyre was a member of the team working on the design of Melbourne's Olympic Swimming Stadium. Also working on this team was structural

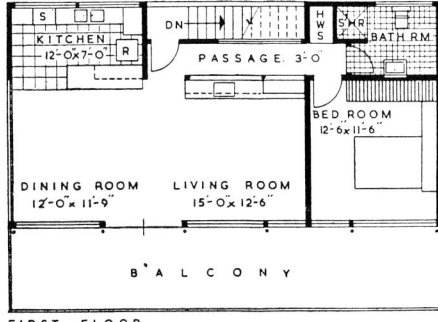

ARCHITECTS AND THEIR WORK •

engineer 'Bill'(W.L.) Irwin. David McKinna, a steel fabricator/rigger from McKinna Brothers, the contractors who built the house, was also involved. Assisted by such expertise, considerations of economy, and the necessary elevation above the 1934 flood level, McIntyre's unique design became a reality.

As the McIntyre family grew, the house underwent a series of changes, starting with the roofing-in and glazing of the two end decks in 1959. From the second photograph (below right) we can see that, in its evolved form, the McIntyre house continued to be a most dramatic building — a house in the treetops.

The partnership of Peter and Dione McIntyre was formed in 1954 following Dione's graduation, Peter having graduated from the University of Melbourne in 1949. Unorthodox shapes and unusual methods of construction produced some very imaginative houses, including the 1954 Snelleman house in Keam Street, Ivanhoe, which gently stepped down its site in a bold curve. Preservation of two large eucalypts and the fall of the land were influential elements in the shape of the house (see plan on page 123). Robin Boyd wrote of Melbourne's architectural world in the decade after the war, 'What enthusiasm abounded when the latest Peter McIntyre or Kevin Borland house was unveiled. It was the European revolution happening all over again, a generation later. What sensations, what excitement, what inexperience.'[19]

In those days married women architects were new to the field in Victoria — a number of single women had entered the profession in the inter-war years. Phyllis Murphy and Dione McIntyre both managed careers and families, each achieving more than thirty years of uninterrupted practice.[20]

Dione McIntyre (then Dione Cohen) had been inspired by a house design

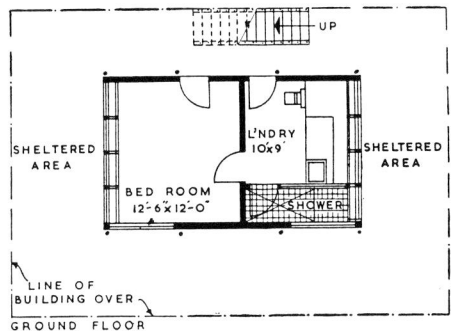

• An example of the structuralist approach is seen in this house overlooking Port Phillip Bay at Dromana, designed by David Chancellor and Rex Patrick in 1956 (see plans above).

Australian Homemaker, May 1957

• *Below:* The River House, Kew, Victoria, Peter McIntyre, 1953–55.

PHOTOGRAPH: THE AUTHOR.

103

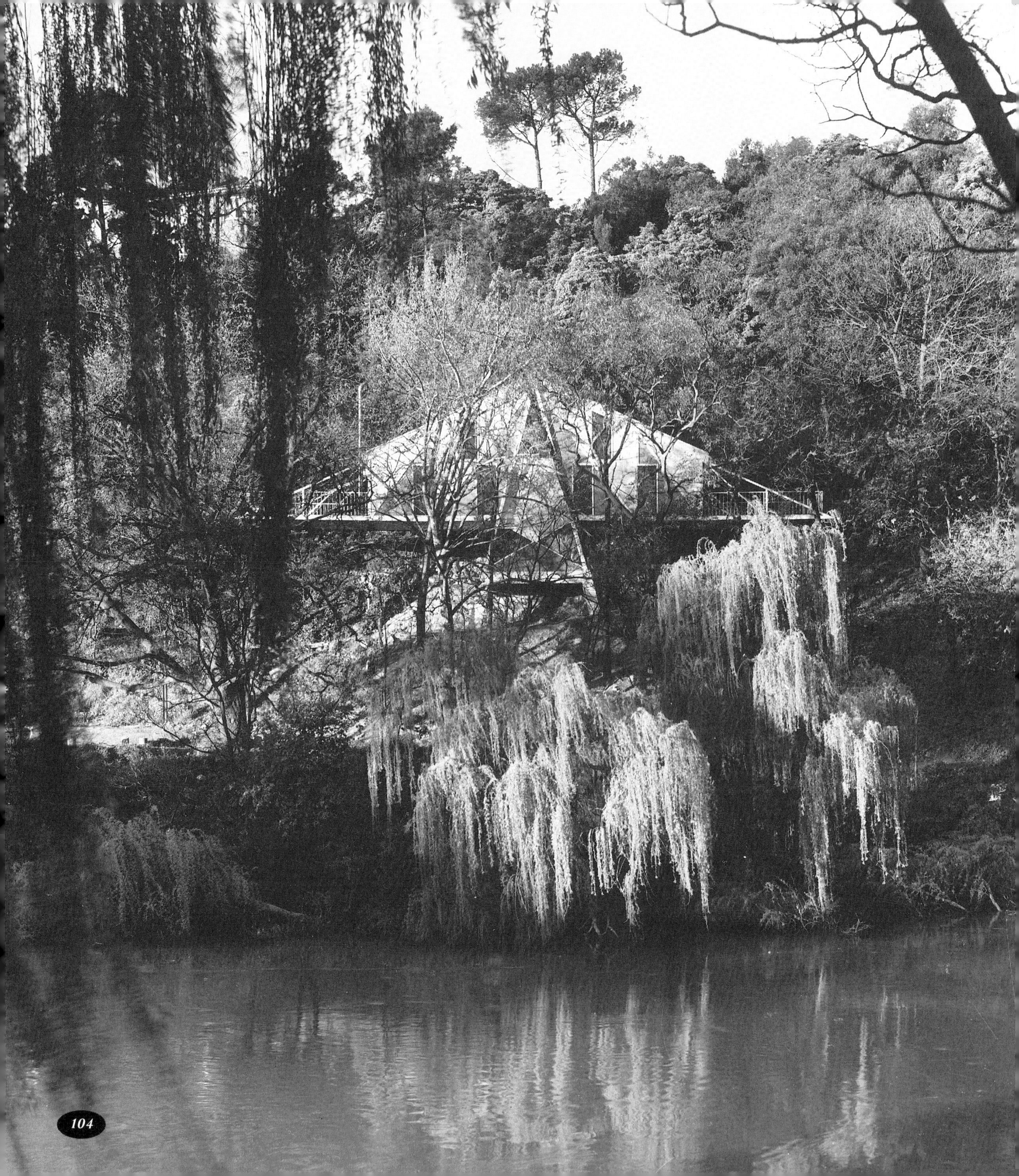

• *Opposite*: The River House, Kew, Victoria; architect, Peter McIntyre, 1953–55.

PHOTOGRAPH: WOLFGANG SIEVERS

• *Right and below*: The sparse functionalist approach is well illustrated in this 1951 house at Studley Park, Melbourne, designed for Frank and Bea Burns by John and Phyllis Murphy.

COLLECTION: JOHN AND PHYLLIS MURPHY

published in the *Age* Small Home Service based on Peter McIntyre's design of the Beulah Bush Nursing Hospital. She became his assistant as a final year student in 1953 at the time when he was working with John and Phyllis Murphy, Kevin Borland and Bill Irwin on the Olympic Swimming Stadium. Dione and Peter McIntyre married in the following year.

Phyllis Murphy was born Phyllis Slater in Melbourne in 1924. Educated at Korowa Church of England Girls' Grammar School and the Methodist Ladies' College, she began an architecture course at the Melbourne Technical College (later RMIT) in 1942. In 1945 and 1946 she worked for the firm of Yuncken, Freeman Brothers, Griffiths & Simpson; then in 1947 travelled overseas with John Murphy. She joined the architecture course at the University of Melbourne in 1948, completing it in 1949. In 1950 she married John Murphy and they established their practice in the same year.[21]

Born in Melbourne in 1920, John Murphy was educated at eight schools including Malvern Grammar School. He commenced the architecture course at Swinburne Technical College in 1938 and in 1939 worked with his father at Cowper, Murphy & Appleford. From 1940 to 1944 he was in the Army Survey Corps, travelling to the Middle East in 1941 and to New Guinea in 1943. Discharged in 1944, he began a full-time architecture course at Melbourne Technical College. He subsequently studied architecture at the University of Melbourne, completing the course in 1950.

The partnership of John and Phyllis Murphy was noted for its domestic work in the 1950s and early '60s. It has been observed that their houses were not typical of the 'Melbourne School', evidencing a kinship with expressionism.[22] There was no experimental geometry, but rather a concern for rational design with a sympathy for the human dimension. They shared the contemporary demands of providing a sense of spaciousness within the limited area prescribed by post-war restrictions and material shortages. One characteristic in their work was the flush gable end which is traced to ideas gained in their observation of post-war housing in Sweden and England.[23]

The Murphy's 1951 house for Frank and Bea Burns in The Belvedere, Studley Park, Melbourne, can be seen in the photographs on this page, as a trim, modern, functional design, reflecting the era of austerity. Plain surfaces, large window areas and a low-pitched roof without eaves are in marked contrast with the excess of featurism which was rampant in that decade. Crisp detailing was also notable in the 1955 Mather house in Valley Parade, Glen Iris, but this time a dramatic note is introduced in the steep pitch of the skillion roof (see next page).

With growing interest in Australia's colonial tradition the verandah returned to

AUSTRALIAN HOUSES OF THE FORTIES & FIFTIES

• House in Valley Parade, Glen Iris, designed in 1955 for Dr and Mrs Keith Mather by John and Phyllis Murphy.

COLLECTION: JOHN AND PHYLLIS MURPHY

• *Opposite*: Richardson house Blackfriars Close, Toorak, Victoria, 1954; architect, Robin Boyd.

PHOTOGRAPH: WOLFGANG SIEVERS, 1955

functional domestic architecture. John and Phyllis Murphy made it one of their signatures and were early figures in an Australia-wide movement to recognise the valuable aspects of traditional vernacular architecture. *Home Beautiful*'s issue for December 1956 featured an article by Gerald Stewart boldly headed 'Verandah Stages a Comeback'. Discussing his design for the Shannon house in Boundary Street, Wahroonga, on Sydney's North Shore, Arthur Baldwinson comments 'The colonial verandah has proved its worth and I believe it should be carried on as a living tradition.'[24]

Baldwinson & Booth included verandahs in a number of houses at Wahroonga, as did Sydney Ancher at Pymble and St Ives. Slender steel posts were used in the Shannon house which was an L-shaped plan with the verandah on two sides of a courtyard. In the 1951 Slater house in the Melbourne suburb of Canterbury, John and Phyllis Murphy included slender steel verandah posts, whereas in the 1954 Hickey house in Kooyongkoot Road, Hawthorn, they chose traditional square wooden posts. Many architects achieved the effect of having a verandah through the use of terraces and balconies sheltered by widely projecting eaves. In two-storey residences, the lower level would be sheltered by the upstairs balcony.

Because of their associations with gloomy interiors, verandahs were rejected by many architects who were committed to European modernism. But walls of glass in Australian heatwave conditions were not always as appropriate as they were in cold climate regions. It is interesting to note that the 1949–54 Rose family house at Turramurra, designed by Harry Seidler, included a terrace sheltered by the main roof which served exactly the same function as a verandah.

In 1956, Hobart architect Esmond Dorney built an unusual steel-framed house in Churchill Avenue, Sandy Bay. Its 'butterfly' roof was curved with a pergola/sunshade extending beyond the eaves (see page 59). At the same period, Shugg & Moon designed a house for a site overlooking the Derwent River at the foot of Mt Direction about ten kilometres north of Hobart. A simple rectangular plan included a low-pitched gable roof extended to form a carport and a very large area where the framework became a pergola supported by slim steel posts.[25]

A house designed to maximise winter sunshine was built at Devonport, Tasmania, in 1958 by Bush, Haslock, Parkes, Shugg & Moon. Its rectangular plan was centred on a large courtyard with the house actually being in two blocks, one with two living areas (including an open-plan kitchen) and the other with four bedrooms, a bathroom and utility area. North-facing walls were fully glazed as were three sides of the courtyard, the fourth being open to the north. The outside walls on three sides were brick to six feet (1830 mm) with high windows. A porch at the northern end of the courtyard was roofed in corrugated plastic.[26]

The 1958 house at the corner of Allenby Road and Adelma Road, Dalkeith, Western Australia, by Raymond Jones was a large house built on a small block. As can be seen from the photograph on page 108, it presented an interesting roofline of two low-pitched skillions broken in the

ARCHITECTS AND THEIR WORK

• *Above*: Raymond Jones designed this house for a relatively small block on the corner of Allenby and Adelma roads, Dalkeith, a Perth suburb, in 1958.

PHOTOGRAPH: FRITZ KOS

centre by a short angle near the point of entry. Three bedrooms, a living area, and kitchen/dining area all looked onto a terrace and courtyard at the rear of the house. There were actually two large living areas, one 25 ft × 18 ft (7625 mm × 5490 mm) opening into a second one of 31 ft × 14 ft (9455 mm × 4270 mm). The main walls were of cavity bricks and plastered with timber partitions between the smaller rooms. Fibrous plaster ceilings generally followed the roofline. Some rooms had timber-panelled ceilings. Window frames and joinery were in jarrah with a natural finish. Having designed the house next door, the architect was offered the opportunity to continue the roof in the same plane.[27]

The stylised, low-pitched skillion was introduced to Perth in 1948 when architect Eric Leach caused a stir by building his own house in oiled timber and brick on what seemed an impossibly steep site in Saunders Street, Mosman Park. He created a series of floors stepping down the slope which overlooked Mosman Bay.[28] Timber was not generally seen in Perth's fashionable areas.

Historians point out that Perth architects were enthusiastic in their acceptance of the International style from the 1950s, following the acclaim given to the early Harry Seidler houses. Certainly there were many cube-form designs with window walls, but it is interesting to find that more direct influences were also involved. Geoffrey Summerhayes began studying architecture in 1946. In 1951–52 he travelled to the United States and studied under Marcel Breuer and Buckminster Fuller. He also visited Walter Gropius at his home, as well as Frank Lloyd Wright's Taliesin East and Taliesin West. He recalls that when he returned to Perth his father was very nervous of him applying 'flat roof, glass box ideas picked up in the USA.'[29] The 1956 new wing for the Ahern house (right) was given a shallowly curved roof, large areas of glass and sliding timber louvre screens.

Adelaide architect Russell Ellis built a two-storey cube-form brick house at Springfield, South Australia, in 1947. Designed as his own family residence, it was set on an elevated site overlooking Adelaide and the sea beyond. A wall of glass in the living room included doors opening to a slate-paved terrace (see plan opposite). The upstairs bedrooms and bathroom were given access to a spacious

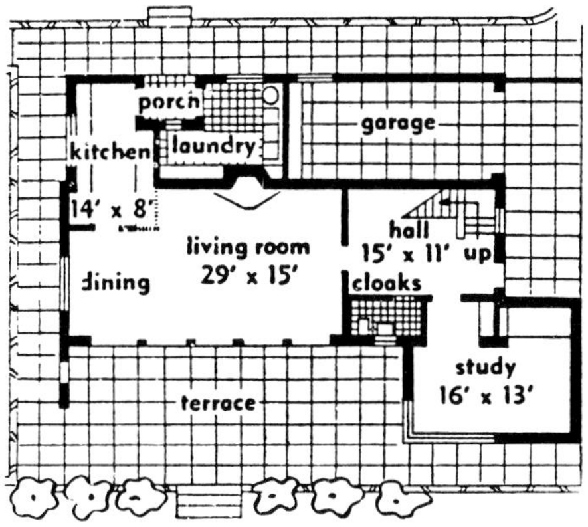

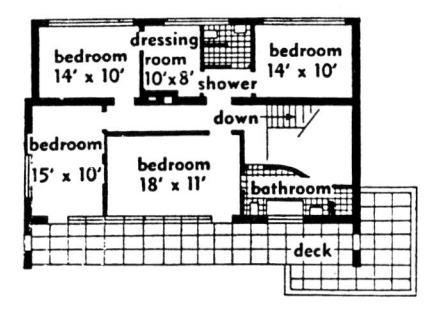

ARCHITECTS AND THEIR WORK

• Plan for house built at Springfield, South Australia, in 1947 by Russell Ellis.

• *Below*: Robin Boyd designed this North Adelaide house in 1955 for fellow architect Gavin Walkley.
COURTESY: GAVIN WALKLEY

• *Below Left*: In 1956, Perth architect Geoffrey Summerhayes created this new wing for the Ahern house.
COURTESY: GEOFFREY SUMMERHAYES

deck which was sheltered by a cantilevered roof. External walls were painted pale oyster grey, with recessed walls under the balcony and the roof a salmon colour. A garage was designed to be an integral part of the house.[30] Trees were highly valued on the Springfield Estate and the Ellis residence was given a north-facing aspect on a site which had eucalypts, pines, olives and an almond grove.

Architects associated with modern functional houses in South Australia include Jack Cheesman, Maurice Doley, Brian Polomka, Gavin Walkley, Robert Dickson and Brian Claridge. It is interesting to note that Robin Boyd designed a house for Gavin Walkley which was built in 1956, at 26 Palmer Place, North Adelaide. This design is believed to be Boyd's only South Australian building.[31]

Queensland in the post-war era provided an exciting challenge for architects looking to create modern functional houses which were well suited to the climate. Many such houses were designed and built, adding a new dimension to Queensland's regional heritage. At St Lucia, inexpensive building blocks in a well-wooded, elevated setting overlooking the Brisbane River were a natural attraction for younger architects. In houses for themselves and for their clients they created a diversity of thoughtful designs, some reflecting earlier regional styles, others offering new responses to local conditions. An important group of houses, now classified as 'Post-War Brisbane Regional'[32], were the work of John Dalton, Peter Newell, Hayes & Scott, Peter Heathwood, Douglas & Barnes, Karl Langer, John Hitch, Neville Lund and others.

Peter Newell settled in Queensland in 1946 and is credited with bringing from Victoria the practice of painting brick walls.[33] Light or dark olive greens, greys and pale pinks were favoured, white being somewhat blinding in Queensland's sunlight. As in other states, there were houses influenced by the Victorian Type, with their low-pitched roofs and wide eaves, others hinted at influences from Sydney's North Shore bushland suburbs.

Importantly, there were refreshed visions of the Queensland house, often elevated, and given wide verandahs. The traditional device of suspended screens or panels between the verandah posts were reinstated and in some designs, slatted, adjustable blinds or louvres, either horizontal or vertical were used. International functionalist style had stripped away unnecessary ornamentation and some of these new Queensland houses were flat-roofed cubic forms with large areas of glass. Awning or hopper windows were included in various arrangements, with new versions of the old casement type also seen.[34]

Slatted, external, adjustable sun blinds were incorporated in John Dalton and Peter Heathwood's prizewinning design for the Queensland Plywood Board's 1956 open competition for a plywood display house. This was not an elevated house, but similar cube-form designs were raised. However, these often dispensed with stumps, using brick or concrete piers or walled sections which might be a garage or utility area. John Dalton's own house at Fig Tree Pocket, built in September 1959, evolved from a 1955 project for a house at Ascot.[35]

Born in Leeds, Yorkshire, in 1927, Dalton emigrated to Australia in 1950. He had trained in building and continued studies in this field from 1952 at the University of Queensland where he graduated with a Diploma of Architecture in 1958. Sydney Ancher and Denmark's Arne Jacobsen were his gurus in the 1950s. Having qualified in what was then a very provincial Queensland, he felt that a softer response to the manifestos of Mies van der Rohe, Walter Gropius and others was more suitable. His house at Fig Tree Pocket (see above) included many innovative ideas. Sprinklers played water onto the roof, providing evaporative cooling. Other details included walls which folded away, a central ventillating clerestory and adjustable louvres shading the north face.

Looking back on the post-war era John Dalton has commented that the influence

ARCHITECTS AND THEIR WORK

• *Opposite page*: Architect John Dalton's own house built in the Brisbane suburb of Fig Tree Pocket in 1959 displays a clear concern for regional needs.

COURTESY: JOHN DALTON

• *Right*: Designed for N. Rutledge, by John Dalton in 1955, this house in the Brisbane suburb of St Lucia was constructed using Burnie Board, both internally and externally.

COURTESY: JOHN DALTON

of the International style was very important in that it made architects look to an Australian response, 'and thereafter rediscover and develop an indigenous philosophy'.[36] Architects in various parts of Australia absorbed and responded to influences and ideas each in their own way. Some followed closely upon those who were setting the directions, others shared as equals, current ideals and theories, without any loss of individual integrity. A few possessed the genius to be able to achieve outstanding works; most were happy to find professional respect, reasonable monetary reward and a feeling of having made some contribution to their community.

Chapter 5 Endnotes

[1] Henry-Russell Hitchcock, *The Pelican history of Art, Architecture: Nineteenth and Twentieth Centuries*, Penguin Books, Middlesex, 1975, p. 524.

[2] ibid, p. 482.

[3] Reyner Banham, *Los Angeles, The Architecture of Four Ecologies*, Penguin Books, Middlesex, 1973, p. 189.

[4] Beyond the 1950s, *The History and Design of the Australian House*, Oxford University Press, Sydney, 1985, p. 146.

[5] Nora Cooper, 'Prizewinner in Sydney', *Australian Home Beautiful*, February 1947, p. 45.

[6] Conrad Hamann, 'The German Connection, Sesquicentenary Essay on German-Victorian Crosscurrents, 1835–1985', Department of German, Monash University, Victoria, 1985, p 55.

[7] ibid.

[8] Hamann, p. 55.

[9] J.M. Freeland, *Architecture in Australia: A History*, Penguin Books, Cheshire, Melbourne, 1968, Ringwood, Victoria, 1972, p. 273.

[10] Donald, Leslie Johnson, *Australian Architecture 1901–51*. Sydney University Press, Sydney, 1980, pp. 177, 178, 179.

[11] Dr Karl Langer, *Sub-Tropical Housing*, Faculty of Engineering, Queensland University Press, 1944.

[12] Peter Newell, 'The House in Queensland. From First Settlement to 1985', Unpublished Master's thesis, University of Queensland, February 1988, vol.1, p. 110.

[13] John P. Mockridge, 'Indoors or Out — As you Wish *Australian Home Beautiful*, December 1947, pp. 10, 11.

[14] Information from John Mockridge in correspondence with the author, 1992.

[15] J.M. Freeland, *The Making of a Profession — A History of the Growth and Work of the Architectural Institutes in Australia*, Angus & Robertson in association with The Royal Australian Institute of Architects, Sydney, 1971, pp. 280, 281.

[16] ibid.

[17] Paul Hennessy, 'Drama in Steel Construction', *Australian Homemaker*, May 1957, pp. 28, 29, 54.

[18] Information from Dione McIntyre in correspondence with the author, 1992.

[19] Robin Boyd, 'The State of Australian Architecture', *Architecture in Australia*, June 1967, p. 459.

[20] Sarah Schoffel, 'Women Architects and Victorian Modern', *Trust News*, National Trust of Australia (Victoria), September 1990.

[21] Information from John and Phyllis Murphy, 1992.

[22] Frank Marioli, 'The Work of John and Phyllis Murphy', unpublished investigation project, University of Melbourne, 1983.

[23] ibid.

[24] Gerald Stewart, 'Verandah Stages a Comeback', *Australian Home Beautiful*, December 1956, p. 25.

[25] *Tasmanian Architect*, Royal Australian Institute of Architects, Tasmanian Chapter, Hobart, Winter 1957, p. 7.

[26] Neil Clerehan, (ed.) *Best Australian Houses — Recent Houses Built by the Royal Australian Institute of Architects*, F.W. Cheshire, Melbourne, 1961.

[27] ibid.

[28] Ian Molyneux, *Looking Around Perth: A Guide to the Architecture of Perth and Surrounding Towns*, Wescolour Press, Fremantle East, 1981, p. 69.

[29] Recollections from Geoffrey E. Summerhayes in correspondence with the author, 1992.

[30] Mary Jane Seymour, 'Trees were Treasured', *Australian Home Beautiful*, September 1948, pp. 28–31, 44.

[31] Information from Gavin Walkley in correspondence with the author, 1992.

[32] R. Apperly, R. Irving, & P. Reynolds, *A Pictorial Guide to Identifying Australian Architecture*, Angus & Robertson, North Ryde, NSW, 1989, p. 222.

[33] Boyd, p. 204.

[34] *Buildings of Queensland*, Royal Australian Institute of Architects, Queensland Chapter, Jacaranda Press, Brisbane, 1959.

[35] Information from John Dalton in correspondence with the author, 1992.

CHAPTER SIX

Defining the Styles

WE CLASSIFY VARIOUS TYPES and styles of architecture as a means of furthering our understanding of the intentions, conditions and fashions of a given era. Houses of the 1940s and '50s were a complex mixture, ranging from plain austerity to high fashion, from functionalist to featuristic. The boundaries, as ever, were not clearly defined, although it was as easy then as it is now to identify one house as 'colonial' and another as 'modern' or 'contemporary'. To be preoccupied with pigeon-holing every house into a style could mean missing important aspects of individual character. If classifications given to styles, types or specific details of domestic architecture are a key to a deepening interest and further investigation, then it is a worthwhile pursuit.

Many architects committed to functionalism in the period under review were convinced that stylism was dead and that future generations would recognise their wisdom in this matter. With hindsight we can see their work as a readily identifiable style, while perhaps agreeing that they were not inclined to borrow from history as others did. Terms such as 'Modern style' need to be reviewed because they make no sense when applied to what is now an old building. 'Moderne' on the other hand represents a defined period style.

Houses can be placed into various categories based on their size, shape, materials and stylistic or philosophical origins. The following review is based on currently accepted classifications or, where necessary, on a descriptive term used in the period from 1940 to 1960.

Popular or vernacular architecture is only partially covered in the standard works available up to this time. In the following pages I will discuss both architect-designed houses and those not designed by architects, in terms of roof-type and ground plan or layout.

• ROOFLINES •

— Hipped Roof —

This is an ancient type which dates back to simple thatch-roofed huts. The classical form in Renaissance buildings was used in England for houses in the style now described as Georgian. Both Georgian and Classical influences affected roof types in Australia throughout the 19th century and well into this century through Georgian Revival styles. The asymmetrical hipped roof in typical suburban houses can also be linked to the 'Prairie House' and the work of Frank Lloyd Wright, Walter Burley Griffin and their associates. Low-pitched hip roofs with wide eaves are seen in Frank Lloyd Wright's Prairie House which appeared in the American magazine the *Ladies' Home Journal*, in

DEFINING THE STYLES

• *Opposite page*: A classic suburban style drawn at the beginning of the 1940s.

COLLECTION: COMMONWEALTH BANK ARCHIVES, VICTORIA

• A mixture of hip, gable and skillion roofs is seen in this 1957 photograph of Alkoo Circle, Chigwell, Tasmania.

COURTESY: STATE OFFICES LIBRARY, HOBART, TASMANIA

• *Opposite page*: Well-kept 1958 house in the Perth suburb of Floreat Park. Designed by J.W. Johnson, it echoes similar work seen in other parts of Australia, and in particular that of Harry Seidler.

PHOTOGRAPH: PETA TOWNSING

1900. In Australia, from 1914, Walter Burley Griffin designed houses which were influential, including a number with low-pitched hip roofs with wide eaves.

Post-war austerity reduced the eaves in ordinary suburban houses but as conditions improved and restrictions were lifted they returned. Clad in tiles, corrugated iron or asbestos-cement, the hipped roof became a standard type in the suburbs of Australian cities.

— Gabled Roof —

Another ancient type, most notably associated with the Gothic tradition. In cold climate regions, steeply pitched gable roofs were ideal for throwing off heavy snow. In warmer regions the pitch was lower, and in many Australian houses in this century it was reduced to very low angles. Old English or Tudor style demanded high-pitched roofs as did American colonial styles, such as Cape Cod. The California Bungalow influence made the low-pitched gable popular from the First World War era, including the use of wide eaves. Architects used low-pitched gable roofs in simple functional houses in the 1940s and '50s. Ordinary suburban houses were generally given a less adventurous gable of around 30 degrees from the horizontal.

— Skillion Roof —

Also referred to as monopitch, the skillion had long been a common form in vernacular architecture but was taken up by 20th-century architects in their drive to discard unnecessary elements. Why have a gable or hipped roof when a low-pitched skillion would do the job? In houses influenced by the International style such a roof might have no eaves. In other 'Contemporary' designs, wide eaves would provide shade and shelter. From the late 1940s the use of various low-pitched skillion roofs became increasingly popular and by the 1960s was a common suburban type.

— Butterfly Roof —

This was one of the styles of the post-war era that builders soon borrowed from architects' designs. Houses with butterfly roofs were admired in the suburbs as being somewhat daring and obviously 'modern'. This was probably because they contrasted with the downward angles and earthbound look of conventional hip or gable roofs. The butterfly, with its central valley, had an upward dynamic quality and like many houses with skillion roofs displayed large areas of wall. These were often given uninspired window treatments which made them look unbalanced or like a face with an unusually high forehead.

— Flat Roof —

In many warm climate regions of the world the flat roof has long been used in vernacular and sophisticated architecture. It is often hidden behind a parapet and in many cases it is a living space. In the early 20th century it was adopted by the European modernists as part of their movement toward stark cubic forms. The flat-roofed look had been achieved in commercial architecture from the 1880s, notably in Chicago. Frank Lloyd Wright worked in the Chicago offices of Louis Sullivan and included flat roofs in his designs from early this century. Walter Burley Griffin was known for his flat roofs in houses built in the 1920s and '30s, but was derided because some developed leaks.[1] Griffin's flat roofs were often constructed to be used as recreation areas. Houses based on the cube form European functionalist style gained popularity in Australia from the 1930s. These also made use of flat roofs as outdoor living areas.

Difficulties in achieving a leak-proof, well-drained construction kept the flat roof out of the average suburban builder's bag of tricks. They might manage a low-pitched skillion hidden behind a parapet, but most people wanted a roof they could see, preferably loaded down with tiles to give a clear impression of money well spent.

• LAYOUTS •

— L-shaped Plan —

To introduce more light into rooms than possible in the traditional rectangle, with perhaps a single room partially extended, architects moved toward a linear approach. Wings one room wide, some with a well-glazed passage linking them along an external wall, offered a variety of possibilities for the shape of the house. By far the most popular was the L-shaped plan. Already established as an alternative style by the late 1930s, it was increasingly popular after the war. There were a number of variations, with the most distinctive emphasising the wing parallel to the direction of the block of land. A typical example is seen at right.

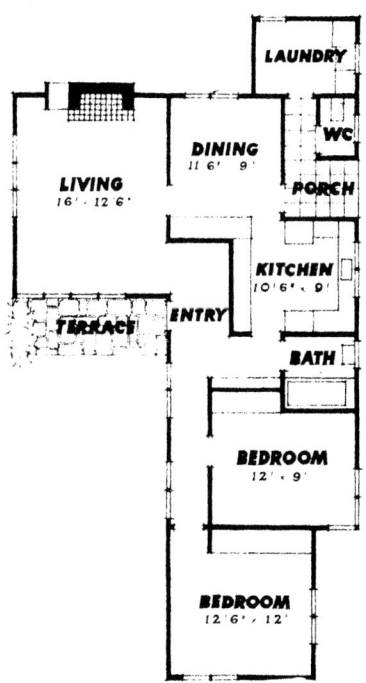

— U-shaped Plan —

Older houses of the courtyard type followed this shape. In the post-war era the open part of the U could face the street or the backyard. Ideally it would be oriented to catch the sun, with windows facing the courtyard or inner area. Some examples included a pergola with a deciduous vine to give shade in the hotter months.

— H-shaped Plan —

Related to the previous shape, the H was a favourite with architects in the 1940s and '50s, because it allowed them more freedom in arrangements of rooms. In the example illustrated on page 116 the two blocks are linked by a fully glazed breezeway which uses louvres to provide flexibility. In some designs the central link was the dining or living room, with

• *Right*: Contemporary design offered by the Western Australian State Housing Commission in 1956.

COURTESY: HOMES WEST

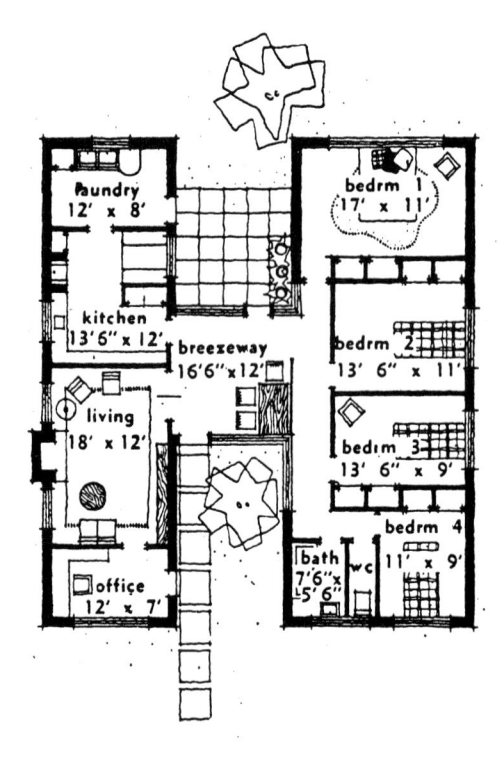

• *Above*: This H-shaped plan is also a version of the type described as 'bi-nuclear'; its two blocks are joined by a fully glazed 'breezeway'.
Australian Home Beautiful, April, 1950.

• *Right*: Courtyard plan, 1950s.

perhaps a hallway as the main throughway. An article entitled 'Use the Breeze' was included in the April 1950 issue of the *Australian Home Beautiful*. Architect Hume Sherrard writes:

A popular feature in southern parts of America is the breezeway, which is a covered porch joining two parts of a house and so planned that the prevailing breeze blows through it. The breezeway is often the connecting link between the living and sleeping parts of the house and acts as an entrance porch where one may sit in the shade, fanned by a breeze blowing through the porch.

— T-shaped Plan —

This shape was given various orientations and in some cases evolved through an extension being added to an L-shape. A closely related plan is the cruciform. In another variation of the T-shape, the living room was kept well away from the rest of the house at the foot of the T, being joined to it by a wide hallway.

— Enclosed Courtyard Plan —

Generally found in architect designs, this shape provided a source of light and an interesting accent in a square-shaped plan. Roy Grounds included a circular enclosed courtyard as a focal point in a 1953 house in Toorak, Victoria.[2]

DEFINING THE STYLES

• Horseshoe-shaped house at Rostella Road, Dilston, a suburb of Launceston, built in 1954 by architect Edward R. 'Ted' Ashton. This dramatic house, in a wonderful setting overlooking the Tamar, reflects the interest in experimental geometry seen in Victoria in the same era.
COURTESY: THE EXAMINER (LAUNCESTON)

• *Below:* The origins of the term 'waterfall style' are evident in the chimney of this 1950s house in Central Victoria.

PHOTOGRAPH: THE AUTHOR

• *Opposite right*: Suburban homes in the Hobart suburb of New Town, c.1950.

COLLECTION: ARCHIVES OFFICE OF TASMANIA

• *Opposite*: This chimney suggests Skyscraper Moderne rather than a waterfall.

PHOTOGRAPH: THE AUTHOR

• STYLES •

— Waterfall Front —

If cube forms dominated functionalist architecture, curved and cylindrical forms were also important. Curved corners and streamlined shapes represented a dynamic new age. Fashionable modern houses in the 1930s were sometimes described as being like ocean liners, with walls, windows and balconies all sweeping around corners. By the 1940s these details were well entrenched as part of a popular suburban style referred to as 'Waterfall' or 'Waterfall Front'. The waterfall idea came from the use of descending curves in chimneys, fence pillars and other vertical elements. Robin Boyd noted that three was 'the key to decorative smartness'.[3] Three steps were typically used for the waterfall effect and parallel lines often went in threes.

Substantial brick houses were the outstanding examples of the Waterfall style in the suburbs. To emphasise the overall theme of horizontality, bands of brickwork were alternated with bands of stucco, usually painted off-white, cream, buff or ochre. In other versions bands of darker-coloured bricks, sometimes machine-textured, would alternate with lighter bricks, such as cream or salmon.

— International Style —

Many permutations can be identified within the broader compass of the evolving International style. Materials such as reinforced concrete, steel frames, walls of glass and every detail stripped down to a pure functional form were the essence of this style. At its core it was a commitment to honesty in the use of materials and a belief that people's needs in the modern world would be centred around technology.

Many houses designed by architects in Australia adopted the superficial features of this style, but were often not far removed in their planning from conservative schemes. Ordinary suburban houses incorporated some influences of the International style, such as large window areas and some aspects of rational planning. But it remained essentially a cerebral style, best handled by architects who were well versed in the theory.

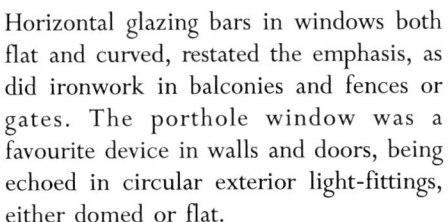

Horizontal glazing bars in windows both flat and curved, restated the emphasis, as did ironwork in balconies and fences or gates. The porthole window was a favourite device in walls and doors, being echoed in circular exterior light-fittings, either domed or flat.

The term 'Waterfall Front' attests to the superficial nature of many examples. It was often just another example of 'facadism' where modernistic detail was applied to a basically conservative brick villa. There was no understanding of the notion of designing 'in the round' which was essential to a truly functional building in the International style. The use of a traditional hipped roof with Marseilles tiles suited the builders and their clients who wanted something seen to be modern, but also comfortably solid.

— Waterfall Austerity —

A simplified version of the Waterfall Front, incorporating a few fashionable details, developed in the immediate post-war years — due to a lack of funds and available materials. The most common type was the timber-framed house clad in asbestos-cement which used curved sheets on the corners of the front rooms. Other examples were built in rendered brick, Mt Gambier stone or concrete. As previously noted, the austerity style was very plain and the only other concession to fashion might be a curved, flat-roofed porch or some waterfall details in metal railings. Most austerity designs with curved corners were not able to include curved windows in the budget and so made do with ordinary wood or steel-framed flat windows placed centrally in the time-honoured fashion. They might manage a 'Chicago-style' window, a large fixed central 'landscape' window with narrow opening sashes on each side.

— Conventional Suburban Style —

By the 1930s there were increasing numbers of suburban bungalows which, while not radically modern in their design, were basically free of non-functional details from period styles such as California Bungalow, Spanish Mission or Tudor. The roof was a medium pitch, either hipped, gabled or hip and gable. Walls were plain, and chimneys basically plain, and the only concession to decoration might be in relation to the porch and front entrance. The classic type of the post-war era was the double- or triple-fronted house with tile roof, small front porch and plain windows in wood or steel. The plan is often described as an asymmetrical set-back or step-back design and evolved from the 19th-century house, with a projecting front room.

Brick and brick-veneer were considered the ideal for standard suburban houses (also called bungalows) and the basic design has continued to be popular right up to the present day. Weatherboard, asbestos-cement, cement block, stone and concrete were all used in the 1940s and '50s, but in the long run brick has eclipsed all other materials. Clay or cement tiles were, as they still are, the popular roofing, and typically the eaves were boxed (sheeted horizontally) rather than showing exposed rafters, as was fashionable for rustic bungalow designs in the 1920s.

In the inter-war years, tile roofs of blended colours became fashionable.

• Colonial-style house, Castlemaine, Victoria, designed for Harry and Billie Blake by Melbourne architect Harry Winbush in 1946.

PHOTOGRAPH: THE AUTHOR

Variations on this decorative treatment continued in the post-war era. Decorative effects in the brickwork included using darker bricks for window sills, as string courses, as coping for low walls, chimneys and fences and in the area below floor-level. Patterns of raised bricks on wall surfaces were also used to break up areas. Sometimes a brick garage would be attached to the house; in other cases it would be separate.

— Georgian Revival Style —

Usually chosen by the affluent as a refined and dignified period style, Georgian Revival or Neo Georgian gathered favour from the early 20th century. It was seen as a tasteful alternative to the excesses of Queen Anne and Old English. The traditional concern for proportions, plain surfaces, fine details and fresh but subdued colour schemes made it acceptable to architects who believed in functionalism but could not convince their clients to build in the newest styles. Windows were small-paned and generally given louvred shutters. Doorways with solid panelled doors had delicate fanlights and sidelights and sometimes a classical porch or perhaps an entablature with pilasters. In the 1940s and '50s, houses in Georgian style were usually in cream brick or painted brick, with woodwork painted off-white, cream or ivory. The shutters might be apple green, blue-grey, buff or cream. Slates, shingle tiles or Marseilles tiles in selected colours were favoured for the roof.

— English Style —

By the post-war era Old English or Tudor style had lost its place as one of the fashionable styles. Restrictions and shortages of materials would only allow a simplified version and in some cases it was only seen in details such as a porch, the treatment of a gable or chimney and in the use of leadlight in the windows. The elaborate examples with many gables, half-timbering and other picturesque details had been reduced by the 1930s to a fairly severe all-brick construction, often given areas of stucco with trimmings in dark brown manganese bricks. The traditional steep gables were reduced, sometimes to a reasonably low pitch and some were given hip roofs.

— Colonial Style —

There were a number of streams of influence within the general category termed Colonial style. Australia's own colonial tradition was rediscovered early this century as part of a Georgian revival influenced by the work of architects in Britain and the United States. William Hardy Wilson, a Sydney architect, was inspired by what he had seen overseas to search out our early buildings, and in 1923 he published *Old Colonial Architecture in New South Wales and Tasmania*. This gave further impetus to the acceptance of Georgian and Colonial Georgian for new houses. Books, magazines and films from the United States increased popular interest in American Colonial style so that by 1940 it was seen in many parts of Australia and in the post-war years was considered by many to be acceptable for anything from suburban houses to substantial town or country residences.

In the hands of knowledgeable and highly-trained architects in the United States it was thoughtfully interpreted, but when taken up by builders and 'designers' could be reduced to a mixed bag of 'Colonial' features, with the original proportions and intentions lost. Australia mostly received the watered-down suburban version of American Colonial,

DEFINING THE STYLES

• *Right*: 'Tasbestos' flat sheet and 'Trojan' tiles were used on this 1956 L-shaped house in the Railton housing scheme of the Tasmanian Housing Department.

COLLECTION: STATE OFFICES LIBRARY, HOBART, TASMANIA

• *Below:* Design for a cottage, Edna Walling. *Cottage and Garden in Australia, 1947.*

where details such as small-paned windows with shutters, cupolas with weathervanes, dormer windows and fretted wooden valances were applied to ordinary house designs or even stretched out in long 'ranch- style' schemes. One important effect of the American Colonial revival was that it gave a new respectability to weatherboards. Australians had mostly associated them with old vernacular buildings and lesser versions of fashionable styles. Now the crisp white walls with contrasting shutters were highly desirable.

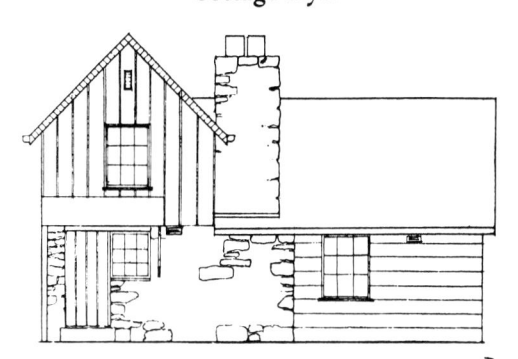

— Cottage Style —

From the 1920s, Edna Walling had reached a wide audience through her writing in the *Australian Home Beautiful*. She championed cottage gardens and, in particular, old perennials. Regularly seen in her articles were photographs of the cottages on her Bickleigh Vale Estate at Mooroolbark, Victoria, including their simple interiors. In 1947 her book *Cottage and Garden in Australia* was published and became an important influence for anyone seeking a traditional approach to basic domestic architecture. Edna Walling cottages were generally compact structures, usually with steep roofs which often included attic rooms. Chimneys and sometimes the walls were of local freestone and roofs were clad in shingles, corrugated iron or asbestos-cement. Exterior walls were typically clad in vertical boarding, with cover straps over each joint. In some designs weatherboards were used.

In keeping with the cottage tradition, windows and doors were glazed with small panes. The standard window used was the six-paned casement, a classic type for cottages in the British Isles. Edna Walling's enthusiasm for simple romantic cottages and woodland gardens appealed to those who were not greatly impressed by the stark forms and hard edges of modernism.

The *Australian Home Beautiful*'s January 1947 issue featured a spacious artist's cottage at Stirling West in the Adelaide Hills. Built of timber on a base of local freestone, it had two stone chimneys and stone verandah columns. Log cabins were also a popular subject at this time.

— Post-war Austerity —

A product of necessity rather than the ideals of those who espoused modern functionalism, houses reflecting post-war austerity tended to be stark, uninspired answers to the conditions which prevailed. They were the average Australian house stripped to its bare essentials, a basic assembly of walls, roof, floor, windows and doors. Many were simple boxes others L-shaped or double fronted. The front porch was minimal, and the eaves were reduced so that very little shelter was offered. If larger windows could be found they would be included, but generally the standard balanced sashes in pairs was used and in utility areas and sleepouts, glass louvres predominated.

Architects designed houses using the same materials within the same restrictions, and usually proved that good design is possible even under such conditions. Prefabrication added to the range of austerity houses a mixture of designs, some successful others less so. Improving conditions saw additions and alterations to many austerity designs, but

• Sketch for brick veneer house at Mentone, Victoria, John Mockridge 1947 (see page 100).

Brick-veneer house at Mentone.

enough survive to remind us of an important time when Australia was reconstructing itself and facing a new era.

— Post-war Contemporary —

When people spoke of having a contemporary house in the 1940s and '50s they meant that it was not in one of the traditional styles. In 1952 the New South Wales Chapter of the Royal Australian Institute of Architects held an exhibition. Architects in attendance conducted a survey of the visitors and came up with some interesting results.[4] Three out of every four people said they wanted houses which 'looked modern' and had 'a lot of glass'.

Flat roofs drew a higher vote than the conventional pitched roofs, and it was proclaimed by Walter Bunning, chairman of the exhibition committee, that the quiz showed a decisive victory for contemporary architecture in the battle with traditional designs. However, we might take into account that the sample was not necessarily a wide cross-section of the community. Most likely it was the interested and better-informed who would attend such an exhibition, but it is nevertheless an insight into the debate at that time.

The results of the survey show that while the flat roof drew 36.9 per cent of the votes the pitched roof was close behind with 34.6 per cent. The vote for a house which 'looked modern' was 77.3 per cent, but then again 64.2 per cent also wanted it to look 'homely'. The high vote for brick construction (47 per cent compared with only 15.4 per cent for timber) was said to partly reflect local government restrictions which meant that the largest proportion of houses seen in the exhibition was brick.

Mr C. Lembke, director of the Timber Development Association, felt that the vote for timber was 'reasonably satisfactory' in view of the history of the timber home in Sydney. Local authorities were by then giving favourable consideration to timber houses and the state had ruled that no more 'brick areas' were to be declared. 'For me the lesson of the Quiz is that we shall try to evolve a modern type of timber home with plenty of glass, something on the line of that found in California.'[5]

'Contemporary' in the post-war era might mean a flat roof, but also included butterfly, skillion and low-pitched hip or gable roofs. Large areas of glass were a key element basically derived from International style. Materials varied from traditional types such as brick, timber, stone, *pise* and mud-brick, to steel,

• Holiday house at Olinda, Victoria; architect John Mockridge, 1947.

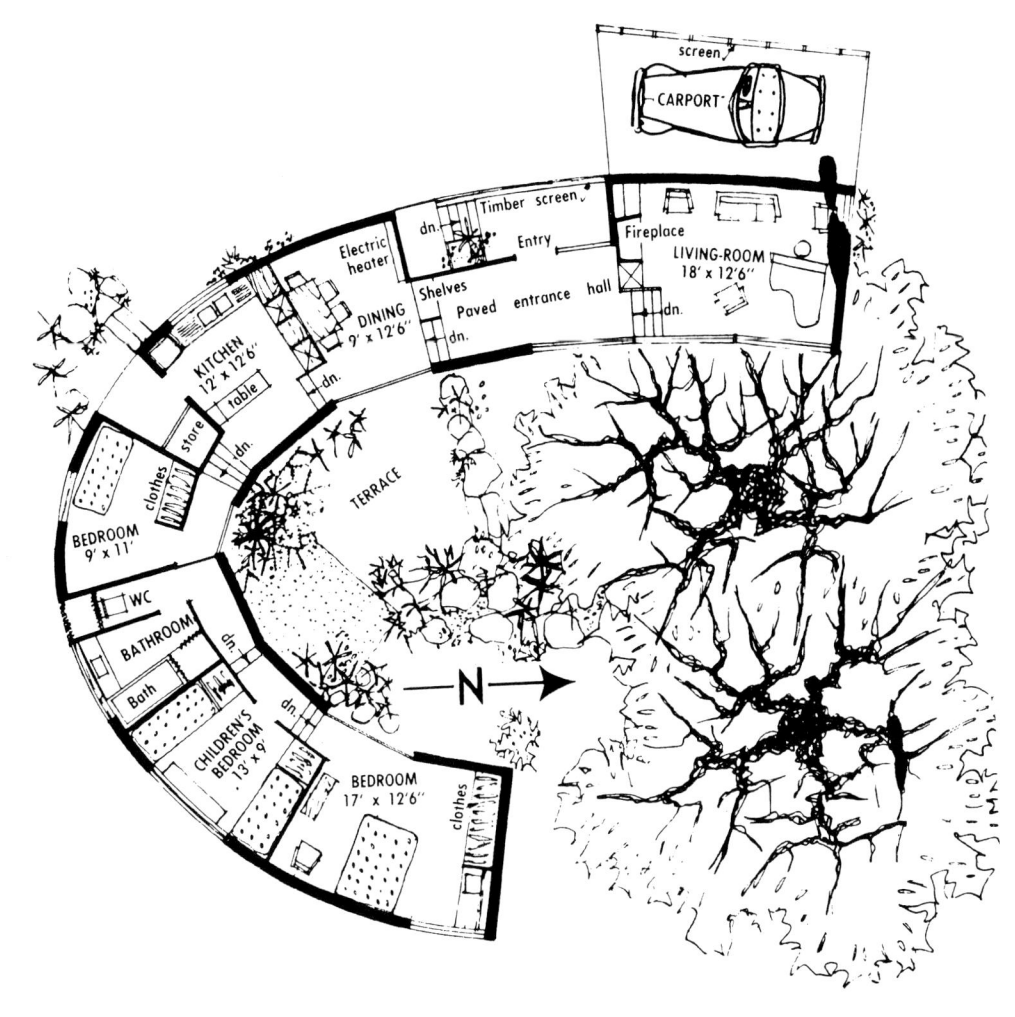

DEFINING THE STYLES

• Realisation of the possibilities in a sloping site with mature trees is seen in the 1954 Snelleman house in Keam Street, Ivanhoe, Victoria. Architect Peter McIntyre designed this residence to sweep down a series of levels curving around and up again.

Australian Home Beautiful, January 1956

• *Below*: House at Mentone, Victoria; architect John Mockridge, 1947.

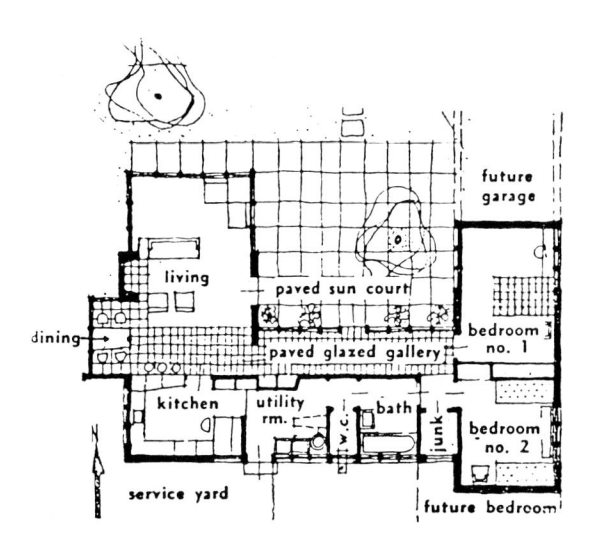

aluminium, plastic, fibre-glass, reinforced concrete and the whole range of sheeting. The term 'contemporary' could also cover designs from sophisticated functionalist cube forms to those endowed with all the latest fashionable details. Decor might vary from an imaginative and thoughtful use of colours, textures and well-designed furniture and furnishings to a featuristic conglomeration of clashing colours, bizarre patterns and latest fads in furniture, fittings and knick-knacks.

— Organic or Environmental —

Although not widely recognised or even understood in the period under review, the philosophy of creating modern houses which had an organic relationship with their environment was at an important stage of development. In essence, this meant selecting both materials and a design to harmonise with a chosen natural setting or one which had a natural character. This philosophy was at odds with ordinary suburban developments which usually began with the removal of any existing natural vegetation. In bushland areas on the fringes of towns and cities, many important 'organic' houses were built in the 1940s and '50s and these are now recognised as important steps in the movement toward wider acceptance of environmental awareness (see chapter 7.)

— Ranch Style —

Magazines and Hollywood films did a lot to promote the Ranch-style house. In the *Australian Home Beautiful*'s issue for October 1945 there is a two-page feature entitled, 'A Modern Ranch-Type Home in America'. Illustrations show a long, low nine-roomed house which is made up of two angled wings linked by a large living room. 'This style, known as the Californian ranch type, is becoming very popular for country homes in the U.S.A. in those States where the prevailing weather conditions are suitable.' Built in white painted brick and weatherboard with blue-green shutters, it had a shingle roof.

This type of structure evolved from the traditional single-storey *rancho* which was usually a series of rooms each opening onto a long verandah. Architects in California adapted the style to modern needs and included new features, such as large glass picture windows. The old courtyard from the Spanish Colonial

123

• *Opposite*: Robin Boyd's own house built in Melbourne's South Yarra in 1959 is a notable example of the structuralist approach.
PHOTOGRAPH: MARK STRIZIC

background became a patio and the verandah an outdoor room.

Angled wings were included in a Ranch-style house built at Wahroonga, north of Sydney, in around 1950. Mr and Mrs Albert Losch chose this Californian style for its informality and spaciousness. Architect John Brogan drew the plans. The exterior was rough-cast, white-washed brick with a low-pitched tiled roof. In keeping with the idea of ranch-house informality, the verandah posts and framework were whitewashed rough hewn posts. 'The huge picture windows have deep window sills where gay pot plants are placed, and in one corner of the house, there is a well established cactus garden.'[6] Mr and Mrs Losch had been to Mexico and had brought back a brilliantly striped rug which complemented the soft yellow walls of the living room.

In September 1956, the magazine *Australian Homemaker* featured a four-page article on Bing Crosby's holiday retreat overlooking Lake Hayden in Idaho. Bing had built 'a long, low log cabin which could be any ranch-style home in Australia.' The Small Homes Service (NSW) had offered the *Australian Home Beautiful*'s readers in April 1955, 'a "Ranch-style" plan for country clients. Suggested as ideal for a hillside farmhouse, township residence or shady homestead for the hot inland, it was designed to be built in three stages. It is ironic that Australia's own tradition of long, low verandahed houses was largely ignored in the rush to borrow from American models.

— Regional Styles —

Architectural guides currently recognise two regional styles in Australian domestic architecture in the period from 1940 to 1960. The Post-war Melbourne Regional house typically shared characteristics with the Ranch style in that it was a single storey with a narrow, linear plan. Influences from houses on the West Coast of the United States are in fact given as a possible influence.[7] Horizontality was emphasised through the use of low-pitched gable roofs with wide eaves and slim bargeboards. Brickwork, bagged and painted, or boarding oiled or varnished, were combined with large areas of glass. Variations used flat or low-pitched skillion roofs.

Houses grouped under Post-war Brisbane Regional shared with their Melbourne counterparts the essential influence of modern functionalist architecture. Importantly, they also looked to a regional integrity and in the Brisbane area this meant designs suitable for a warm, humid climate. Low cube-form houses on ground level or raised up, were given verandahs with blinds, screens or panels between the posts (see previous chapter). Modern elements included large areas of glass, flat or low-pitched roofs, and the use of steel and reinforced concrete.

— Geometrical Designs —

Experimentation was an exciting prospect in the post-war era and was made possible by a wider acceptance on the part of clients of less conservative possibilities. At a time when all that was new and boldly modern was celebrated by much of the community, houses with circular, triangular, and other unusual plan shapes gained great notoriety. Melbourne was the region for unusual geometric styles, but round houses appeared in picturesque settings in many parts of Australia. Most were architect-designed but others were the efforts of builders and owner-builders who were inspired to see if they could follow examples they had seen. Unusual geometry also appeared in other aspects of design, such as the use of bold structural forms (see previous chapter).

— Structuralist Influence —

Architects of the 'Melbourne School' in the 1940s and '50s sometimes chose unusual styles of house construction. Robin Boyd, Peter McIntyre, Roy Grounds, David Chancellor and others created houses where the structure was expressed as an important visual aspect (see also Chapter 5). Robin Boyd's own house of 1959, built on a sloping site in Melbourne's fashionable South Yarra, was given a tensile roof which employed a series of cables strung between steel uprights. The children's and adults' areas were separated by a glass-walled courtyard.[8] It was a house where living and private spaces were divided by changes of level rather than using traditional walls to create boxed-in rooms. The unusual roof and general structure was clearly evident from both without and within.

DEFINING THE STYLES

• Perspective and plan for a 'contemporary'-style house offered by the Queensland Housing Commission in the 1950s.
COLLECTION: QUEENSLAND DEPARTMENT OF HOUSING, LOCAL GOVERNMENT AND PLANNING

• *Opposite page*: Mud-brick-making, Eltham, Victoria, 1947. Gordon Ford stamps mud into a brick mould while Laurie Mayfield (left), Sonia Skipper, Alistair Knox and Tony Jackson look on.

— **Tropical or Subtropical Style** —

Apart from the houses defined as post-war Brisbane Regional, there were houses built in Queensland and the Northern territory in the 1940s and '50s which can be seen to have distinctive characteristics. In many parts of Queensland from the south-east up to Cairns and beyond, there were versions of the traditional house now generally called a 'Queenslander'. In the inter-war years the War Service Homes Commission and the State Advances Corporation of Queensland as well as private companies offered catalogues of house designs, the majority of which were designed for tropical conditions. After the war basic versions of many of these designs were built. Details such as verandahs or porches, casement windows, stained weatherboards and the idea of building up on stumps to various heights still held on, although, up to 1952, restrictions on area made any sizeable verandah or porch a luxury. Those who favoured 'high-set' houses were at least given some compensation when stairs and landings were excluded from floor area calculations.

Cross ventilation through the use of banks of casement or louvre windows was a standard method of coping with tropical conditions and in the post-war years the awning sash or hopper window was increasingly used.

Progressive architects in the 1940s and '50s made a vital contribution to the revival of rational design for the tropical and subtropical house. An outstanding example of modern functionalist ideals expressed in a regional style was a house built in Darwin in the Northern Territory in the late 1950s.[9] Architect Stuart McIntosh chose 'in-line' planning with cross-ventilation for a house elevated on steel columns. The entire northern elevation was a long, slim rectangle of steel louvres and the southern elevation was given a full-length balcony. No glazed windows were used and rooms were given access to the balcony through a wall of insect screens with sliding panels. An open-plan living, dining and kitchen area occupied the western end of the house and bedrooms were at the eastern end to avoid the late afternoon sun.[10]

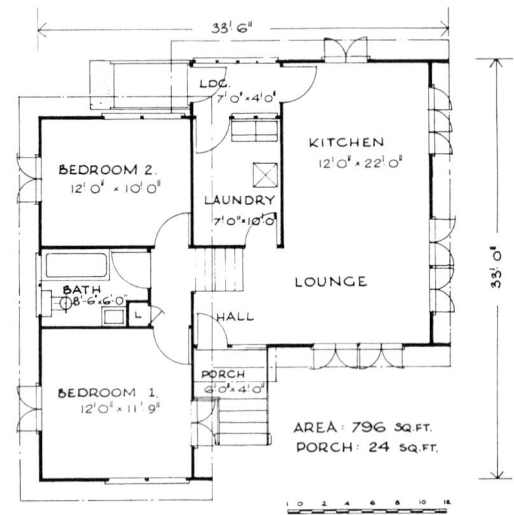

Chapter 6 Endnotes

[1] James Birrell, *Walter Burley Griffin*, University of Queensland Press, Brisbane, 1964, p. 183.

[2] J. M. Freeland, *Architecture in Australia: A History*, Penguin Books, Ringwood, Victoria, 1972, p. 274.

[3] Robin Boyd, *Australia's Home*, Melbourne University Press, Melbourne, 1952, p. 89.

[4] Keith Newman, quoted in 'A Vintage year in Our Home Design', *Australian Home Beautiful*, November, 1952, pp. 64-66.

[5] C. Lembke, quoted in 'A Vintage Year in Our Home Design', *Australian Home Beautiful*, November, 1952, p. 66.

[6] Wahroonga Ranch House, *Australian House and Garden*, January 1952, p. 47.

[7] R. Apperly, R. Irving, & P. Reynolds, *A Pictorial Guide to Identifying Australian Architecture, Styles and Towns from 1788 to the Present*, Angus & Robertson, Sydney, 1989, p. 218.

[8] Beyond the 1950s, *The History and Design of the Australian House*, Compiled by Robert Irving, Oxford University Press, Melbourne, 1985, p. 150.

[9] Neil Clerehan, (ed.), *Best Australian Houses: Recent Houses Built by Members of The Royal Australian Architects*, F. W. Cheshire, Melbourne, 1961.

[10] ibid.

CHAPTER SEVEN
Environmental Influences

LIVING IN A SOCIETY where environmental concerns are a part of everyday life makes it difficult for younger generations to imagine a time when only a few farsighted people were attempting to re-define the relationship between humanity and the earth. This question has engaged thinkers for thousands of years, but for most of the population in post-war Australia progress was a continuation of the pioneering ethos. The future through technology and science promised limitless development. Thankfully, there were those who realised the importance of learning about our natural heritage, of coming to terms with Australia's unique character.

Finding less intrusive ways to dwell in natural or semi-natural surroundings became an exciting challenge. The 1940s and '50s were a significant period when houses built as a response to the environment were opening up new directions.

Two distinctive types of domestic architecture are represented in this field of interest. On the one hand we have the houses which used natural materials for reasons of economy and harmony. Builders of such houses had no great desire for their work to be seen as sophisticated contemporary architecture. On the other, there were houses which included both traditional and modern materials and were designed by architects thoroughly versed in the International aesthetic. Between the two extremes were different permutations, but all possessed one central philosophy, the belief in the importance of an organic relationship between the house and its environment.

Artists, architects, craftspeople, writers, poets, utopians and all the other kinds of people who observe the relationship between civilisation and the natural world had begun to question the advance of industrialised society in the second half of the 19th century. The British Arts and Crafts Movement and many groups of idealists influenced by its philosophies believed among other things in the importance of craftsmanship and in the need for integrity in the design of everything, from houses and furniture to cutlery and fabrics. In reaction to the grim factories and growing urbanisation there

Australian Home Beautiful, June 1948

• *Left*: The first building at Montsalvat, Eltham, Victoria, erected in 1935–36. This was constructed using *pise de terre* (rammed earth), but as the colony grew, adobe (mud-brick), stone and brick all found a place.

PHOTOGRAPH: ROBERT HADDEN

• *Opposite page*: Mud-brick house of Peter and Cecile Glass, John Street, Eltham, Victoria. This innovative two-storey structure was completed in 1959. Built by Alistair Knox and his team, it was designed by Peter Glass who worked with Knox as a draftsman for many years. While the ground floor area was only nine squares, the living area was a dramatic space two storeys high, with a gallery serving the upstairs bedrooms.

PHOTOGRAPH: MARK STRIZIC

also developed a new emphasis on the dignity of the individual and the ideal of a closer relationship with nature.

Arts and Crafts architects discovered the simple beauty of vernacular architecture, with its use of traditional materials and functional form. William Morris, a dominant figure in the British movement, had suggested that buildings should be an intrinsic part of their environment and that materials should be used with due regard for their integrity.[1] American architects and craftspeople took up the principles and ideals espoused by their counterparts in Britain and adapted them to conditions in the United States. Frank Lloyd Wright, who respected both handcraft and the value of the machine, created new kinds of houses which re-stated the importance of the relationship between a building and its natural setting. Similar aims were realised in the Californian houses of Charles and Henry Greene which influenced California bungalows early this century.

Houses, bungalows and cottages in Australia, which were a faithful reflection of Arts and Crafts ideals, generally settled comfortably into natural settings or woodland gardens. The work of the great American architect Frank Lloyd Wright was understood and admired by a growing number of Australian architects. His associates Walter Burley Griffin and Marion Mahony lived here between 1914 and 1936, leaving a legacy of outstanding buildings, including many houses carefully designed to harmonise with their environment.

The influences of rational planning and a respect for traditional materials were seen in the work of the architect Archibald C. MacKnight who built earth-walled houses in northern Victoria and the Riverina from early this century. In 1909 he built his own house of *pise-de-terre* in Victoria's Rutherglen district.[2] His son Charles A. MacKnight joined him in the practice and between them they contributed to the body of knowledge which supported the wider acceptance of earth building from the 1940s.

In its June 1942 issue, the *Australian Home Beautiful* included an article headed, 'What is Pise-de-terre?' It began:

In these days of restrictions on building and building materials it is worthwhile considering the use of one of the most ancient known building materials — earth ... Even today there are millions of people living in earthen dwellings in China, Africa and other lands. England, too, has old houses whose walls consist of rammed earth (*pise-de-terre*), and many readers have seen the picturesque adobe homes and missions in Mexico and California.

It then discusses various aspects of earth construction, noting that, 'the pioneers built houses of earth — mostly of mud bricks — particularly in alluvial gold field areas where soil was most suitable.'

An important aspect of construction, the matter of foundations, is referred to and the MacKnights use of reinforced concrete as foundations for difficult ground is discussed. Excerpts from two reports on *pise* and soil stabilisation from England and America appeared in the April 1943 issue of the magazine. Soil stabilisation was the mixing of cement with earth which A.C. MacKnight describes as 'the half-way house between Pise and Concrete' and he also comments 'The description of Pise methods in the report contains nothing new to us and omits many things which have become common practice here'.

From the early 1930s Justus Jorgensen and his followers at the Montsalvat Artists' Colony in Eltham, Victoria, had been using *pise-de-terre* to construct the first romantic buildings of what has become a mecca for those interested in traditional

ENVIRONMENTAL INFLUENCES

• Stairwell and lower level of the mudbrick house and studio at Eltham, Victoria, designed and built for artist Phyl Busst by Alistair Knox in 1948.

PHOTOGRAPH: MARK STRIZIC

crafts. Another advocate of *pise-de-terre* was John M. Harcourt who also settled in Eltham in the 1930s. He became a great proponent of *pise* construction and built numerous houses. His article in the *Australian Home Beautiful's* January 1946 issue was entitled, 'Natural Earth as Building Material, Pise-de-terre, Cob and Mud Brick Methods Explained'. It is a long and detailed review with emphasis on practical directions for working with mud-bricks. A pivotal figure in the acceptance of mud-brick for modern environmentally conscious houses was Alistair Knox, builder, designer and noted advocate. Born in the Melbourne suburb of Middle Park in 1912, he began work in a bank at the beginning of the Depression. His first visit to the Jorgensen Art Colony was in 1940 when he and an architect friend rode out to Eltham from Eaglemont.[3] On that and subsequent visits he became fascinated by the building techniques used at Montsalvat. Apart from the early *pise* structures there were others in mud-brick or adobe, including the studio erected in 1935. This also had an upper storey of wattle and daub.

After three years in the Australian Navy during the war Knox returned to the bank and part-time study in building practice and theory at Melbourne Technical College. While doing the course he befriended Eltham artist, Matcham Skipper, who was also attending. Links with Eltham and Montsalvat were rekindled, leading to a return visit in 1946, after a gap of some four years.

Knox began his first house in 1946 while midway through his studies. This and a second house were in timber, but in 1947, at a time when building materials were in desperately short supply, he agreed to design and erect a small mud-brick house at Lower Plenty, near Eltham. Frank English, a returned serviceman, had admired mud-brick buildings while in the Middle East and had enough deferred pay to build a low-cost dwelling. Knox enlisted the help of Sonia Skipper who had gained years of experience in mud-brick building at Montsalvat. She ably took charge of the working crew — not an easy task as some of them were only moderately enthused with the idea of real work.[4]

One important barrier faced Alistair Knox and his first mud-brick house — the need to obtain permission from the Shire of Eltham to build a dwelling in that material. The Jelbarts, Harcourts and the 'Jorgensen Colony' had all built in mud-brick, but permits were obtained with few questions asked. John Harcourt had completed a large house of stone and mud-brick by 1945. In the January 1946 article, he notes that the Secretary of the Shire of Eltham was authorised to issue permits without consulting the council, 'provided plans and specifications comply with general building regulations.' By 1947 the secretary had retired and the temporary engineer was handling building matters. After badgering him each week, Knox finally got word that his plan for a complete mud-brick house was on the council's agenda but that his permit would probably not be forthcoming. He realised his only chance of convincing them lay in a pamphlet by G. F. Middleton, called 'Earth Wall Construction', recently published by the Commonwealth Experimental Building Station.[5] Enquiries revealed that copies had just arrived from Sydney and so he caught the first train into Melbourne, acquired about ten copies and was back in Eltham by about 2 pm. When he reached the shire office he was just in time to catch the councillors returning from lunch, ready to continue their monthly meeting. Some were casually discussing his application to build in mud-brick so he handed each one a copy of the pamphlet — with the result that when the meeting resumed the building was approved.

From that time, mud-brick houses were increasingly seen around Eltham, in

ENVIRONMENTAL INFLUENCES

• The interior of the Busst house, Eltham, Victoria, contrasts with the conventional schemes of the same period.

PHOTOGRAPH: MARK STRIZIC

other parts of Victoria and in natural surroundings in other states. That first house by Alistair Knox was a simple rectangle with a skillion roof and a large walk-in fireplace or inglenook. A series of french windows, interspaced with piers 3 ft × 2 ft (915 mm × 710 mm), made up the north elevation and were shaded in the heat of the day by the widely projecting eaves. Poles of Yellow-box (*Eucalyptus melliodora*) 25 feet long were supported by piers, two of which were extended to form the inglenook. The walls were nine inches thick and, along with the piers, were on concrete footings. Flooring was conventional tongue and grooved on joists with bearers and stumps. For the roof, flooring boards were fixed to 5 inch × 2 inch (127 mm × 50 mm) hardwood, then covered with insulating foil followed by layers of malthoid and finally water-worn creek gravel, floated in bitumen.[6]

When asked why he built with mud-brick rather than *pise*, Knox said he believed they were a more flexible form — they were modular, while a wall of rammed earth was monolithic. 'You could even build a round house with mud-bricks, but you'd have your work cut out to do it in *pise*.'[7] He also noted that mud-bricks were not only an answer to the building problem but fitted admirably into the Australian landscape.

A much larger house followed his first effort. It was a brave and important step, as it began the use of the concrete slab in conjunction with mud-brick. Phyl Busst, an amateur painter associated with the Eltham Artists' Colony, engaged Alistair

Opposite: Architect Peter Muller's own house, Whale Beach, New South Wales, 1955.

Australian Home Beautiful, June 1960

Knox in 1948 to build a residence-cum-studio. When completed it fitted snugly into the hillside, with both lower and upper storeys given access to ground level. It also included curved walls which were to be seen in many later mud-brick houses. The upstairs bedroom/studio opened onto a balcony which was above the living room.

Concrete for the slab was handmixed by two men, Eltham identities Horrie Judd and Gordon Ford. The entire job which required fifty-two bags of cement, along with twenty tons of screenings and sand, was done in a single day.[8] Gordon Ford started on his own mud-brick house in 1947 and by the early 1950s had begun his long career as a landscaper.

In 1949, Alistair Knox befriended composer and music critic Dorian Le Gallienne. This led to Le Gallienne and his lifelong companion Dick Downing asking Knox to design and construct a mud-brick weekend house for them on their bushland property adjoining the Yarra River at Eltham. These two men possessed a deep sense of a whole landscape and its relationship to humanity. Their thinking had an important effect on Alistair Knox:

Like everyone else at this time, I was itching to be clever in design. It was Dorian's explanations which caused me to slow down and think in simple, timeless proportions — to relate to the powerful landscape, rather than try to outdo it.[9]

The first of four Knox structures on the property was a simple rectangular plan with a concrete plinth capping each mud-brick wall. Set into these concrete beams was a system of rafters which formed scissor trusses. It was a technique inspired by the Church of England at Maldon in Victoria's goldfields region. The ceiling ridge gave the impression of being unsupported and, like a church, the entire interior was open to view except for some partitions which were a mere seven feet (2135 mm) high. Windows in the gables captured the landscape and thoughtful planting brought it even closer.

Knox was busy throughout the 1950s designing and building. In 1962, having taken a hard look at the balance sheets, he changed direction and concentrated on designing. While mud-brick or adobe became very popular, the system of *pise-de-terre* or rammed earth was still found most suitable in regions where the proportion of clay in the soil was less than 50 per cent. The ideal for *pise* was 70 per cent of sand and 30 per cent of clay. For mud-brick the proportions were reversed. An article by S. G. Andrews, entitled 'Adobe or Pise — Economical Houses', appeared in the May 1950 issue of *Australian House and Garden*. It discussed two houses, one an owner-built adobe house built in 1948-49 at Montmorency, near Eltham, and the other in *pise* at Baulkham Hills, New South Wales. The latter was currently under construction.[10]

Many architects in the post-war years were creating houses in bushland settings. Robin Boyd noted that there was a distinctive 'Warrandyte Style' which he saw as a logical extension of the fundamental ideals seen in the Californian Bungalow.[11] Such houses had walls of vertical boards, rubble stone or adobe, low-gabled or skillion roofs, large 'studio' windows and the basic services. Warrandyte was a traditional picnic spot, a small township on the Yarra upstream from Eltham. It shared with that place a reputation as an area for artists and craftspeople. Architects Best Overend, Robert Eggleston and Fritz Janeba were among those associated with the area.

Architect Kenneth McDonald in his 1954 book, *The New Australian Home*, noted the growing consciousness of the relationship between houses and the environment:

Sometimes the modern house sits up on its site like a camera focused on a view or, in other instances, the house spreads itself out, rambling and nestling closely into the contours of the land. But in all instances, there is a harmony between the environment and the well-designed house.[12]

Houses which incorporated natural materials as an important key to their integration with a setting, but which were also unashamedly modern, represent an important advance in environmental consciousness in Australia. Walter Burley Griffin, with his passion for the natural landscape, made a notable contribution. His early designs for Sydney's unique Castlecrag development, which began in 1921, used native stone for solid masonry walls. These seemed to grow out of the rocky crags so that the houses were integrated with the wooded bluffs overlooking Middle Harbour.

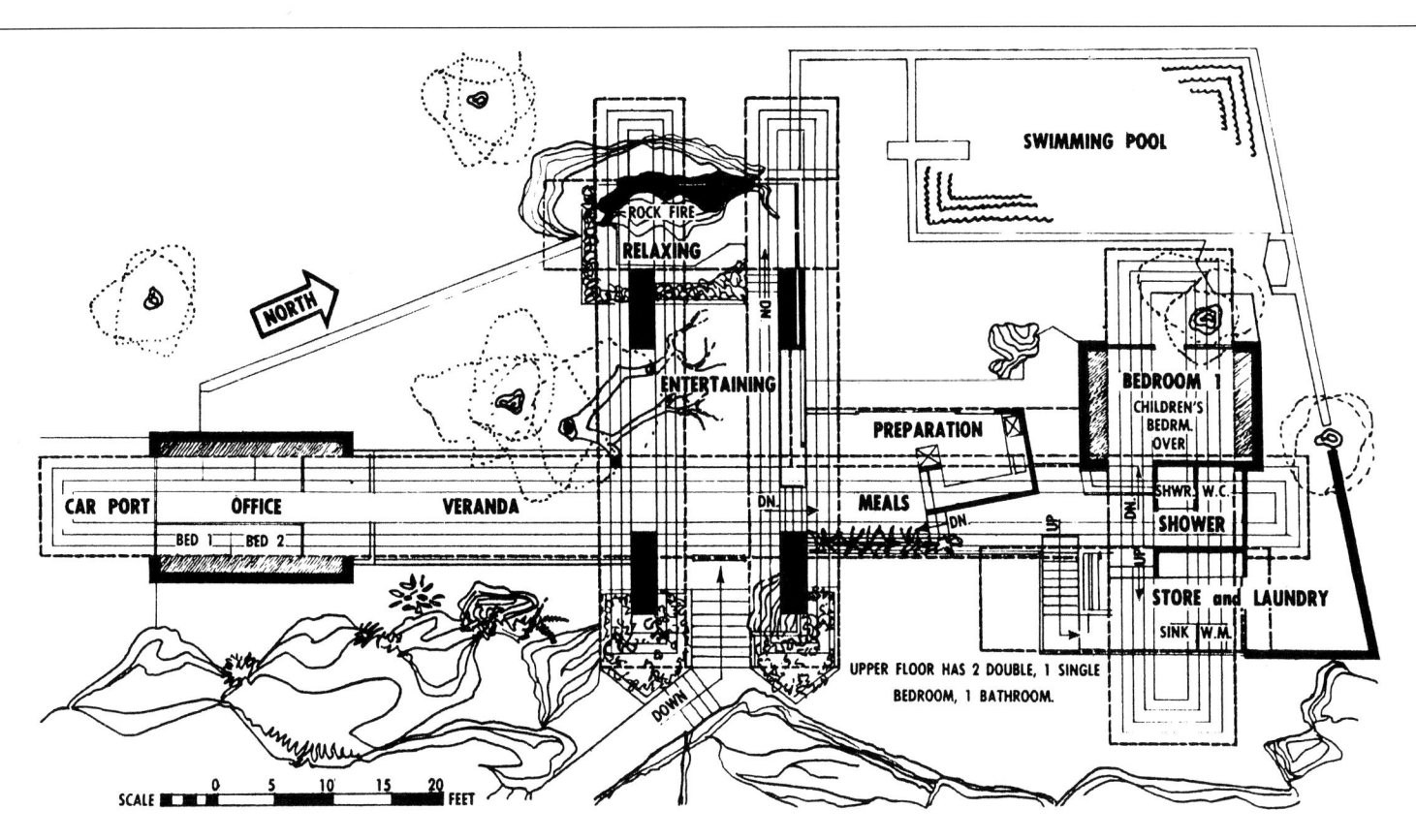

In the 1950s, architect Peter Muller, also a man imbued with a deep sensitivity to the environment, created a series of exciting houses in natural settings. His first commission, the 1953 Audette house in Edinburgh Road, Castlecrag, was designed on three axes, with its horizontality emphasised by broad sweeps of untreated timber. The walls of the upper level were sheltered by widely projecting eaves, an echo of the work of Frank Lloyd Wright, as were the interpenetrating forms which recalled the famous Fallingwater at Bear Run, Pennsylvania. In all subsequent work, Muller displayed a clearer independence, a strongly individual response to the Australian landscape.

Born in Adelaide in 1927, Peter Muller was educated at St Peter's School, and from 1944 to 1948 at the University of Adelaide. In the period from 1945 to 1948 he was also studying at the South Australian School of Mines and Industries. During the years 1950 and 1951 he attended the University of Pennsylvania where he received a Master of Architecture.[13] He began practising as an independent architect in Sydney soon after returning from overseas in 1952. Noted for his determination to use natural materials, he avoided synthetic finishes and designed each house to be in harmony with its surroundings.

Muller's own house, built in Bynya Road, Whale Beach, New South Wales, in 1955, was, as can be seen from the plan above, made up of a long axis, intersected by a central transverse axis. The latter included the entrance and areas for entertaining and relaxing. A second transverse axis intersected the bedrooms along with the storeroom and laundry. In the relaxing area, the fireplace was a shell of natural rock, perfectly integrated by means of having the floor-to-ceiling plate-glass windows fitted to its contours. A long panel of reinforced glass made up part of the roof over the entertaining area. By night, floodlights mounted in the branches of a large overhanging tree created patterns on the carpeted floor below. The roof structure of the central living area projected well beyond the glassed-in fireplace outcrop and was supported by four rectangular piers of grey cement brick. The colour of the bricks harmonised with the bark of the gum trees.

This unusual and imaginative house was so well integrated into the steep site overlooking Pittwater that, from the road above, it was only glimpsed through the screen of trees and partly obscured by outcrops of rock. Interior colours varied from grey to buff, ochre, brown and russet, with a white brick wall in the dining area. Natural colour in the polished wood added to the generally warm tonings. The office was separated from the house by a flat-roofed verandah or gallery with the roof projection forming a carport.

For the 1955 Walcott house, which was on land adjoining the Muller property in Whale Beach, the theme of a dominant

• AUSTRALIAN HOUSES OF THE FORTIES & FIFTIES

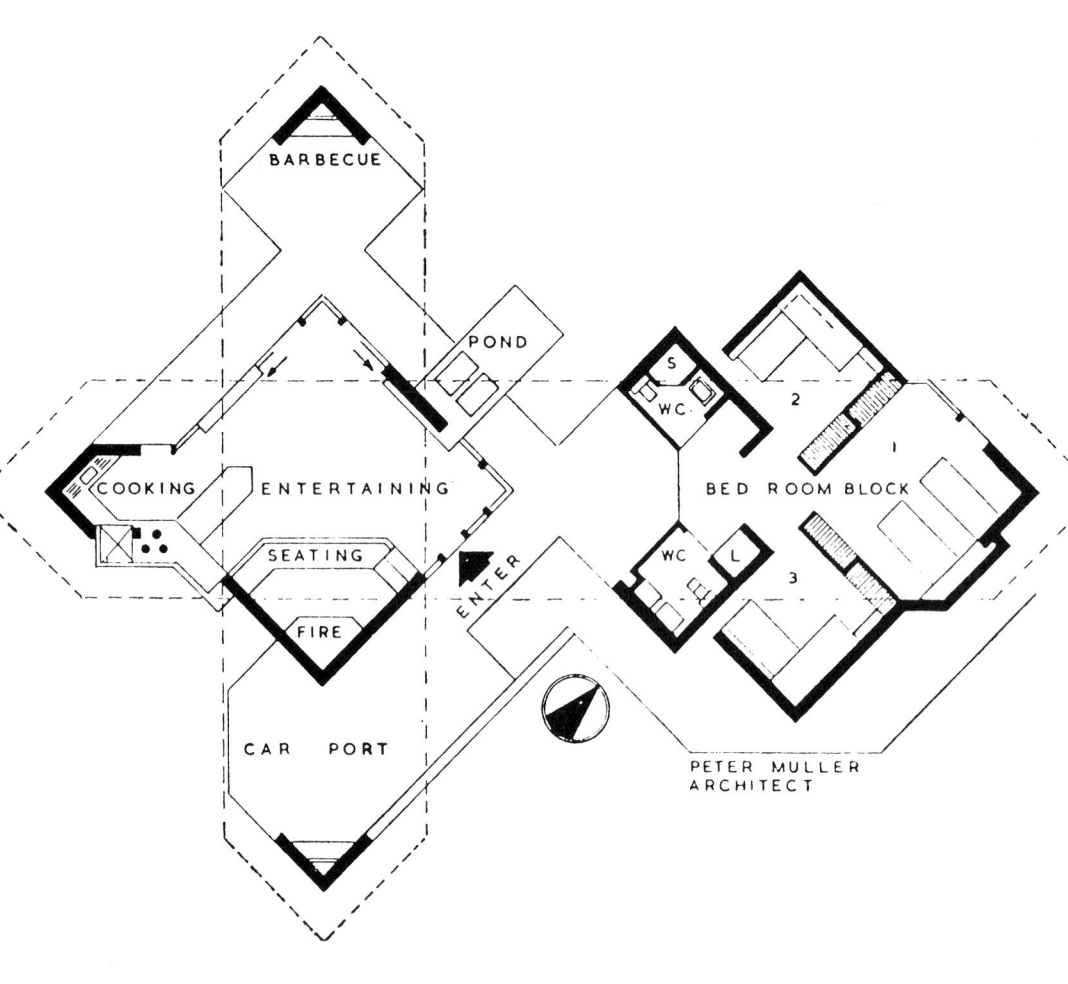

• *Left and below*: The 1956 Walcott house, Palm Beach, New South Wales; architect, Peter Muller.

The Australian Homemaker, May 1957

axis was continued but used overlapping and connected squares set on the diagonal. We can see from the plan on the left that the entertaining area was separated from the block which contained the bedrooms. The roof was made up as 14 ft × 7 ft (4270 mm × 2135 mm) prefabricated panels which included wooden framework and plywood skin. The underside was polished and varnished before being transported to the site. After being assembled and bolted into position the waterproof membrane was added, the whole operation taking less than two days.[14]

Peter Muller included a number of interesting details in this compact and unpretentious house. There was a sunken fireplace area with built-in seating and a cantilevered dining table. For summer living, glass wall panels were designed to slide into brick piers giving open access to the roofed-over barbecue area.

On a large scale and in a prominent position, Muller's 1956 Richardson house at Sydney's Palm Beach was a triumphant integration of a modern functional house with a challenging natural site. Considered one of his most accomplished works, this romantic design strikes a perfect balance between the stark geometry of a house conspicuous in the landscape, and the type which is almost completely camouflaged in its setting. It seems to emerge from the sandstone cliff, the long narrow house clinging to the rocky upper level, with curved or semi-circular projections in stone and concrete descending to the lower level. Access to the waterfront was by means of an elevator or lift. A cantilevered balcony curved around the central projection at the upper level, offering a sweeping panorama of water and timbered hillsides.

For the interior, a unity of form was achieved by re-stating the circle in the form of substantial round pillars and a translucent turquoise-green fibreglass dome, with solid white discs linked by small red discs forming the roof to the living area.[15] Through houses such as this, Peter Muller became a notable influence for a younger generation of architects. Some historians consider the Gunning house of 1960 in Edinburgh Road, Castlecrag, to be the culmination of his ideas on domestic architecture.[16]

Another Sydney architect whose work reflected the philosophy of an 'organic' relationship between a house and its site was Bruce Rickard. He built houses in the late 1950s and beyond which clearly demonstrated a deep concern for a sensitive relationship with the environment. Frank Lloyd Wright was an acknowledged influence, but, as in the case of Peter Muller, Rickard's individual integrity was always beyond question.[17] Writing on the state of Australian architecture in 1967, Robin Boyd picked up on the link between the rustic California Bungalow and the materials used in the Sydney region for organic houses. He noted, 'the same rugged, ragged clinker bricks and earthy colouring and nutty crunchy textures.'[18]

Possibly the ultimate organic relationship between a house and its site was manifested in the stone house built at Warrandyte, Victoria, by artist Danila Vassilieff, in 1940. Blasting a site on a steep hillside with a creek below, he used the huge blocks of stones for the walls. Further supplies were gained from the hillside opposite with all the small chips and silica used to fill a terrace. Wynne Scott, writing in the *Australian Home Beautiful* of October 1949, described the house which was aptly named 'Stonygrad'.[19] 'Trees, set in the stone floor, support the roof, and trees (one could hardly call them logs) form the tremendous beams, which are covered with split logs.' Bark was placed over the split logs, then stone chips and a coat of cement. This extraordinary house continued to grow over many years and when proclaimed finished in 1946, was crowned with an old Melbourne cable tram.[20]

As this house mellowed it was certainly an example of the philosophy that harmony with the environment is achieved through the use of natural materials. From around 1950, however, there was a powerful demonstration of a very different approach. In the eastern United States, architect Philip C. Johnson built his own residence in a woodland setting at New Canaan, Connecticut, in 1949–50. It was the International style in domestic architecture, evolved to become a prismatic cube, a house entirely walled in glass. Only the bathroom was enclosed, with ranges of cupboards serving as divisions for other spaces but not reaching the ceiling.[21] Mies van der Rohe created a similar house and shared with Johnson the view that a glass-walled cube form in a woodland setting offers a more sympathetic and integrated relationship than the quest for harmony through the choice of natural or rustic materials and selected forms.[22]

A complete acceptance of this approach was only likely in Australia if conditions were similar. Cold climate woodlands are very different from typical Australian bush in the heat of summer with bushfire threatening. Walls of glass were readily accepted in the 1940s and '50s, but wide eaves and other forms of shelter were generally found essential, at least for the walls most exposed to the sun. Using natural or planted vegetation as shelter was an alternative choice.

South Australian architect Brian Claridge created a three-level house on a steep, thickly-wooded site at Crafers in the Adelaide Hills. Built in 1959, it was a cube-form structure, with large areas of glass. Shelter from the sun was provided by the trees which were in close proximity on all sides. When mirrored in the glass, trees and sky merged with the house in a perfect integration. Window mullions echoed the verticals of the tree trunks with a bold contrast provided by the horizontal boarding of the terrace.[23]

Houses designed by architects who were aware of the two extremes of approach to domestic architecture in a natural or naturalistic environment were most typically made up of influences ranging across the spectrum. Even fairly average works were far more likely to

• AUSTRALIAN HOUSES OF THE FORTIES & FIFTIES

• *Opposite*: The integration of a house built with natural materials and an unspoiled bushland setting was beginning to find wider approval in the 1950s.

PHOTOGRAPH: MARK STRIZIC

display an environmental consciousness, a sense of place, than any of the thousands of mundane suburban boxes built on sites thoroughly cleared of trees and other vegetation before development. Stone and natural timbers, combined with new materials, large areas of glass, intelligent planning and the latest services and equipment could add up to a very successful house, completely functional and aesthetically right for its time and place. A blend of natural and introduced vegetation made a perfect setting for a 1958 house at Marryatville, South Australia. Designed by architect Maurice Doley as his own residence, it was on a sloping site with a creek a few metres away from its stone foundations. In fact, stones from the creek were placed in the masonry walls of the outdoor living areas which was actually an open-fronted room below the main level.[24] From the creek, the house was seen through a screen of trees, its natural timber and stonework giving it a unity with its site. Walls of rustic stone blocks were generally without eaves but in other areas the flat roof was projected well out to shelter walls of glass.

Oiled or stained timber and stonework of various kinds were increasingly popular throughout Australia in the 1950s. Builders and owner-builders seeing their use in architect-designed houses began to incorporate them in the same manner, but rarely with the same finesse. Edna Walling, carrying through more direct influences from the Arts and Crafts movement, had celebrated field stone and unpainted timber from the 1920s and through her writings had reached a wide public. The rising popularity of the 'native' garden was due to a number of people, including Edna Walling. She encouraged the ideal of simple cottages in woodland settings and this was paralleled in suburban or other settings where complete or additional plantings of trees and shrubs recreated the feeling of a natural environment.

If the 1940s and '50s brings to mind austere houses with austere gardens or featuristic suburban villas with manicured lawns, gaudy flowers, 'specimen' trees and obedient shrubs, let us not forget that it was also an important era in the emergence of environmental consciousness.

Chapter 7 Endnotes

[1] Steven Adams, *The Arts & Crafts Movement*, New Burlington Books, London, 1987, p. 88.
[2] 'Builder', 'What is Pise-de-terre?' *Australian Home Beautiful*, June 1942, p. 16.
[3] Alistair Knox, *Living in the Environment*, Mullaya Publications, 1975, published by Compendium Pty Ltd, Birregurra South, Victoria, 1978, p. 8.
[4] ibid., p. 21.
[5] G. F. Middleton, 'Earth Wall Construction', *Experimental Building Station Bulletin* no.5, North Ryde, NSW, 1946.
[6] Esme Johnston, 'Built from the good earth', *Australian Home Beautiful*, June 1948, p. 28.
[7] ibid.
[8] ibid.
[9] ibid., p. 42.
[10] S. G. Andrews, 'Adobe or Pise, Economical Houses', *Australian House and Garden*, May 1950, pp. 38, 39, 88, 89.
[11] Boyd, Robin, *Australia's Home*, Melbourne University Press, 1952, p. 201.
[12] Kenneth McDonald, *The New Australian Home*, published by Kenneth McDonald, Melbourne, 1954.
[13] Muriel Emanuel (ed.), *Contemporary Architects*, Macmillan Press. London, 1980.
[14] 'Other People's Homes', *Australian Homemaker*, May 1957, p. 38.
[15] Beyond the 1950s, *The History and Design of the Australian House*, Oxford University Press, Sydney, 1985, p. 146.
[16] Kenneth Frampton & Philip Drew, *Harry Seidler: Four Decades of Architecture*, Thames & Hudson, London, 1992.
[17] R. Apperly, R. Irving & P. Reynolds, *A pictorial Guide to Identifying Australian Architecture*, Angus & Robertson, Sydney, 1989, p. 236.
[18] Robin Boyd, 'The State of Australian Architecture', *Architecture in Australia*, June 1967, p. 463.
[19] Wynne Scott, '"Stonygrad" — Home in a Quarry', *Australian Home Beautiful*, October 1949, pp. 27, 76, 77.
[20] Felicity St John Moore, *Vassilieff and His Art*, Melbourne, 1982, p. 72.
[21] Henry Russell Hitchcock, *The Pelican History of Art, Architecture: Nineteenth and Twentieth Centuries*, Penguin Books, Baltimore, USA, 1975, p. 570.
[22] Donald Leslie Johnson, *Australian Architecture 1901–51: Sources of Modernism*, Sydney University Press, Sydney, 1980, p. 168.
[23] 'Houses Around Adelaide', pamphlet published by Royal Australian Institute of Architects, South Australian Chapter, Adelaide, 1964, p. 29.
[24] Neil Clerehan (ed.), *Best Australian Houses: Recent Houses Built by Members of The Royal Australian Institute of Architecture*, F. W. Cheshire, Melbourne, 1961.

CHAPTER EIGHT
Gardens for Everyone

A GARDEN OF SOME DESCRIPTION has always been an essential part of the Australian dream of a house on a block of land. In the 1940s and '50s that ideal was achieved by a larger percentage of the population than ever before. Interest in gardening varied from a minimal upkeep to the lifetime passion of the dedicated enthusiast. However, more pressing issues kept many people away from gardening in those decades. As has been noted, many in the services during the war daydreamed of peaceful home gardens, making plans for future schemes, picturing images of family life in both house and garden. Couples caught up in the struggle to buy or build their own home were anxious to get started, but it was often some time before they could afford to devote much time to gardening.

Many family albums show that slow but magical transformation, with early photographs of the house sitting forlornly in its setting — in contrast to those taken a few years later, when the edges have been softened with trees and shrubs reaching up. Finally, with family grown up, the house sits proudly in a mature garden. The whole area has changed. Our garden began in 1949 with a row of stones to delineate the front boundary. In that bushland area there was no need to create barriers. With plants and cuttings from family and friends, and a few packets of seeds, the long adventure began. Even after almost four-and-a-half decades there are still many flowers from the earliest years. Big old-fashioned, sunny-faced nasturtiums have thrived, happily re-seeding themselves. A hedge of Lorraine Lea roses bespeaks another era. Sheltered corners are home to many tender plants. Thoughtfully, my parents spared the gums and the native cherries so that the garden became a blend of indigenous and introduced plants.

What kind of gardens were typical of the 1940s and '50s? That question might broadly be answered with a simple description, but like all eras there was a great diversity of ideals and interests. Typically, the front gardens of houses built in that period included large areas of lawn, beds of bright flowers and useful shrubs, and one or more ornamental trees. The side gardens would depend on available space, but could have some tender plants on the sheltered side and

• *Opposite page*: Recently completed Townsing residence Federal Street, Cottesloe, Western Australia, April 1946. This two-bedroom brick house on limestone foundations was one of the designs made available by the State Housing Commission of Western Australia.
COURTESY: FRAN TOWNSING

• Bird's-eye views were often produced by *Australian Home Beautiful*'s staff artist to dramatically illustrate designs by Olive Mellor.

Australian Home Beautiful, July 1948

sunlovers on the other. Further shrubs and trees might find a place, but often there was a driveway or a carport or garage. Magazines devoted special issues to the carport and there were many suggestions for making it blend with the garden. Trellis panels were home to climbing plants, and planter boxes or a garden bed along one side also helped.

To divide the front area from the backyard there were screens in the form of trelliswork, trimmed hedges, shrubs or perhaps a wing fence or wall in brick or stone. All the published plans as well as pictorial evidence and clear memories tell us that the vegetable garden was still an important aspect of the backyard, as were the fruit trees and, depending on the region, one or more selected vines. Grapes and passionfruit were favourites but there were also berries. My mother's attempts to manage a strawberry harvest were frustrated more by children than marauding birds. In many parts of Australia, the lemon tree was considered essential and was usually subject to periods of concern and attention not generally given to other garden subjects.

Before blocks of land were whittled down to the typical 'pocket handkerchief' of recent decades there was always room for one or two substantial sheds, a good area of lawn and, of course, space for a clothes line. Many people kept on with the traditional long lines raised and lowered by means of wooden 'props'. From the 1920s the standard rotary clothes hoist had been gaining popularity. Gilbert Toyne of East Malvern, Victoria, marketed

• The Rotoscythe was an expensive rotary mower advertised in the *Australian Home Beautiful* in December 1948.

his patented designs from 1924.¹ In the 1930s he added the hydraulic hoist to the range. Manufacture ceased during the war, but from early 1946, Toyne's standard rotary clothes hoists were again available.² Other firms began manufacture and names such as Hills, David and Aldo were familiar, with the 'Hills Hoist' becoming the best known.

Increasing emphasis on outdoor life had been an important factor in the demand for larger areas of lawn which is noted from the early decades of this century. For ordinary sized gardens, the handmower remained the most commonly used tool, with sophisticated motor-driven models for those who could afford them. All this was to change when Mervyn Victor Richardson of Concord, New South Wales, created his first rotary motor mower in 1952. The 'Victa Rotomo' revolutionised domestic lawn maintenance and by 1956 some 60 000 Victas were being made and sold each year.³ It is interesting to note that most of the design details seen in rotary motor mowers from this time were already present in the 'Rotoscythe' offered by Finlay Brothers of Melbourne in 1948 (see right). Motor mowers proliferated at the time when Australians, now more mobile than ever, were keen to speed up the jobs at home and head off for trips and holidays in the family car. Many people were pleased to be able to devote any energy saved to other work in the garden, while others simply took to relaxing on the patio.

Apart from variations on the well-kept average garden there were wild gardens, cottage gardens, semi-formal and formal gardens, subtropical and tropical gardens, bush gardens, utility gardens and places where plantspeople created prizewinning flowers, fruits or vegetables.

Bold statements in the form of 'featuristic' details were a part of Australia's suburban scene in the 1940s and '50s. Gardens often reflected this fashion, with bright flowers of every hue and shrubs and trees chosen for the boldness of their colour and texture, or again for their sumptuous flowers. Concrete animals, gnomes, Aboriginal figures and sleeping Mexicans vied with wishing wells, concrete or stone baskets and various tubs or urns. But this was only part of the story — there were many simple, unpretentious gardens and definable streams of influence from various traditions. The important trends were the increasing acceptance of Australian plants and a new relationship between indoor and outdoor living. Patios and outdoor living areas brought more furniture and other comforts to the outside and, by means of window walls with doors and sliding panels, the garden was visually more a part of life indoors. To add to that feeling, indoor plants came back into favour. With the same materials, for example brick, stone or timber, seen both outdoors and indoors the relationship was further enhanced.

Wartime restrictions had a number of effects on gardens and gardeners. Apart from the need to support the war effort with vegetable gardens, and many amateur and professional gardeners being otherwise occupied, the magazines shrank to a limited number of pages printed on newsprint. Books were scarce and again affected by restrictions. Somehow, Oxford University Press managed to publish Edna Walling's delightful book *Gardens in Australia* in 1943, with a second edition in 1944.

Various horticultural societies and garden clubs managed to continue some activities through the war years and, once the war was over, were there to foster the rising generation of gardeners. Seed-growers and nurserymen made up for lost time and many businesses expanded dramatically over the next few decades. A bewildering array of advertising tempted both professional and amateur gardeners to bigger, brighter or more unusual plants, with some flowers such as the gladioli becoming almost a mania. Pages and pages of the gardening magazines were devoted to the latest gladioli, dahlias and other favourites. A writer in the May 1951 issue of the *Australian Garden Lover*, reviewing the newer varieties of that year, commented: 'It would be a brave man indeed who would say definitely which are the best of the newer additions to Glad-dom . . .'

Other very popular flowers were carnations, roses, chrysanthemums, daffodils, irises, poppies, delphiniums, begonias, sweet peas, lupins, pansies, stocks, hyacinths and the various kinds of lilies. Camellias, rhododendrons and azaleas had a great following in regions suited to them, as did the favourite old-fashioned perennials. Cacti and succulents were popular enough to be represented by a national society, with many sunbaked rock gardens filled with these fascinating plants. Specialist nurseries continued to offer all sorts of rare and interesting plants. Ornamental trees and shrubs to suit all kinds of gardens and all manner of conditions were available in the post-war years.

Fashions or popular directions in gardening can be broadly traced, with many less obvious influences interwoven in the whole fabric of horticulture. Writers were in a powerful position to shape and direct popular taste. In books, magazines and newspaper columns their words were inspiring, informative and, at times, critical. The two main forces were those who championed the competition garden and prizewinning blooms, and the sometimes diametrically opposed writers who encouraged sensitive design and at times an almost spiritual approach. Both sides were rich in knowledge and each belonged to respected traditions. Some writers occupied the middle ground and, while accepting the popular taste for bright colours and 'showy' designs, also endeavoured to inspire their readers to extend the possibilities of their gardening interest.

Competitions, along with festivals or shows, were greeted with mixed responses. Many people, who worked to create gardens which were reflective of the wider understanding of gardening as an art, were not impressed by the aggressive and yet often uninspired competitive garden, or the notion that the largest blooms, the greatest assembly of plants or the gaudiest combinations of colours were the best. Edna Walling and Jocelyn Brown were both outstanding garden designers, influential through their writing, who were far removed from these beliefs.

Subjects covered in magazines wholly or partially devoted to horticulture included seeds, plants, bulbs, shrubs, trees, tools, sprays, manures, mowers, cultivators, hoses and garden furniture, ornaments or structures. Planting guides or calendars were important as were cultural hints and all facets of maintenance. General news and the reports from societies and clubs found an important place. Correspondence and the writing of regular contributors were also essential ingredients.

Well-known writer and naturalist Jean Galbraith contributed to the *Australian Garden Lover* from 1926 to 1976 under the pen-name 'Correa' and shared with her readers a passionate love for plants and a deep respect for the natural environment. She also wrote of her world of people and places, bringing a gentle humanity to the sometimes sombre practicality of the sprays and bone-dust brigade. Published by the Melbourne-based Horticultural Press, the *Australian Garden Lover* began in 1925 and ceased in 1979. A similar magazine, the *Home Gardener*, published in Melbourne by Mitchell and Casey, was extant from 1917

• *Opposite page*: Shrubs and trees in a variety of shapes provide important contrast with the plain lines of this suburban house of the 1950s.
COLLECTION: STATE OFFICES LIBRARY, HOBART, TASMANIA.

• Garden plans by Olive Mellor.
Australian Home Beautiful, May 1946

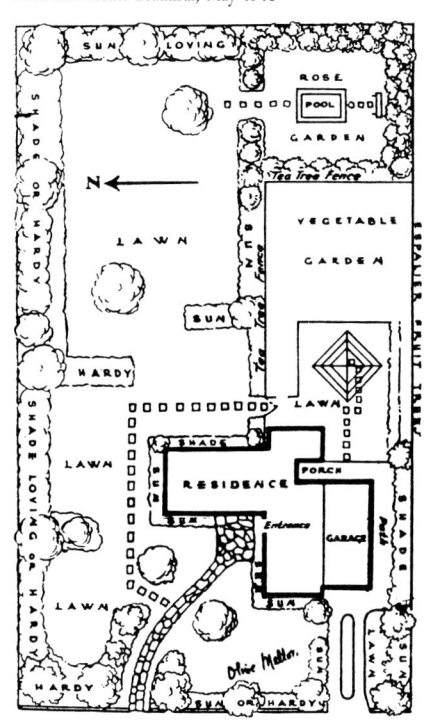

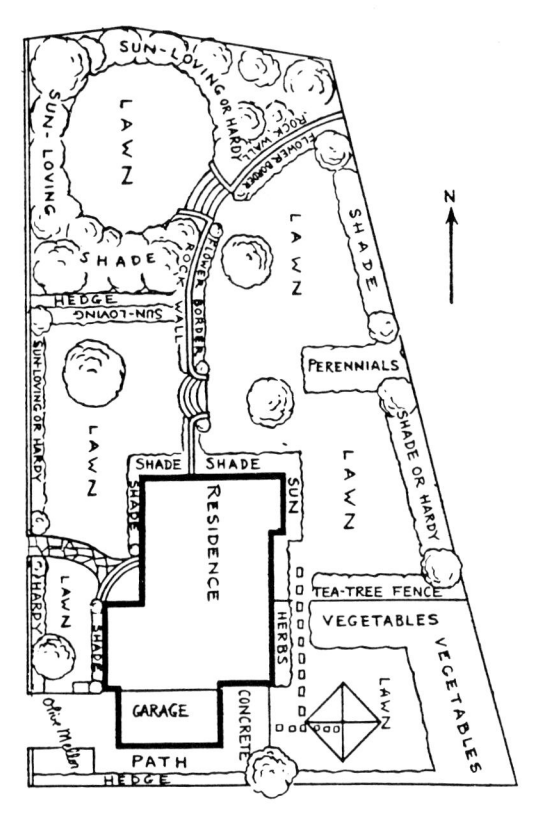

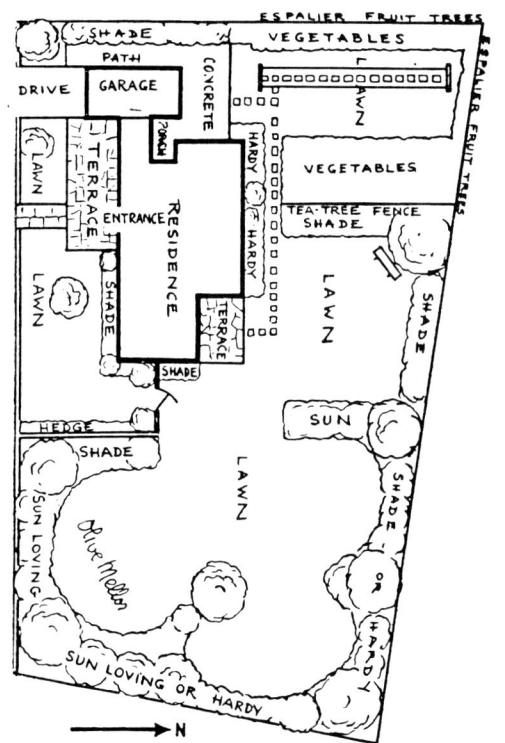

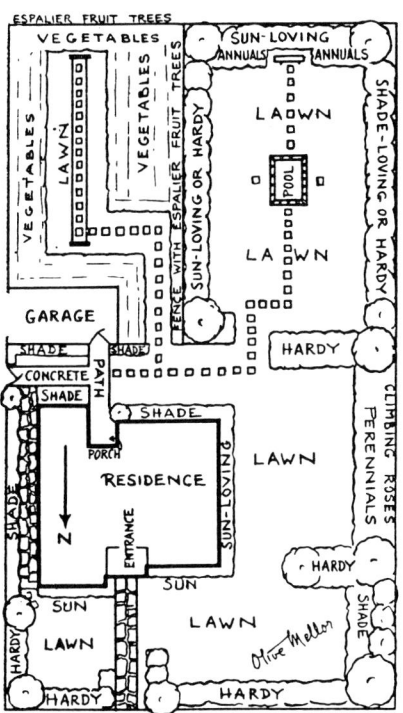

to 1954. The longtime-editor of this magazine was Thomas A. Browne who, in 1947, moved to the *Home Beautiful*.[4]

Edna Walling began writing for the *Australian Home Beautiful* in 1925 when it was still called the *Australian Home Builder*. It changed its name in October of that year. Her regular contributions continued, with just a few breaks, for twenty-six years. Her column, 'A Letter to Garden Lovers', began in 1937 and ceased in 1950. In this period we can trace her increasing interest in using Australian plants. Late in 1940 she wrote:

Once when we were wandering over the cliffs at Peterborough we noticed a little mauve and pink daisy growing in the turf itself and we learnt it was *Brachycombe graminea*, and have since found it to be a treasure I would never like to be without.[5]

That same 'Letter' also included a photograph of an unmade road densely bounded in natural vegetation. Her 1952 book, *The Australian Roadside,* was an early plea for conservation and brought together the thoughts expressed over many years. Throughout the 1940s Walling's writing for *Home Beautiful* was a mixture of practical ideas for garden design along with planting suggestions and possibilities for small details. If she championed birches, rowans, medlars, hawthorns, prunus, oaks and maples, she increasingly urged her readers to value the native cypresses (*Callitris*), eucalypts, native cherries (*Exocarpus*) and tea-tree (*Leptospermum*).

• Old-fashioned handmowers were gradually replaced by rotary motormowers from the mid-1950s.

COLLECTION: THE AUTHOR

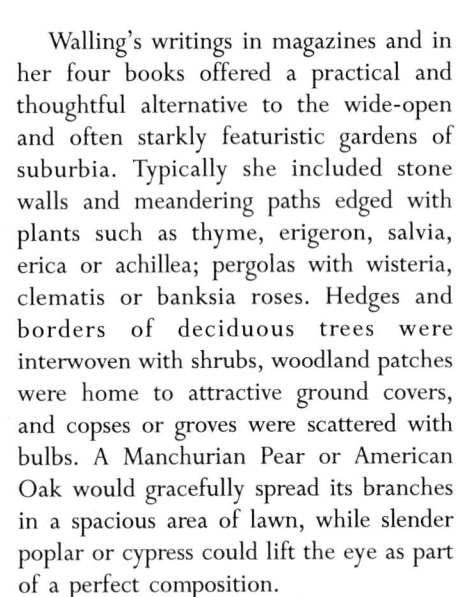

Walling's writings in magazines and in her four books offered a practical and thoughtful alternative to the wide-open and often starkly featuristic gardens of suburbia. Typically she included stone walls and meandering paths edged with plants such as thyme, erigeron, salvia, erica or achillea; pergolas with wisteria, clematis or banksia roses. Hedges and borders of deciduous trees were interwoven with shrubs, woodland patches were home to attractive ground covers, and copses or groves were scattered with bulbs. A Manchurian Pear or American Oak would gracefully spread its branches in a spacious area of lawn, while slender poplar or cypress could lift the eye as part of a perfect composition.

Home Beautiful's other regular contributor over many years was Olive Mellor (1891–1978). Her influence on the general range of household gardens in the 1940s and '50s was probably second to none. She wrote on a great diversity of topics from garden design to constructing a pool, from vegetables to tree pruning and herbs to cacti. An important service for readers offered selected individual designs which were also inspiring and informative for other readers. The published designs were based on material from readers, such as block plans, photographs and information about views and areas to be screened. In most cases the whole scheme was illustrated as a dramatic bird's-eye view. Care was taken to offer sound, practical design which included responses to the ideas and wishes of those who had requested help.

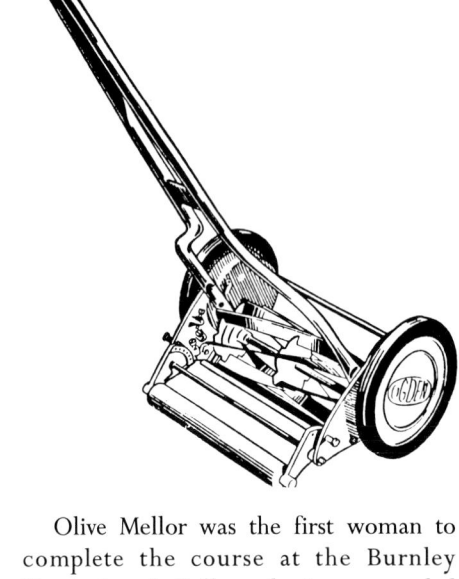

Olive Mellor was the first woman to complete the course at the Burnley Horticultural College, having persuaded the Minister for Agriculture to allow her to study fulltime. Before that, women had been allowed to attend lectures, but not to do the practical work.[6] Mellor became the first woman lecturer on the Burnley staff and in 1917 had Edna Walling as one of her students.[7] Ill health forced her to retire in 1920 and she subsequently designed gardens privately before becoming a writer for *Home Beautiful* in the mid-1930s.

In later life she recalled designing some 500 gardens during her career, many of which would have been for the readers of the magazine.[8] As can be seen by the examples shown on page 143, her designs were quietly assured, giving consideration to people's current needs as well as long-term requirements. Every aspect received careful consideration, with plants skilfully chosen on individual merit and not out of demands to be fashionable. Her comprehensive articles would often include a number of plans along with plant lists for five climate zones. Her contribution to the important 1939 *Australian Gardening of To-Day* was entitled 'Planning a Native Garden':

> Only twice during the years in which I have been making gardens have I been asked to plan a native garden, and yet, in our own natural flora, we have a wonderful field to draw from, limited at present far more than it should be; for business men cannot afford to produce goods that are not saleable, and though nurserymen are gradually educating the public by introducing a few more of our own trees and shrubs each year, we are still only beginning to appreciate the value of our native plants.[9]

Mellor's suggested plan is a simple and basically informal one for a suburban allotment. The eighty or more plants listed include three favourites from New Zealand: cordyline, phormium and corokia. In an interesting reversal of the situation in the 1940s and '50s, where a few Australian plants were gradually included in most gardens, she suggests a blend which fifty years later is often seen.

The plants used, are, of course, indigenous, but annuals and perennials could well be introduced to the scheme, particularly the more natural sorts such as forget-me-nots, alyssum, English daisies, aquilegias, foxgloves, lobelia, mignonette, nepeta, scabious, portulaca, Virginia stocks, cynoglossum and linaria; but not such flowers as pompous looking dahlias.[10]

• George Althofer of Dripstone near Wellington in New South Wales established his Nindethana nursery in 1938. He played an important role in increasing the range of native plants available to Australian gardeners.

COLLECTION: THE AUTHOR

The 768-page *Australian Gardening To-Day* was an essential reference for dedicated gardeners in the 1940s and '50s. Along with Olive Mellor's contribution we find Professor E. G. Waterhouse writing on 'Domestic Gardening as an Art'; Edna Walling on garden design; J. L. Provan on soils and fertilizers; R. T. M. Pescott on insect control; Dr A. S. Thomas on roses in Australia; E. E. Pescott on citrus culture; Edwin Ashby on native shrubs; Charles Barrett on ferns; R. V. Pritchard on rockwork and rock plants; W. A. Somerset on fruit trees; R. E. Boardman on the vegetable garden; Alex Smith on garden carpentry, and many others. Gladioli, dahlias, chrysanthemums, carnations, orchids and cacti were all treated individually. There is also a chapter on herbaceous border plants by Harold Sergeant. More than half of the book is devoted to an encyclopaedia of garden plants, including for that time 'the widest and most accurate description of native flora obtainable'.[11]

Influential books in the post-war era included the 1948 *Shrubs and Trees for Australian Gardens* by Ernest E. Lord and *Australian Plants for the Garden: A Handbook on the Cultivation of Australian Trees, Shrubs, Other Flowering Plants and Ferns*, by Thistle Y. Harris, published in 1953. In the latter work, readers were offered a practical but imaginative approach to the use of native plants.[12] Some seventeen garden plans to suit a range of sites drew on Edna Walling's expertise — she contributed 'base garden plans'.[13] Lord's *Shrubs and Trees for Australian Gardens* went into a second edition in 1950 and a third in 1956. In its completely revised form (by J. H. Willis), it continues to be an invaluable reference.[14]

By the 1950s there were several nurseries specialising in native plants and enough encouragement in books, magazines and newspaper columns to build the momentum into a popular acceptance of Australian plants or of complete native gardens. If, by 1960, there was a clear trend developing, the great swing was yet to come. Edna Walling had virtually given up using exotic plants in her garden designs by the early 1950s, but was by then only directly influential through her books and her designs. Professionally she was associated with the noted landscaper and designer Ellis Stones (1895–1975) whose work in the 1940s and '50s and beyond was an important contribution towards the emergence of an 'Australian' garden. In later years, Stones (affectionately known as 'Rocky') gave credit to Edna Walling for playing an important role in shifting the balance toward Australian plants.[15]

Rockeries and rockwork have been an important part of the gardening world for hundreds of years. With the increasing interest in wild or naturalistic gardens in the second half of the 19th century, a more realistic use of natural rocks was demanded. The writings of Gertrude Jekyll, William Robinson and others helped disseminate ideas which were ultimately to influence wild, woodland or bush gardens in Australia. Edna Walling is known to have valued highly her own collection of the works of Gertrude Jekyll.[16] In the 1911 book, *Gardens for Small Country Houses*, by Gertrude Jekyll and Lawrence Weaver, there is a section devoted to rock gardens written by Raymond E. Negus. He makes an important comment which is relevant to the 1940s and '50s:

The rock garden, unlike many other forms of horticulture, is a deliberate imitation of Nature; nine-tenths of our rock gardens, if they imitate Nature at all, imitate her in her least pleasing moods, for they represent formless heaps of rubble. Every stone in the garden should bear a semblance of having been in its place from time immemorial.[17]

If the 'natural' style of gardening had not won wide acceptance in suburbia in the period under review it is important to

• *Below*: Outdoor furniture and plants in tubs and pots were increasingly popular in the post-war years.

PHOTOGRAPH: PETA TOWNSING

restate that architects in general were sympathetic, and quite a few were keen advocates. Ellis Stones designed a number of gardens for houses by Melbourne architects Grounds, Romberg & Boyd.[18] For the 1954 Richardson house by Robin Boyd, he used large boulders to enhance the natural character of the site and as a means to retain the soil on the steep slopes. The house was a bridge-like structure spanning a creek, and represented the ideal of a functional dwelling and its setting being in perfect harmony. Apparently it was in this period that Ellis Stones began using timber as well as stone for construction work.[19]

As well as carefully placed rocks and naturalistic plantings in his garden designs, there were pools and miniature waterfalls, informal retaining walls, random paving, simple steps of natural stone and various sorts of walls. Many of these gardens were on a relatively large scale and typically were a mixture of native and exotic plants. Stones wrote two articles for *Home Beautiful* in 1946 which discussed both formal and natural stonework. In one he shows how the end of a retaining wall can be finished with a bold outcrop of rocks.[20] In the second article a formal pool is the focal point of a 'more-or-less informal' layout.[21] He also shows how an apparent outcrop of rocks is an ideal border to an informal pool and comments that, 'In making a pool the choice lies between formal and informal and that choice will probably determined by the size and character of the garden.'

Apart from the use of natural-style outcrops, rock gardens or rockeries were constructed for growing collections of alpine plants and, as previously mentioned, for cacti and succulents. An inspiration to many was that well-known work, *My Rock-Garden*, by Reginald Farrer. First published in 1907, it was reprinted many times, including the years 1942, 1945 and 1946.[22] Australian writers alerted readers to the need to adapt designs to local conditions. Alpine plants suggested for rock gardens included arenaria, saxifraga, cistus, sempervivum, hypericum, saponaria, dianthus, thymus, lithospermum and phlox.

Much of the stonework in gardens in the 1940s and '50s was in the form of 'crazy paving' or walls veneered with flat stone. Those interested in maximising its featuristic character chose multi-coloured stones such as slate from Castlemaine in Victoria. Individual pieces in pink, beige, cream, ochre, brown, blue-grey and grey were combined to create patterns which at times resembled a bright wallpaper. In some examples the stone was cut into squares and rectangles of various sizes so that a 'contemporary' geometric pattern was possible. This was no doubt inspired by the popular geometric designs seen in textiles and in cube-form architecture. Those examples are in turn traced to earlier influences, such as the paintings of Piet Mondrian.

Patios, courtyards and terraces were paved in stone, brick or concrete. Wooden

GARDENS FOR EVERYONE

• Modern courtyard garden, Western Australia, 1950s.

PHOTOGRAPH: FRITZ KOS

• *Below right*: Fashionable stonework was generally flat pieces fixed to a base of concrete or brickwork.

PHOTOGRAPH: THE AUTHOR

or concrete tubs, often brightly painted, were planted with all sorts of ornamental conifers, flowering shrubs, bright annuals and perennials, or interesting succulents. Pergolas of all sizes were very fashionable and typically were attached to the house to provide some shelter for a paved area. Respite from the hot summer sun was given by wisteria, ornamental grape and other deciduous vines. The freestanding pergola had been favoured by garden designers from around the turn-of-the-century. Gertrude Jekyll included them in her designs and wrote in 1902. 'It is only of comparatively late years that we have borrowed the pergola from the gardens of Italy.'[23] Edna Walling included them in her work with some very long ones sheltering paths or walks. Sydney-based designer Jocelyn Brown also recognised their worth and we can see one in her garden plan published in the March 1942 issue of the *Home* (see page 148). It is marked 'for climbing roses and vines', and is an extensive construction with fourteen pairs of uprights.

Many front gardens featured a lamp on a post, with perhaps the house name or number displayed on it. For a Colonial-style house this would be in a traditional design. Painted wagon wheels were placed against walls or fences or flanked the driveway gates of properties where the owners were looking to add a rural or ranch house touch. Swans and storks in concrete echoed the birdlife of great gardens. Car tyres were cut and painted to become baskets or, again, the favoured swan.

147

• AUSTRALIAN HOUSES OF THE FORTIES & FIFTIES

• *Below*: This garden plan by noted Sydney-based garden designer Jocelyn Brown was published in the March 1942 issue of the *Home*. It continues the sophisticated formal approach made so popular by Gertrude Jekyll around the turn of the century.

• *Opposite page*: Brick fences were often given details such as courses of dark manganese bricks to match the house.

COLLECTION: COMMONWEALTH BANK ARCHIVES, VICTORIA

• *Below opposite*: Brick veneer house, Chigwell, Tasmania, 1957. Woven wire fences were widely used in the 1940s and '50s, both with wooden or metal posts and rails, and sometimes with a combination of the two.

COLLECTION: STATE OFFICES LIBRARY, HOBART, TASMANIA

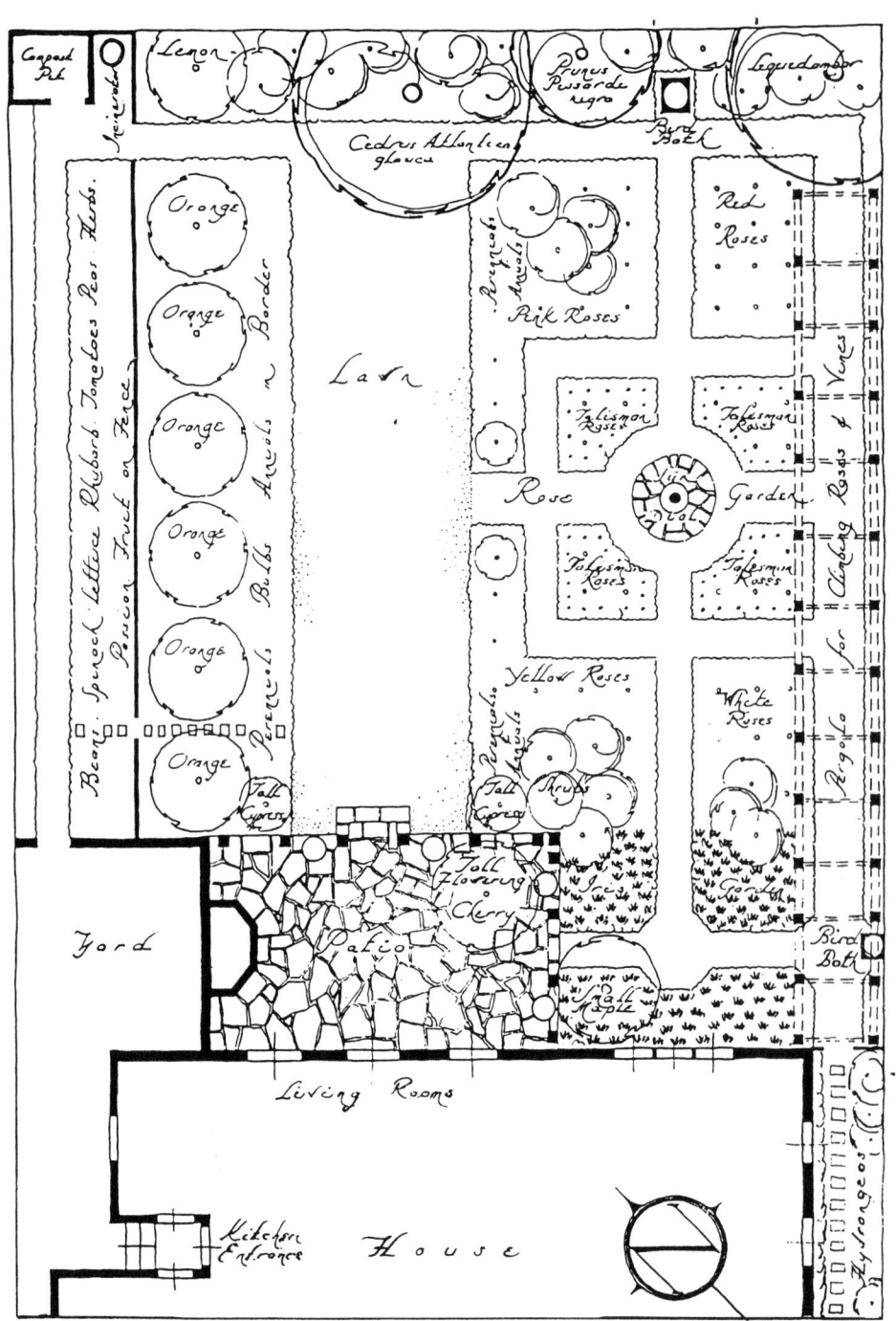

• PATHS AND DRIVEWAYS •

Many gardeners continued the traditional use of stone, brick or gravel for paths and other such areas, but for a large percentage of householders concrete was seen as cost effective and easy to maintain. Standard concrete edging for garden beds was also considered ideal, particularly as it was an aid to the achieving perfectly trimmed lawn edges. Concrete paving blocks or flags were an in-between solution and when thoughtfully placed were considered acceptable — even by the architects and landscapers who were not usually happy with large areas of concrete paving. The standard concrete paving flag was 12 inches (300 mm) square. Edna Walling suggested random pavers in freestone shapes which were cast in the ground then turned over to display a natural texture. Crazy paving made from broken sections of concrete was also used.

The fashion for curved paths is noted throughout this century. In suburban front gardens one or two paths would intersect the front lawn and lead to the front porch. A meandering path of stepping stones set in the lawn was a popular device and appears in many garden designs. But they were found to be unsatisfactory in high traffic areas, as it was difficult to space them to suit everyone's stride.

• WALLS, FENCES & GATES •

Front gardens, with their chosen designs in fences and gates, have long been an essential part of the presentation of the house. In the 1940s and '50s, typical front fences were in brick, concrete block, stone or timber. The woven wire fence of the inter-war period was now only seen in the standard 'Cyclone' chain-link type. The brickwork in fences, including gateposts and piers, was generally designed to match the brickwork of the house. A great range of variations were created from the plainest construction to decorative Moderne. In many examples 'wrought iron' was incorporated, forming panels between brick piers. These panels would match the gates, and often the balustrading of the porch.

Timber fences were the logical choice for timber houses, although they were also used for brick houses. Colonial or Georgian Revival styles in timber or brick were often given a traditional picket fence. Fashion decreed simple pickets with square or pointed tops, shorter and a little wider than the type associated with Victorian or Federation houses. When consciously based on authentic colonial designs, picket fences would follow the original proportions. Other variations were picket fences with a capping rail, a continuation of an inter-war type, and the short picket used above a brick or stone base. The latter type was often in the form of panels between masonry piers.

The so-called 'ranch style' fence of horizontal boards fixed to posts was a universal type, varying from the austerity pattern of three boards, and around two feet in height, to the more substantial versions with five or six or more horizontal boards. When privacy was desired, high fences of vertical boards or brushwood were used. Sometimes these were in the form of panels between piers of brick or stone and raised on a base of the same material. Apart from the ubiquitous paling fence on boundaries, there were different kinds of dividing fences or screens within the garden in both timber and masonry. Brushwood and vertical or horizontal boards were popular, as were fashionable perforated concrete blocks.

As mentioned earlier, various forms of trellis were also used. These screens were softened by climbers such as *Hardenbergia violacea*, *Kennedia nigricans*, *Solanum jasminoides*, *Wisteria sinensis*, *bougainvillea glabra* 'Sanderana', *Jasminum grandiflorum*, *Clematis montana* var. *rubens* and the floriferous *Pelargonium peltatum*.

Hedges of suitable shrubs continued to be valued where they would be both useful and decorative. High dense hedges on the street frontage had lost out to that pride in home ownership which wanted both house and garden to be seen by all. Average householders were keen to get the basic garden maintenance done, preferring other uses for leisure time to laboriously trimming a hedge. However, a 'hedge' of modern shrub roses was seen as worth the effort, given the annual display of gorgeous blooms.

• ROSES •

Shrub and standard roses have, throughout this century, held their position as favourite plants for the traditional garden. In the 1940s and '50s there was a continuation of the popular interest seen in the inter-war years. Without doubt the best known rose of that era was Madame A. Meilland, released in 1945 and popularly called Peace.

• *Opposite*: Suburban gardens in Western Australia in the 1950s. The front fence was not favoured by many householders in suburban Perth.

PHOTOGRAPH: FRITZ KOS

• *Right*: Pride in a well-kept garden is evident in these elderly people's homes at Chigwell, Tasmania, in the late 1950s.

COLLECTION: STATE OFFICES LIBRARY, HOBART, TASMANIA

New releases vied with established favourites, the overall demand being for large blooms or masses of smaller blooms such as the polyantha roses or the floribundas which are like polyanthas but have larger flowers. Shrub roses can range from a large bush to a dwarf plant. Standard roses, those on a single trunk, also continued to be popular. Pillar roses grown up posts or over pergolas held a place as did the climbers which were generally seen on fences. Notable favourite roses seen in many parts of Australia in the period under review included Crimson Glory, Lorraine Lee, Golden Dawn, Mrs Herbert Stevens, Sutters Gold, Helen Traubel, President Herbert Hoover, Una Wallace, Talisman, Comtesse Vandal, Texas Centennial, Etoile de Hollande, Editor McFarland, Ophelia, Speks Yellow, Chrysler Imperial, Madame A. Meilland (Peace), Charlotte Armstrong, Ena Harkness, Virgo, Elite, Tzigane and Picture.

Australia in the post-war years had the perfect combination of conditions for a great upsurge of interest in gardening. With secure employment, shorter working hours, increasing prosperity, greater home ownership and a proliferation of nurseries and gardening publications, the future was assured. A widening of the range of possibilities was also taking place with groups and individuals forging directions which were to enrich our gardening culture in the decades to follow.

Chapter 8 Endnotes

[1] Peter Cuffley, *Australian Houses of the '20s & '30s*, The Five Mile Press, Fitzroy, Victoria, 1989, p. 6.
[2] *Australian Home Beautiful*, May 1946, p. 44.
[3] *Made In Australia — A Sourcebook of all Things Australian*, William Heinemann Australia, Melbourne, 1986, p. 15.
[4] Anne Latreille, *The Natural Garden, Ellis Stones: His Life and Work*, Viking O'Neil, Penguin Books, Ringwood, Victoria, 1990, p. 77.
[5] Edna Walling, 'A Letter to Garden Lovers', *Australian Home Beautiful*, February 1940.
[6] Information from Margaret Mellor in correspondence with the author, 1992.
[7] ibid.
[8] Peter Watts, *The Gardens of Edna Walling*, Women's Committee of the National Trust of Australia (Victoria) Melbourne, 1981, p. 66.
[9] Olive Mellor, *Planning a Native Garden, Australian Gardening To-Day Illustrated, Sun News-Pictorial*, Melbourne, 1939, p. 73.
[10] ibid.
[11] W.A. Shum, (ed.), *Australian Gardening of To-Day Illustrated, Sun News-Pictorial*, Melbourne, 1939, p. 4.
[12] Thistle Y. Harris, *Australian Plants for the Garden: A Handbook on the Cultivation of Australian Trees, Shrubs, Other Flowering Plants and Ferns*. Angus & Robertson, Sydney, 1953.
[13] Latreille, p. 83.
[14] Ernest E. Lord & J. H. Willis, *Shrubs and Trees for Australian Gardens*, Lothian Publishing Company Pty Ltd, Melbourne, 1982.
[15] Latreille, p. 87.
[16] Peter Watts, *The Gardens of Edna Walling*, The National Trust of Australia (Victoria), Melbourne, 1981, p. 30.
[17] Raymond E. Negus, 'Rock Gardens', Gardens for Small Country Houses, Gertrude Jekyll and Lawrence Weaver, *English Country Life*, London, 1911, p. 240.
[18] Latreille, p. 110.
[19] ibid.
[20] Ellis Stones, 'Boulders and Borders', *Australian Home Beautiful*, July 1946, pp. 20-21.
[21] Ellis Stones, 'Pools — Formal and Natural', *Australian Home Beautiful*, September 1946, p. 9-11.
[22] Reginald Farrer, *My Rock-Garden*, Edward Arnold & Co., London, 1946.
[23] Gertrude Jekyll, 'The Pergola in English Gardens, Its Making and Planting'. *Journal of the Royal Horticultural Society*, vol. xxvii, 1902.

CHAPTER NINE
Interior Design

ROOMS OF MANY COLOURS, ballerina lampshades, lush arrangements of gladioli and dahlias, flights of ceramic ducks. Is that really how Australian house interiors were in the post-war years? Well, many certainly fitted that image, but quite a few were different, some coolly modern, others organic, cottagey, colonial or a dignified Georgian. The design and decoration of interiors at any given period is likely to vary considerably across the socio-economic spectrum. Those two decades from 1940 to 1960 offer some extraordinary contrasts in taste and in the realisation of ideals. Most people were consciously looking to achieve comfort and some reflection of their own personalities. Comfort was always possible, but for those constrained by economic and social conditions there was little chance of stepping aside from products and ideas shaped by popular fashion.

Architects, furniture designers, interior decorators, artists and journalists all agreed in the 1940s that Australian domestic interiors were generally well behind the standards set in other parts of the world. Many of the expatriates who returned to Australia at the outbreak of the Second World War were disappointed to find the stores filled with outdated and uninspired furniture and furnishings. Interior decorator Margaret Lord, recalling her impressions on returning in 1940, wrote:

> It seemed that anyone setting out to furnish a house from ready-made furniture would have to choose between a pseudo-traditional style — something vaguely Jacobean or Georgian — or, if more adventurous, a rather phony modern style in blond wood with splayed legs. This was generally referred to as "Swedish Modern".[1]

Conservative taste and lack of information about international developments in interior design conspired to make most Australian houses comfortably pedestrian. Cultural isolation was only beginning to break down through developments in communications and transport, so that ideas and fashions still arrived late and tended to retain their hold on the wider community long after they had been superseded in their countries of origin. However, a small group of talented Australians, including individuals seeking

● Architect Bryce Mortlock designed a courtyard house with an all-purpose room leading off the general living area.
Australian Homemaker, February 1957

• A comfortable 'contemporary' sitting room of the 1950s.
COLLECTION: ARCHIVES OFFICE OF TASMANIA

their own inspiration and direction, did manage to create interiors which reflected international standards in modern functional design.

The war caused many changes and developments for the whole community. It may have virtually halted domestic building and interior design, but it also engendered fresh ideas about houses and commonsense planning. One of the recollections for many directly involved in the war was that thoughts were often focused on how life might be when the world was again at peace. As has been noted, those in the services, enduring all kinds of living conditions — including horrific prisoner of war camps — naturally day-dreamed of home and family life. However, what is really extraordinary is that Margaret Lord's 1944 book, *Interior Decoration, A Guide to Furnishing the Australian Home*, even found its way to prisoners behind the Japanese lines. Hundreds of copies were included in parcels dropped from aircraft.[2]

Other service personnel applied for a correspondence course in interior decoration through Army Education and were sent a copy of the book. When originally planning the course Margaret Lord thought it would mostly appeal to women on the homefront or in the services. She was surprised to find that most of the students were men.

I was kept constantly in touch with people living and studying under great difficulties, sailors at sea, soldiers in the mud of New Guinea, or in the heat of northern Australia, all of whom were still interested and optimistic enough about the future to want to learn about interior decoration.[3]

AUSTRALIAN HOUSES OF THE FORTIES & FIFTIES

• *Opposite page*: In the sitting room of the 1959 Waks house at Northbridge, New South Wales, Harry Seidler used indirect lighting to create a striking effect.
PHOTOGRAPH: MAX DUPAIN
COURTESY: MAX DUPAIN AND ASSOCIATES PTY LTD

• *Below*: Ideas for fireplace surrounds.
Australian Home Beautiful, May 1958

In the 1930s there had been a growing appreciation that efficient modern houses should have well-lit, functional interiors which benefited from such technological advances as electrical appliances and easily maintained surfaces. The kitchen, bathroom and utility areas were first to receive such attention and were given brighter, fresher colours such as cream and green or white and blue, while living rooms and bedrooms often stayed shadowy and cosy with their autumn tonings and dark stained woodwork and furniture. Houses influenced directly or indirectly by the International style were given large windows throughout so that, with dark surfaces banished, and plain furniture and furnishings, they felt light and airy.

An awareness of progressive ideas in interior design often made life difficult in the 1940s because it usually meant having to search for good design in furniture, furnishings, appliances and other household items. For some the only answer was to have furniture and fittings made to order by one of the handful of craftsman/designers who were available. Fashionable 'Art Moderne' design of the thirties continued to influence popular mass-produced furniture right up to the 1950s. This was pastiche modernism, with veneers liberally applied, 'waterfall' curves and chrome-plated fittings. In spite of the Bauhaus ideals of creating clean, functional design by a process of subtraction the popular lounge suites were usually elephantine, with very wide arms and sombre fabrics.

The mantel and fireplace were simpler than their 1920s counterparts but in average houses were still awkwardly 'Moderne', often featuring machine-textured 'tapestry' bricks or perhaps the streamlined effect in pre-moulded plaster with curved corners. Details in the general plasterwork such as cornices, central ceiling panels and curtain pelmets also carried over the influence of Moderne style, with waves, zig-zags, sunbursts and stylised plant forms. Carpets and rugs might also echo similar origins in geometric 'jazz age' design, or could really confuse the eye by introducing the traditional floral patterns to the room. In 1949 Daryl Lindsay, the Director of the National Gallery of Victoria, wrote:

Generally speaking, the sitting room of most of our small houses is overcrowded and many of the things in it are fighting with each other for notice. The carpets, chair coverings and curtains all have different patterns and sometimes different colours.[4]

At this time architects were designing unfussy interiors with a variety of arrangements in the disposition of rooms. Emphasis was on open-planning for the living areas, including well-designed kitchens. Surfaces were plain, with furniture kept to a minimum mostly through choice, but in some cases as part of the general austerity of the immediate post-war years. Architect and writer Neil Clerehan observed in 1961 that some modern houses of the 1950s were, 'almost depressingly bare inside'. Pointing to the popular vision of furniture as status symbols, he applauds the ease of maintenance in the architect-designed functionalist interior but notes that, in certain cases, 'this new bareness has been smugly adopted as the structure itself replaces the suite as the family status symbol.'[5]

One aspect of rational design which did find wide acceptance throughout the community was the use of built-in furniture. There was nothing new in the idea, as even 19th-century houses and cottages sometimes had built-in cupboards and bookcases. But from the years before the Second World War there was an increasing tendency to discard free-standing furniture such as the kitchen dresser in favour of cupboards built in modular form and fixed as a continuous unit. Mary Jane Seymour in the October 1947 *Home Beautiful* wrote:

Built-in furniture is the logical answer to a number of problems created by modern living. Houses are smaller than they used to be and every inch of floor space must be used to the best advantage but neither is there time to spare for the leisurely "turning out" operations of former days. Anyhow, there is no-one to do it, domestic help being practically non-existent.[6]

The article criticises heavy pieces of furniture which 'require much energy to move and are simply a nuisance on cleaning day, and often they do not justify in usefulness the amount of space they occupy'. Built-in furniture in the form of cupboards, buffets, wardrobes, desks, beds and even radio cabinets are all suggested.

• AUSTRALIAN HOUSES OF THE FORTIES & FIFTIES

INTERIOR DESIGN

• Opposite page: Art Moderne tiled fireplace in a sitting room in the late 1940s.
Australian Home Beautiful, December 1948

• *Right*: Modern household appliances were gradually made more accessible throughout the 1940s and '50s.
COLLECTION: THE AUTHOR

'No longer need the housewife be haunted by the thought of dust and cobwebs accumulating in hidden places, for all these have been eliminated.'

Modern electrical appliances such as kettles, jugs, fans, toasters, food mixers, vacuum cleaners, floor polishers, washing machines, refrigerators and new designs in gas, electric or solid fuel stoves were an essential part of the revolution which took place in average households in the 1940s and '50s. For many families such things represented hopes only slowly realised. Lavish advertisements and images of family life in films and later on television were a constant reminder of the consumerist ideal. Most of the popular electric appliances had been around for some time but high prices kept them out of the average household. With rising standards of living pushing up sales and production the field became competitive and brought goods, once considered luxuries, within reach. The gas or electric hot-water service took up a large percentage of advertising space in the 1940s and '50s, with householders generally expecting to have hot water plumbed to a number of points.

— Kitchens —

Stainless steel kitchen sinks mounted on a modern 'built-in' cupboard base became a familiar type in the post-war years. A modern version of the porcelain-enamelled cast iron sink as well as those in acrylic were also seen. Designs included the standard single central bowl, twin central bowls and single left- or right-hand bowl. Ceramic tiles, plastic laminate or surfaced sheeting provided an easily maintained backing for the sink and benches. If hot water was not piped from a centralised hot-water service a small instantaneous gas or electric unit would be fixed to the wall above the sink. Cream and green had been popular colours for kitchens in the 1930s and held favour until overtaken by the proliferation of newly-fashionable hues. Brighter colours in kitchens were typically first seen in floor tiles or linoleums and plastic laminate bench and table tops. To add to the effect, richly coloured plastic canisters began to replace the older type in painted tinplate. In the late 1940s, blues, blue-greys and cherry reds on floors and benches were combined with pale lemon, buff or light grey walls. As the 1950s advanced the colours and colour combinations became more vibrant.

Simple kitchen settings, usually of Australian hardwood, continued to be available even toward the end of the 1950s. The tables were given plastic laminate tops and the chairs laminate backs. Woodwork was given a standard cream lacquer finish, or it might be stained a light oak colour. Settings of chromium-plated steel with 'Laminex' or 'Formica' tops and vinyl upholstery were in great demand in the 1950s and, as proof of their sturdy quality, have survived in large numbers.

A typical kitchen of the 1950s could have bright curtains in an abstract or semi-abstract pattern, some with frilly 'crossovers' of Terylene or muslin. Small indoor plants and ornaments occupied various shelves or shadow boxes, and decorative plates were hung on the wall. Miniature pots in scrolled metal wall-fittings held plants or plastic flowers and foliage. There was also likely to be an electric wall clock, a kitchen stool, a Mixmaster, the toaster, electric jug or kettle and perhaps a mantel radio. On the sink was a plastic-coated metal dishrack and, on the bench or table, a bowl or basket of fruit. Washable enamel paints were a common wall treatment, but there were also washable kitchen wallpapers, gaily patterned with suitably cheerful designs. Ice-chests, originally concealed in cabinets of varnished timber, were now of enamelled metal but still square-shaped. Refrigerators went through a similar evolution but somehow by the 1950s they had become puffed up with curved shapes, like the latest cars, making them

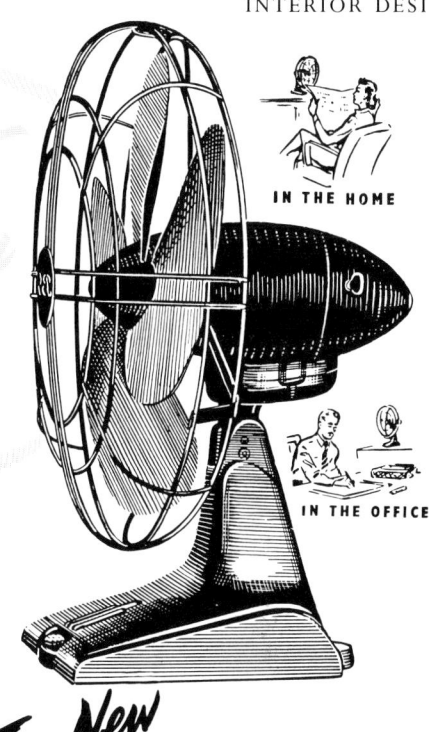

A Summer breeze — when and where you want it

IN THE HOME

IN THE OFFICE

The New **B.G.E.** ELECTRIC FAN

157

PRICE CONTROL IN THE KITCHEN!

• *Below*: Aga stove early 1940s.
COLLECTION: THE AUTHOR

impossible to fit in snugly as modular units. They dominated the kitchen at a time when gas and electric stoves were increasingly fitted as units rather than standing alone in the space once taken up by the wood-fire stove. Extractor fans and range hoods replaced the chimney. In rural areas the classic slow-combustion stove proudly kept its place as the heart of the kitchen. England's famed AGA was well advertised in Australia in the 1940s and '50s. Gas and electric ranges varied in their design but shared the same evolutionary path. They were usually classed as upright, elevated or cabinet type but there were also side-by-side twin ovens or side-by-side ovens, and hotplates. Fully automatic elevated electric ranges with glass-panelled oven doors were advertised as a great advance in 1957.[7]

Various forms of 'breakfast nook' were included in kitchen designs, having gained popularity in the pre-war years. A row of stools placed along an 'island bench' was used as a 'breakfast bar' in some houses in the 1950s. Wall cupboards with glass doors provided an opportunity to display decorative kitchenware and various ornaments. A suspended unit with glass doors on both sides could be placed over an island bench or, in some cases, open shelves might be similarly used.

— Bathrooms —

Bathrooms covered a wide range of possibilities from the smallest or most austere designs to highly luxurious creations. Handbasins and baths were of pressed steel or cast iron, finished with a baked enamel, or glazed earthenware. Galvanised sheet-metal baths were still being sold in some areas; there were also models in stainless steel and, from the late '40s, in acrylic. Coloured bathroom suites were available in the 1930s, but became much more commonplace in the post-war years. Typically the colours offered were cream, green, blue and pink, along with the traditional white or, for a striking effect, black. For a neater appearance, the pedestal handbasin was ideal; it concealed the plumbing. The built-in bath with glazed tiles or imitation tiling in sheet form was also seen as a neater choice. Floor surfaces included rubber, terrazzo, ceramic tiles, linoleum, vinyl tiles, cork, asphalt, magnesite or even concrete sealed with paving paint. Patterns in tiles and linoleums were usually large squares in 'checkerboard' patterns of contrasting colours. When applied to the walls, ceramic or imitation tiling would be carried to a height of at least four feet (1220 mm).

• Architects John and Phyllis Murphy designed this kitchen for the 1955 Saphin house in the Melbourne suburb of Brighton.

PHOTOGRAPH: WOLFGANG SIEVERS
COURTESY: JOHN AND PHYLLIS MURPHY

Glass shower screens for the bath or for a separate shower recess often continued the 1930s fashion for etched or sand-blasted decorative effects. Fish blowing bubbles as they swam through wavy seaweed was a popular design. Built-in radiators and perhaps a heated towel rail were to be found in better-quality schemes. A large mirror was seen as ideal but often only a small one was provided. Wall cabinets and ordinary towel rails or hooks were standard fittings. Small fittings included toothbrush, tumbler, soap and toilet-roll holders. The lever- or pushbutton-operated, low-level flushing cistern was offered in colours to match the whole suite in the 1950s. Sewerage and septic tanks were taking over from the pan system in most places.

— Laundries —

Wood-fired coppers were an all-too-familiar aspect of household life for many people in the period under review. The hand wringer was still doing service and the essential 'copper stick' was used for both agitating and lifting the washing. Gas and electric coppers at least saved on the effort involved in keeping the fire going. Washing machines in one form or another had been around since the 19th century. By the 1940s they had evolved into two basic types, the cylindrical form with agitator and wringer and the rectangular spinner. The latter type was best known in the Bendix, a front-loading machine with spin-drying action, widely advertised in the post-war years. Top-loading agitator models had an electrically-operated

• Bendix front-loading washing machine of the late 1940s.

COLLECTION: THE AUTHOR

• *Below*: Interior design, early 1950s.

Australian Home Beautiful, September 1953

wringer until the early 1950s when they began to offer a spin-drying function. With an all-in-one capability, some washing machines found their way into the bathroom or even the kitchen. The old detached or semi-detached 'wash-house' was disappearing and the trend was to have the laundry as an integral part of the house. In many cases it was designated a 'utility room' with a new stainless steel 'washtub' to go with the washing machine instead of the old concrete troughs. Here the ironing might also be done and there could be cupboards for the household equipment and possibly linen storage.

— Living and Dining Areas —

As noted in earlier chapters the newer, more flexible planning changed the relationship between areas for preparing and eating food and, in turn, between those areas and the main living space. An additional living space in many houses was the sunroom which gathered popularity from the inter-war years. If there was one clear trend in average houses or in architect designs on every scale, it was an increasing demand to break from the formalities of earlier times. Houses of a more formal Georgian style, or with similar pretentions, would retain the earlier character, but in 'contemporary' schemes the furniture, furnishings and general decor were part of a new, freer society. From 1956, television added further impetus to the informality, with an increase in hours spent in the main living area. Meals once served in the kitchen or dining area were now eaten in the living room.

Simplification of the mantelpiece or fireplace surround was a notable direction in the 1940s and '50s. However, that was not the whole story for, in many houses, a new horizontal emphasis extended the mantelpiece as part of a wide panel of brick or stonework. Further horizontality was achieved through the use of shelves or cupboards flanking the fireplace or heater surround. In organic or rustic designs the chimney and fireplace often became a massive construction, perhaps part of an entire stone or brick wall. The copper fireplace canopy was also a favoured element for 'contemporary' houses, both in cone and pyramidal forms. If television became the focal point, the fireplace or heater held its important status in cooler weather. Log fires have always had a particular appeal, but for those who demanded efficiency there were the new slow-combustion heaters with a small 'window' in the door to allow a glimpse of the familiar flames. Some of the well-known names were Convair, Wonder-Heat and Kumfort (Metters).

Gas heaters with imitation burning logs in an old-style grate were a compromise for those who found it hard to let go of the romance of the open fire. Other models were simply functional and were available with a suitably modern surround. Choosing the wall surrounding the fireplace or heater as the 'feature' wall possessed a certain logic. In many houses it was given emphasis by having it panelled with vertical boards. Apart from the alternative possibility of making a feature of a single wall of stone or exposed brick, the cheapest answer was to choose a striking paint colour, quite different from those on the other walls. With wall lamps, a picture or two and other decorative touches it was considered a satisfactory 'feature'.

INTERIOR DESIGN

• *Below*: Collectors' pieces from the 1930s, '40s and '50s are at home in such an appropriate setting.
PHOTOGRAPH: THE AUTHOR

• *Below*: Bold and imaginative colour schemes were suggested for contemporary homes.
Australian Home Beautiful, September 1953

From the 1920s the trend towards more compact houses which were less expensive to build had gradually reduced the number of chimneys to one or two, whereas in earlier times most rooms would have an open fireplace. Electric, gas or kerosene radiators and heaters could be used, generally with the chimney retained for the living room and perhaps a second chimney for the stove in the kitchen. For affluent households there was central heating but for most Australians this was still something read about in books and magazines.

Increasing the size and quantity of windows offered new possibilities for indoor plants. The earlier favourites had been chosen to cope with often rather dim interiors, but now with a flood of daylight there were many plants which would thrive indoors. Amongst the favourites were the philodendrons, monsteras, brassias and portulacas as well as ferns and palms. Plants in pots might be individually placed or arranged in groups. Some climbed up a screen of open framework or lattice, others were grouped in rectangular planters.

Furniture in the living and dining areas included lounge chairs and usually a couch or sofa, the sideboard and possibly storage cupboards, dining table and chairs, coffee table, magazine rack, bookshelves, television set, a standard lamp and a radiogram. Interiors clearly influenced by the International style were sparse and functional, with any decorative effect coming from carefully chosen colours, patterns and textures or from a few items such as a modern painting or print in a plain frame, an interesting vase with a flower arrangement, an indoor plant or perhaps a small sculpture. Melbourne-based interior decorator Edna Horton Lewis in her 1948 book, *Furnishing on a Budget*, restates the value of commonsense functionalism but is also prepared to advance the less rigid, friendlier approach which eventually eclipsed the so-called 'operating theatre style'.

What is it that gives a homely, welcoming look to a house: that most enviable of all achievements in interior decoration? It is certainly not a matter of costly fabrics and furnishings, or anything that only wealth can supply. On the contrary, it is largely a matter of assembling the simple needs of everyday living into a restful and pleasing composition, and of avoiding anything that inclines toward the pretentious.[8]

Opposite page: Decorative 'wrought iron' screen doors provided an important focal point. These examples are from a 'Page' Catalogue of the late 1950s.

COLLECTION: THE AUTHOR

— Bedrooms —

If the living areas could represent a broad spectrum of ideas, so could the bedrooms. On average, bedrooms were less cluttered than they had been early in the century and this principle was carried to the extreme of an ultra-functionalist design with a plain bed, built-in furniture and simplicity in every detail. By contrast, the romantic period-style bedroom could be well endowed with furniture and decorative elements varying from quality antiques to the popular 'Queen Ann' suites. Floral fabrics were often chosen as suitably old-fashioned or 'feminine' and when combined with a floral carpet were enough to drive the dedicated modernist to distraction.

Apart from the bed which could vary in design depending on the occupants of the room there would typically be a chest of drawers or a dressing table, or both. In master bedrooms and most others a mirror was essential, and despite the call for more built-in furniture the freestanding wardrobe remained popular. Some master bedrooms boasted a four-piece suite with twin wardrobes in highly figured Russian birch or maple veneer. Such schemes were likely to have curtains to match the bedspreads and venetian blinds in a selected colour.

Children's bedrooms have always tended to be relatively plain. With space often at a premium, double-decker bunks were a popular choice. Woven wire mattress bases were still the common type although some benefited from centre supports with spiral springs. The innerspring mattress was gaining popularity. A bedhead with bookshelf was ideal not only for favourite books, but also for treasured possessions. Sleeping in sparse conditions in some form of sleepout remained an alternative, particularly for the boys and young men in a family. Teenagers considered themselves fortunate if their parents would let them decorate their rooms with pin-ups of their favourite stars of sport, music and film. Bed lamps were good for encouraging reading, even if much of that was in the form of the latest comics.

A chair and a desk provided a quiet spot for homework, which became a greater burden when television arrived on the scene. Children's serials on the wireless in the late afternoon and early evening were certainly addictive but less so than the mesmerising effect of television. American films and television family shows suggested to young Australians that their bedrooms should more closely follow those of their counterparts in that apparent paradise for teenagers, the United States. Pennant flags, sports trophies and perhaps even a transistor radio or a portable record player would ensure a new status. Girls were very proud of their dressing tables, which were often glass-topped and kidney-shaped, with a skirt of floral chintz.

Two-bedroom houses presented a problem if there were children of both sexes; a sleepout or additional room was the only answer. Sex segregation after the age of eight years was suggested by the Commonwealth Housing Commission in 1946, but indications are that most parents arranged separate rooms before that age.[9] In architect-designed houses there was often a new approach to the placement of bedrooms. As noted in earlier chapters they could be in a separate wing, with the living areas accessed via a linking sunroom, passageway or breezeway. In some cases the children's rooms were zoned to provide a distinct separation, including space for studying and recreation away from the adults.

— Sunrooms and Other Spaces —

Various kinds of suntraps have been incorporated into house designs over many centuries. Banks of windows and conservatories were found ideal to provide bright, warm areas in houses in the British Isles and were brought to Australia from the early days of settlement. With additional influences from other parts of the world, the sunroom increased in popularity in the early decades of this century. In many cases it was a glassed-in verandah and was furnished with the same sorts of informal furniture as that used on the open verandah and the patio. Indoor plants, cane or wicker chairs, a divan or daybed and a games table were some of the possible inclusions. If a separate sewing room was not provided it was likely that the sewing-machine would be placed in a corner of the sunroom.

Many houses included a study which followed the traditional role of being a place where people could work at a desk or sit and read, away from the general household. In some examples, such as in the 1945 Sydney Ancher house at Killara, New South Wales, the area set aside as a study was an extension of the large open-living area (see page 94). Another special purpose area or room seen in some designs was that set aside for children to play in. With the limitations placed on the floor area of a house up to 1952, it required very careful planning to allow for more than the usual standard rooms. Halls and passages were kept to a minimum or eliminated completely in average plans. However, the glass-walled gallery served as an entrance hall in many of the houses designed by architects.

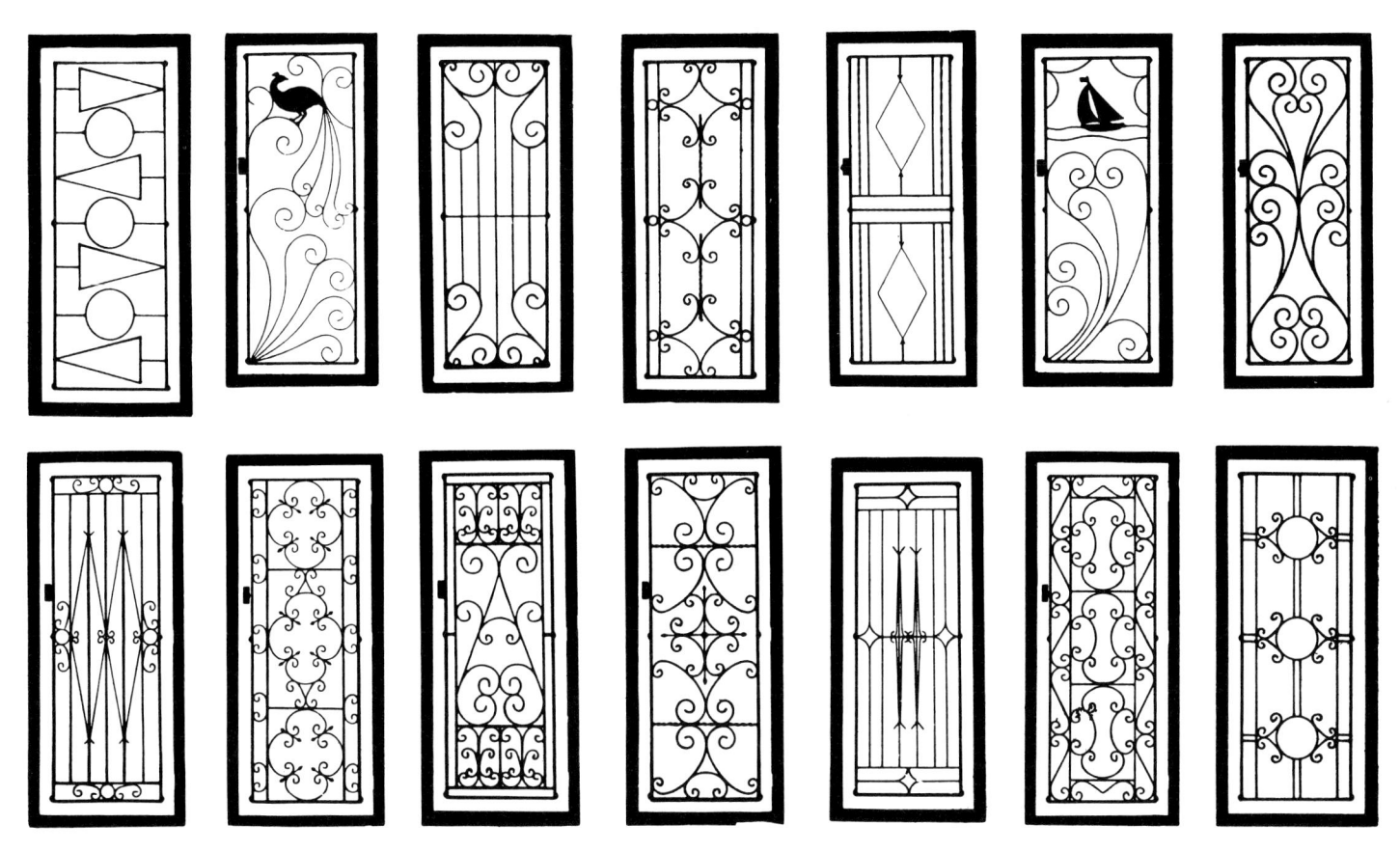

Close study of the evidence to hand suggests that most interiors in Australian houses built in the 1940s and '50s were conservative and low-key rather than exciting or progressive. Only a small number were radical in their conception. If vibrant colours were juxtaposed in striking combinations in many schemes in the latter part of those two decades, there were more years and many more houses in which the decor was subdued, quietly cheerful or perfectly refined.

Designer Margaret Lord wrote in 1944 that interior decoration was the art of designing rooms which comfort the body, please the eye, and interest the mind.

The surroundings in which we spend our time — the rooms in which we work, play or relax — influence our lives immeasurably, not only from the point of view of comfort, but appearance also. We can all remember occasions when we have felt suddenly cheered by entering a pleasant room whose colours were good and whose furniture was simple and well arranged.[10]

Affordable furniture in modern functional designs was increasingly available in the post-war years. If householders felt they could not manage moderately priced ready-made items, there was a wide range of 'home assembly packs'. Besides sections which included 'contemporary' furniture in many department stores there were shops and galleries offering well-designed furniture, fabrics, domestic utensils and a range of decorative items. Again, the overall picture was that modern design, following the standards set by the International aesthetic, was even in the 1950s still struggling to gain universal acceptance in the Australian community.

The 1957 catalogue for the Melbourne firm of Steele and Co. Ltd. offers little in the way of really modern furniture, a fair percentage of 'modernistic' designs and a surprising amount of period pieces, some of which continued the fashions of the 1920s. The top of the range of lounge suites offered was a fully carved,

• AUSTRALIAN HOUSES OF THE FORTIES & FIFTIES

INTERIOR DESIGN

• *Opposite page*: Interior at the courtyard level of Robin Boyd's own house of 1959 (see pages 124 and 125).
PHOTOGRAPH: MARK STRIZIC

• *Right*: Wrought iron was very popular for contemporary-style schemes.
Australian Home Beautiful, June 1959

• *Far right*: Feltex advertisement of 1941.
COURTESY: FELTEX CARPETS LIMITED

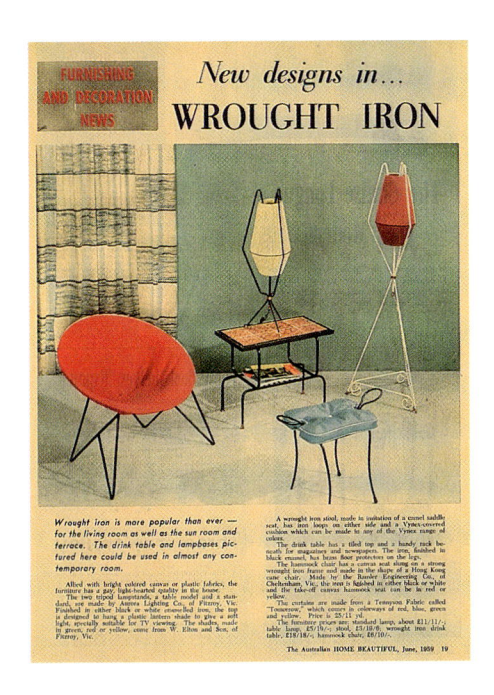

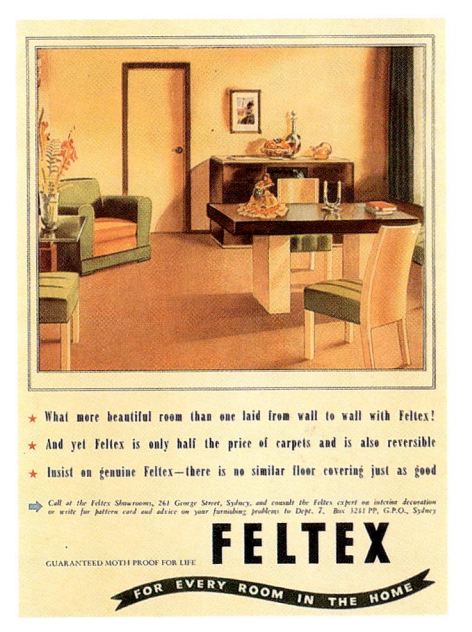

period-style three-piece 'Jacobean' classic. Highly fashionable stores, offering the most expensive furniture and furnishings, generally remained committed to period styles or an eclectic mixture of modern and traditional design. Interior designers who possessed imagination and a passion for good design influenced the affluent upper levels of society toward bolder, more dramatic interiors.

Sydney interior designer Marion Best was known for her colour sense 'of rare quality' and for her sure instinct for decorative design.[11] In 1949 the new Sydney-based journal, *Art and Design*, featured her work, including two colour photographs by Max Dupain. A striking room in her own home is illustrated and described as having three walls of Prussian blue, sprayed with pinky-beige sand, with a fourth wall in mulberry pink. Furniture included a low Chinese magazine table, a bed of lacquer red in a Chinese Chippendale design, Chinese prints and lamp bases and a painting of an oriental dancer by Loudon Sainthill. There was also an antique mirror with red velvet slip in its frame, and all the fabrics were hand-woven.

It was in this house in fashionable Woollahra that, in 1950, seven interior designers met to discuss the formation of a society or association, with the desire to help raise the standard of interior design in this country. Those seven were Marion Best, Margaret Lord, Mary White, Don Johnston, Edmund Dykes, Don Shaw and Stuart Low.[12] Subsequently, the Society of Interior Designers was founded. Members worked in various ways. Some were independent professionals with an office or studio, many had shops and others were consultants in the furnishing departments of large stores.[13]

The identifiable types of interiors in houses built in the 1940s and '50s can be divided into the following basic categories: Conventional, Cottage, Colonial, Georgian Revival, Art Moderne, Eclectic, Organic, International and Contemporary. A brief summary of each follows.

— Conventional —

The majority of houses built in the 1940s and '50s were given interiors which can be identified through shared characteristics. When Barry Humphries created Edna Everage he was thinking of Mrs Average and her world of typical Australian suburbia. Interiors evolved over the two decades from 1940 to 1960 but there were readily recognisable elements, many of which are now enshrined in satire or popular nostalgia.

A large percentage of Australians embraced some aspects of modern design and rejected others. For example, while architects chose plain or subtly patterned carpet, the majority of householders continued to favour exuberant floral Axminsters. If simple modern chairs were chosen, the standard lamp would most likely have a decorated shade trimmed with frills.

There were the popular framed prints of ballerinas, Mediterranean scenes, or the blue-faced woman. Mirrors of all shapes, sometimes with decorative sandblasting, graced the wall above the mantel or the sideboard. Often they were without frames, the edges cut in ripple pattern. Wall lights in brass, aluminium or wood sported shades in parchment or fancy glass. Table lamps offered versions of the standard lamp shades with painted decorations and trimmings of fringing, ruching, cord, ribbon or leather.

The pendant lamps carried over designs made popular in the inter-war years with

165

• Occasional tables from the 1957 Steele and Company catalogue.
COURTESY: JOHN AND PHYLLIS MURPHY

T 359 — TABLE
With 18in. circle top, richly veneered, and finished in mahogany, £6 15 0
Walnut finish £6 10 3

T 357 — TABLE
Period reproduction table in quality finish. Your choice of mahogany or walnut colour. With ball and claw feet and roped edge. £14 11 6

T 363 — TABLE
Attractive free form table, 30in. x 18in. and 15in. high. In walnut, mahogany or natural oak . . . £3 4 6

T 364 — TABLE
Beautifully veneered and featuring chrome frame. 22in. circle, 20in. high. Walnut . . . £9 10 6
Mahogany finish £9 13 6

'bowls' and 'dishes' of opaque glass to diffuse the light. Aluminium-, plastic- and chrome-plated metal were used in various ways to create 'contemporary' or 'traditional' fittings. If there was an entrance hall it could have a fancy pendant fitting, its metal in ivory and gold, the glass panels, champagne with orange relief pattern or dust pink with pink or pale green with green. The telephone table might be contemporary or 'Queen Anne' with a suitable chair or stool, a big black telephone and vase of flowers, real or plastic, or perhaps an artistic dried arrangement.

If the timber trimmings were not painted chalk white or ivory they would be finished in a varnish to a light 'blonde' colour or honey-brown; but sometimes it was the richer brown of the pre-war years. On the mantelpiece could be a Moderne-style clock with veneered case, some ornaments, and a vase with a fresh or dried flower arrangement. An open fire would mean some kind of fire screen. Popular types were wooden framed designs with decorative centre panel. The chrome and glass or chrome and bakelite smoker's stand was considered essential.

When vinyl-coated fabrics became popular in the immediate post-war years chairs, couches and units were covered in this 'easy-care' material. Heavier 'club style' suites continued to have Genoa velvet covering, but might use vinyl for the sides and backs. For proudly displaying china and crystal there were rectangular or bow fronted china cabinets with mirror back and plate glass shelves. An alternative was the 'glory chest', with one glazed section to display prized wedding presents. Veneered buffets were usually part of a six-piece dining setting.

Windows were typically dressed with curtains and venetian blinds, the latter being practical for all sorts of reasons, including the privacy they offered during daylight hours without completely closing off the outside world. Average households adopted a widening range of colours in interior decorating in direct response to the various forms of promotion used by the competing companies who sold plastics, fabrics, wallsheeting, floor and wall tiles, carpets and rugs, and most of all, paints.

— Cottage Style —

Interest in traditional-style cottages, including the decoration of their interiors, held a significant place in domestic design throughout the early decades of this century. Such an interest can be traced to the influence of the British Arts and Crafts Movement and to American interpretations of its philosophies along with a rediscovery of America's own heritage. Added to that we have Australia's Arts and Crafts societies, our own 'colonial revival' and the work of individuals such as Edna Walling. In some ways it is surprising that 'Cottage style' interiors could exist in tandem with Contemporary and International styles, but given closer scrutiny it becomes apparent that the ideals of functional simplicity were often shared. When Cottage style was overly 'cute' or self-consciously romantic it could be seen as distant from modernist ideals, but when it made use of plain objects, fabrics and fitments in a basically unfussy interior the historical links were clear.

Cottage style appealed to certain kinds of people: to those who were artistic and literate but not necessarily affluent, to craftspeople, to idealists who believed in a simple lifestyle, and to collectors of cottage antiques. Holiday houses and bungalows or cottages were often decorated in Cottage style because it could be inexpensive, easily maintained and comfortably informal. Edna Walling's 1947 book, *Cottage and Garden in Australia*, was a timely handbook for devotees of all aspects of cottage life, but there had already been a stream of articles and books over previous decades. Extracts and illustrations from *Old English Household Life* by Gertrude Jekyll and Sydney R. Jones, first published in 1925, were included in an article in the *Australian Home Beautiful*'s April 1947

INTERIOR DESIGN

Above: Open plan living in Perth, c. 1956.
PHOTOGRAPH: FRITZ KOS

issue. *English Cottage Furniture* by F. Gordon Roe, published in 1949, followed by *Windsor Chairs* in 1953, were both influential works.

Various permutations of the Cottage style included the nautical or seaside cottage, the colonial cottage and the types based on classic English models. Wooden furniture ranged from handmade antique chairs, tables, chests, beds, sideboards and dressers to late factory-made cottage chairs or complete reproduction settings. The traditional kitchen dresser, usually in oak, was the perfect foil for old blue and white plates and platters, cups, jugs and teapots, as well as pieces in pewter, copper, brass, wood or earthenware. Windsor chairs were favourites and there were three-legged stools, rush-seated chairs, along with upholstered armchairs such as scroll-arms and wingbacks in floral chintzes.

Floors were usually polished timber, with various traditional rugs or matting, while curtains ranged from muslins, ginghams and chintzes to burlaps and handweaves. Walls might be timber panelled, painted plaster or wallpapered. Favourite colours for walls were soft yellows, soft blues and pale olive greens or various shades of off-white to cream. Old brass candlesticks, lanterns, ships' lamps and kerosene table lamps were often included. Electric lamps were usually wooden or brass wall brackets, pendant fittings or standards with simple shades. Shelves for books, Staffordshire figures, old mantel clocks and other collectables were essential to such schemes. Fire dogs and grates, fire irons, bellows and baskets or large copper or brass tubs, ideal for firewood, were all included. Other suitably decorative cottage pieces were antique spinning-wheels, warming pans, grandfather clocks and the ubiquitous horse brasses.

Framed samplers, antique maps, Baxter prints and old works of art adorned the walls and often a fine patchwork quilt would be found on the double bed with its wooden-posted ends. Chests and small tables, vases of cottage flowers and baskets of fruit all added to the atmosphere. Edna Walling in her 1947 book provided designs for simple chimneys and fireplaces as well as various types of traditional

• Typical pendant light-fitting of the 1940s and early 1950s.

PHOTOGRAPH: THE AUTHOR

cottage doors. Continuing popular acceptance of the Cottage style is evident in the reproduction furniture offered in standard catalogues. If the modernists thought they had pushed the traditional Cottage style to the periphery they were not to know that it would find much wider acceptance in Australia in decades to come.

— Colonial —

Interest in Colonial-style architecture, including appropriate interiors, was subject to continuing influence from the United States beginning early this century. The rediscovery of our own colonial heritage was in part linked to the American experience and at times Australians were somewhat confused as to which tradition they were following. Colonial-style interiors in Australia tended to borrow the form and details of American schemes seen in books and magazines. In the 1940s and '50s, their furnishings varied from sophisticated Georgian to simple cottage designs. Some reproduction 'Early American' was offered in Australia, but often the choice was to restore old furniture available locally. Mass-produced American cottage chairs were often restored and included in interior designs with English country furniture. Easy chairs and couches upholstered in old-fashioned floral fabrics were combined with ladderback or Windsor chairs. The rocking-chair was especially favoured. American cottage clocks were also to be found in local secondhand and antique shops and were often set on a painted Georgian-style mantelpiece with brass candlesticks and pieces of pewter. Polished floors with handmade rugs, four-poster beds with old-fashioned quilts, and side tables with simple electric lamps were some of the key elements. Colours favoured were off-white or ivory with soft blues, greens and pinks, with accents of blue-grey, olive green, gold and russet.

— Georgian Revival —

Throughout the first half of the 20th century Georgian Revival or Neo-Georgian was accepted as a suitably dignified and tasteful style by affluent levels of society in Britain and the United States. In Australia in the inter-war years the upper middle-class were similarly drawn to Georgian style. It remained a significant portion of interior design and decoration throughout the 1940s and '50s, with stores, galleries and antique shops meeting the demand.

Interest in period furniture and, in particular, the styles of the Georgian era was evident in the mounting of an important exhibition in Sydney in 1941. Entitled 'An Englishman's Home', it was a lavish affair by the standards of those times and offered twelve 'rooms' carefully assembled using original pieces from private collections. Included were rooms representing Queen Anne, Early Georgian, Chippendale, Hepplewhite and Adam, Sheraton, Regency, Victorian, Edwardian and 'An Early Pioneer Room.'

Interiors generally referred to as Georgian, or perhaps in some cases Colonial Georgian, naturally varied in scale from sumptuous to moderate. Typically there were antique or reproduction pieces in highly-polished mahogany, good-quality rugs on polished timber floors, and chairs and sofas upholstered in chintzes with delicate floral patterns. Traditional chandeliers and wall-fittings with miniature parchment candle shades provided subdued electric lighting. Full-length curtains of glazed chintz, damask, cretonne, brocade or printed linen were sometimes topped by a pelmet.

Woodwork was generally painted in ivory colour, including the balusters of the traditional staircase. Handrails on the latter were of polished timber as might be

INTERIOR DESIGN

• This informal interior is in the tradition of the rustic hunting lodge or country retreat.

the ends of the steps. Mirrors in gilt 'Adam' frames surmounted the classical-style fireplaces. Doors were painted or polished timber of six-panelled design. Sideboards and tables might have candelabras and artistic flower arrangements in fine quality vases. Brass fire-dogs and fire-irons, mantel clocks in ormolu cases and perhaps a long case or grandfather clock added further to the feeling of an earlier age of grace and good design.

— Art Moderne or Art Deco —

The style originally identified as 'Art Moderne' is generally seen today as synonymous with Art Deco, that sophisticated and often opulent field of modern design which reached the wider world from the mid-1920s. Unlike the functionalist approach of the Bauhaus, Art Moderne combined modern forms with decoration for its own sake. Cubes, 'waterfall' curves, streamlines, sunbursts, zig-zags, skyscraper motifs and portholes were all elements used in the design of interiors. Glass, chromium-plated metal, decorative veneers and timbers, marble, bronze, ivory and ebony were favoured materials.

In many houses built in the 1940s and '50s Art Moderne continued to be an influence. One notable area was in the design and decoration of bathrooms. Striking geometric effects were created through the use of tiles on both the walls and the floors. Some schemes would have a black or green bath with perhaps a bold stepped pattern in black and lilac tiles on

169

• Georgian-style interiors continued to be favoured by those who sought conservative elegance.

Australian Home Beautiful, July 1945

the wall. Handbasins and other items would be square-lined, with an Art Moderne mirror flanked by tubular side lights.

In the living room the fire surround of tiles, brick or plaster, could continue the style as would the furniture with its cube forms, waterfall curves and ornamental veneers. Plasterwork, carpets, rugs and furnishing fabrics also displayed geometric and stylised natural forms. Mirrors again echoed the geometry as did the light-fittings in glass, chrome and aluminium. Wall-fittings with shades of Lalique glass made upward fans of light on textured walls. Glass bricks continued to be highly fashionable, and figured veneers on doors and panelling were also seen. A staircase might have black painted geometric or scroll design iron work. Tables of glass and metal or entirely faced in mirrored glass might carry a stylised figure, a vase of carefully selected flowers and foliage or an elegant lamp.

— Eclectic or Classic Modern —

There were many interiors which could be described as modern in the 1940s and '50s, but were not entirely within the parameters of the International style. Here were schemes which respected the basic precepts of functional design without demanding that all the furniture and furnishings be contemporary. There was even room for the inclusion of purely decorative elements. If a perfectly refined Regency chair looked well with a square-lined modern table, painted brick walls and a slim metal cantilevered floor lamp, then that was quite acceptable. British, Scandinavian and American designers had all found inspiration in traditional furniture, amd collectors prized original examples. Classic design of any age could well become part of a thoughtfully planned eclectic scheme.

That influential work, *The American Woman's New Encyclopedia of Home Decorating*, by Helen Koues, available in Australia throughout the 1950s, offered many examples of eclectic or classic modern interiors. Some tended toward the sparse, coolly cultivated approach, others were warm, woody blends of Colonial or Early American and the environmental influence of such architects as Frank Lloyd Wright. In the 1941 exhibition, 'An Englishman's Home', held in Sydney, Marion Best arranged two modern rooms. The scheme, described as 'Classic Modern', illustrated the adaptation of older furniture to a modern setting. 'This is of particular interest to people who, while living in a modern house or flat, possess furniture of an earlier period.'[14]

Early in 1951 *Home Beautiful*'s Elinor Ward wrote of a new house in the Melbourne suburb of Ivanhoe. It was a neat gabled design of off-white painted brick with a roof of old slates. 'The house has the look of an older, settled building, but it does not copy any style or fashion. It is a very pleasant, unpretentious, contemporary house — with refrigeration and dish-washing machine in the kitchen — combining the best of both worlds.'[15] The large L-shaped living room had walls painted a soft almond green and one was wallpapered. A wide white fireplace had cupboards and bookshelves built into the timber surround and a hearth of stone. Rugs in an 'old rose' colour were on a floor of natural polished wood and the big couch was covered in green-grey linen with two big chairs in 'pure lime' colour.

INTERIOR DESIGN

• An evocation of the 1950s. This interior of a 1958 house in the Perth suburb of Floreat Park displays original Grant Featherston chairs, including R152 and R160 in the Contour range of the early 1950s. On the right in the lower photograph is Featherston's Scape chair of 1960.

PHOTOGRAPHS: PETA TOWNSING

Coral-coloured cushions enlivened the couch. 'Old pieces of furniture are used in the modern interior and fit it beautifully, the dark notes of the wood seeming to tie the colour scheme down and give it value.' It was noted that the simple timeless lines of the several rocking-chairs and an 'old American desk chair' were all in harmony with the contemporary elements in the scheme.

Average interiors may well have developed an eclectic character when old pieces of furniture were included to supplement the few new items purchased with a limited budget. Books and magazines offered advice on refurbishing old furniture, including various attempts at modernisation.

— Organic —

An affinity with nature was the central philosophy of the environmental or organic house, and in most cases the interior was an integral part of the whole ideal. The use of natural materials was a logical choice. However, there was also the careful selection of manufactured materials whose colour, texture and character would be part of a harmonious whole. Both the interior design and the general furnishing and decoration could vary depending on the intentions of the architect and the householder. A mud-brick house could have a plain functional interior, with rendered earth walls, natural timber and perhaps stonework. The furnishings might be an eclectic mixture of traditional and modern, including handcrafted materials

• AUSTRALIAN HOUSES OF THE FORTIES & FIFTIES

• Easily maintained surfaces, adequate storage space and modern appliances were essential elements in the contemporary kitchen of 1950.

COLLECTION: THE AUTHOR

Avant-garde architects and designers chose striking mixtures of colour and form. Panels of cherry red, daffodil yellow and nautical blue were combined with greys, blue-greys, chalk-white or soft greens. Partitions, benches, simple storage cupboards as islands or peninsulas were all used to divide spaces. Shelves were created in many designs as integral forms and might be of wood or glass. Staircases were skeletal with open risers and slim metal or wood handrails. Mirrors were unadorned and in a bedroom the built-in wardrobe might be entirely mirror-faced.

Kitchens were sleek and as efficient as current technology would allow. Cupboards were modular and in light timber, surfaced in plastic laminate or painted. Benchtops of Laminex or Formica could be a soft, neutral shade, a rich colour or dramatic black. Lighting was both direct and indirect. Cone shades on walls or standards were directed both upward and downward to give the desired effect. Concealed fluorescent lighting might be in long troughs or pelmets. Curtains on modern tracks closed off glass walls when privacy or control of light and temperature was desired.

Architect Arthur Baldwinson built a house for himself at Sydney's Lane Cove in 1954 which was a carefully co-ordinated complex of shapes, textures and

such as fabrics and metalwork. Colours favoured tended to be within the range typically found in a natural bushland setting.

Organic or environmental houses which represented a modernistic expression of structure, a greater use of new materials, or new ways to use traditional materials, also achieved harmony through colour, texture form and volume. Glass, timber, metal, concrete and stone, along with various kinds of sheeting and textiles, were all used to create interiors which were dramatically modern and were an essential part of the organic relationship between a house and its environment. Glass walls enhanced this relationship.

— International Style —

Interiors which drew on the International aesthetic exhibited many shared characteristics. Walls and ceilings were generally plain or subtly textured, floors were either in natural timber with rugs or given practical floor coverings. Furniture that was not built-in was representative of the best contemporary design available. Large areas of glass in trim rectangular framing allowed the maximum of natural light. The age of the machine and of new materials was clearly evident in details such as lamps, lights, appliances and fittings.

172

INTERIOR DESIGN

• Traditional 'checkerboard' patterns using striking colour combinations were suitably dynamic for the modern floor of linoleum, rubber or vinyl.

Australian Home Beautiful, September 1948

colours. An article in *Home Beautiful* included the following description:

Some sections of the walls of the L-shaped living room are lined with tallow-wood, and include a built-in cocktail cabinet. Other sections consist of bagged brickwork and are painted a pastel blue-grey, the same colour as the ceiling. The living room includes a bay, timber-walled on two sides, glass-walled on the third, which centres around built-in bookshelves of polished silver ash whose tops are covered with slate slabs, and whose inside surfaces are painted black.[16]

Post-war Contemporary

This was the popular interpretation of the various aspects of 'contemporary' design. In many cases it could be described as a lively, if sometimes disturbing, blend of all that was offering in patterns, textures, colours, shapes and forms. In furniture, it was blonde timbers, chrome tube, black steel rod, splayed legs, square, round, triangular and 'kidney' shapes and the 'super ellipse'. Chairs for informal living were often in organic or capsule forms, perfect for the sprawled or curled up figure watching television. Modernistic abstract patterns in carpets, rugs and various fabrics, if thoughtfully chosen, could offer new exciting harmonies. By the late 1950s, the revolution in paint technology and the promotion of competitive colour ranges ensured that many 'contemporary-style' interiors included striking combinations of vivid hues — achieving an atmosphere thought to be in keeping with a bright new age.

Following the earlier examples created by the architects, stained vertical boards, exposed beams and sections of stonework became highly desirable. In many schemes the plain hardwoods of simpler designs became featuristic 'knotty pine'. Stonework could similarly take on a multi-coloured featuristic air. Modern prints or paintings in angled modern frames were lit by lights with anodised aluminium cone shades. In a truly 'contemporary' house there were few, if any, hints of times gone by unless it was the stylised 'vintage car' or 'horse and carriage' pattern in a fabric or wallpaper.

Chapter 9 Endnotes

[1] Margaret Lord, *A Decorator's World. Living with Art and International Design*, Ure Smith, Sydney, 1969, p. 97.
[2] Lord, p. 107.
[3] ibid.
[4] Daryl Lindsay, 'Our Furnishings Lack Taste', *Australian Home Beautiful*, September 1949, p. 15.
[5] Neil Clerehan, (ed.), *Best Australian Houses: Recent Houses Built by Members of the Royal Australian Institute of Architects*, F. W. Cheshire, Melbourne, 1961.
[6] Mary Jane Seymour, 'Built-in Furniture Not Only Saves Space', *Australian Home Beautiful*, October 1947, p. 32.
[7] Westinghouse advertisement, *Australian Homemaker*, February 1957, p. 5.
[8] Edna Horton Lewis, *Furnishing on a Budget*, Georgian House, Melbourne, 1948, p. 69.
[9] Robin Boyd, *Australia's Home*, Melbourne University Press, Melbourne, 1952, p. 276.
[10] Margaret Lord, *Interior Decoration, A Guide to Furnishing the Australian Home*, Ure Smith Pty. Ltd., Sydney, 1944, p. 2.
[11] 'Marion Best — Interior Designer', *Art and Design 1*, Ure Smith Pty. Ltd., Sydney, 1949, p. 22
[12] Margaret Lord, *A Decorator's World*, p. 185.
[13] ibid.
[14] Nora Cooper, 'The Progress of Modernism, A Decade's Advance in Furniture Design', *Australian Home Beautiful*, June 1941, p. 8.
[15] Elinor Ward, 'It Nestles into a Hillside', *Australian Home Beautiful*, March 1951, p. 37.
[16] Gerald Steward, 'Well-Known Before it Was Built!', *Australian Home Beautiful*, June 1955, p. 19.

173

CHAPTER TEN
Furniture, Furnishings and Fittings

HOPES THAT THE IMMEDIATE post-war years would see a revolution in household furniture were only partially realised. Henry Manne writes on 'Furniture for Peace Time' in *Home Beautiful*'s February 1945 issue. 'It is obvious that the design of homes in the post-war period will call for plain furniture.' Once again espousing the principles of modern functional design, by then widely disseminated for around two decades, he calls for furniture which honestly expresses its purpose, shuns superficial ornamentation, and is free from the bonds of traditional 'period' design. In fact the years from 1945 to 1960 were to witness a continuing battle between 'good modern design' and the popular styles such as Queen Anne, Georgian, Moderne, Colonial and even Jacobean.

Smart Heavy-Duty CHROME CHAIRS & TABLES by K. R. Devling

Chairs 53/6 to 105/-
Tables from £7/19/9 ea

Ideal for lounges, kitchens, sun-rooms — in fact any place where strong, comfortable, modern furniture is needed. These chrome tube steel chairs and tables are available in sets or single units.

• FURNITURE •

As can be expected, there was also factory-made 'Contemporary' furniture which simply borrowed the key elements or details seen in modern design, often without achieving the fundamental qualities inherent in such works. There were, however, examples, where innovative furniture found a wide market through mass-production. One of the best known in Australia is the tubular steel cantilever chair designed in Germany in the mid-1920s by Marcel Breuer. These were produced in Australia by A. G. Healing Limited from 1931. In the 1940s and '50s they were widely advertised by K. R. Devling, who apparently made them under an agreement with Marcel Breuer dating back to the early 1930s.[1] Kitchen settings of four chairs and a table were a popular choice for thoughtfully designed functional interiors.

Just as the influence of International-style architecture arrived in a variety of ways between 1930 and 1960, so too did that of classic modern designs in furniture. A notable example was the simple wood and webbing chair designed for Hans Knoll by Danish-American designer Jens Risom in 1941–42. In the post-war years the original design, along with copies or variations, was seen in Australia. Armchairs, dining chairs and stools were available in kit form in the 1950s, with webbing offered in scarlet, gold, lime, 'ink blue' and forest green.

Webbed chairs of laminated plywood created by Sydney designer Douglas Snelling (1916–1985) in the 1940s were also similar. An interesting idea was the use of a footstool which when attached to a chair created a chaise longue.[2]

Other chair designs mass-produced in the United States and seen in modern Australian houses include the 'Diamond chair' by Harry Bertoia, made by Knoll from 1950, and the 'Sling chair' or 'Hardoy chair', designed in Argentina in 1938 and made by Knoll in the 1940s and '50s. The 1948 'Womb chair' by Finnish-American Eero Saarinen was the archetypal modern easy-chair. An upholstered shell on slim metal legs, its designer named it for the way it so comfortably held a curled-up figure.

Classic furniture designs, familiar through mass-production in the United States, were also created by Charles Eames and George Nelson. Both designers were featured in *Home Beautiful*'s March 1951 issue and the furniture illustrated included

FURNITURE, FURNISHINGS AND FITTINGS

• Apart from the Featherston armchair R160 on the left, this setting includes an original smoker's stand, two fine examples of Wembley ware and a recent production of the coffee table designed in 1944 by American sculptor Isamu Noguchi (1904–1988).

PHOTOGRAPH: PETER TOWNSING

AUSTRALIAN HOUSES OF THE FORTIES & FIFTIES

• *Left*: Functional Products Pty Ltd of Sydney offered furniture designed by Douglas Snelling. In 1955 they announced the Snelling 'B.S.F.' Unit, a modular system of shelves and cupboards, and the Snelling Saran-Webbed Chair.
Australian Homemaker and Handyman, July 1955

• *Below*: Chair designed by Hans Wegner, manufactured in Australia in the 1950s.
Australian Home Beautiful, August 1959

steel-framed Eames Storage Units which were recent designs. While modern Scandinavian furniture continued to emphasise handcrafted timbers, American designers were emphasising technology as a means to mass-production. Fibreglass, plastic, plywood, and the new lightweight metal alloys were all employed, as were new techniques in welding or fixing these materials.

America's new furniture was an important influence, but so too was the diverse range from the Scandinavian countries. Before the war there was a tendency to lump all Scandinavian furniture together under the broad term 'Swedish Modern' and, as has been noted, furniture in light coloured wood with splayed legs was accepted as a standard type. However, Sweden, Finland, Norway and Denmark all produced high-quality furniture, some of which inspired designers throughout the world. Alvar Aalto of Finland and Bruno Mathsson of Sweden both created influential chair designs in bentwood or bent plywood. These designs of the 1920s and '30s were considered modern classics in the post-war era. Scandinavian furniture was widely accepted as the ideal representation of international modernism, and by the 1950s perfectly crafted pieces in teak set a trend in Australia which was to continue for many decades.

Chairs by Danish designer Hans Wegner typified the sophisticated handcrafted look which recalled the ideals of William Morris and his followers. However, in contrast to the original Arts and Crafts rejection of the machine age, the construction of these pieces utilised modern power tools and assembly operations in harmony with handcrafting. Seats were typically of leather, rope, rush, cane or plywood. The design by Hans Wegner, seen above, was manufactured in Australia in the 1950s by Danish De Luxe Pty Ltd and named the 'Denmark' chair. It was made of Australian blackwood (*Acacia melanoxylon*) with a leather-covered seat. The price in 1959 was £39, some five times the price of an average armchair in stained 'Tasmanian oak'.

FURNITURE, FURNISHINGS AND FITTINGS •

• Rose Seidler House, Harry Seidler 1948–50.
COLLECTION: TRACY WATT

SAVE POUNDS! — Make your own Furniture easily and quickly at home with TIMBER-PACKS

The fascinating and profitable hobby of making furniture at home, could until recently, be tackled only by an expert carpenter with a fully equipped home workshop. With TIMBER-PACKS however, any amateur can now make excellent quality modern furniture using only a hammer, screwdriver and a tin of glue. Illustrated on this page are some of the TIMBER-PACK range of over 60 home assembly packs. Each one is accurately pre-cut from selected quality kiln-dried, blonde furniture timbers, all holes are bored and assembly and polishing instructions, screws, nails, etc. are supplied with every pack. You can order from this page by sending cheque or M/O to TIMBER-PACKS PTY. LTD., 539 Chapel St., Sth. Yarra, Vic. Packs can be sent anywhere in Australia. They are delivered to your door in Capital Cities or to your nearest attended railway station in the country. Do not add freight, packs being sent freight collect on delivery. A 16-page catalogue is also available post free on request. In Tasmania write to Charles Davis Ltd., Hobart.

SWEDISH DINING TABLE £9/18/6
With Solid one piece laminated top. Size 4' 6" x 2' 6". Seats 6 comfortably. Very easy to assemble. Also 5' x 2' 8" £10/13/6. 5' 6" x 2' 10" £11/8/6.
WEBBING DINING CHAIRS £3/3/- ea.
Modern, form fitting design. No. 60. Webbing available in Scarlet, Gold, Lime, Ink Blue and Forest Green, 1/6 yd. (18 yds. req. per chair.)

NEST OF TABLES £7/17/6 COMPLETE
or may be purchased separately. No. 49.
Small 18" x 16" 42/6
Medium 27" x 16" 52/6
Large 36" x 16" 62/6
18" high.

CONTEMPORARY LOUNGE CHAIR £6/12/6
A really comfortable chair. No. 62. Matching 2-seat settee £9/18/6. No. 63. Inner-spring loose cushions £4/15/- per set of 2 plus 2¼ yds. 50" material.

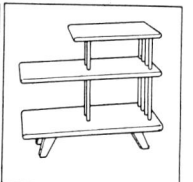

2 FT. BOOKCASE £2/12/6
Modern unit bookcase with 10" wide shelves. No. 48. Also available with three 3' long shelves. No. 47. £3/9/6. Height of shelves is adjustable on both units.

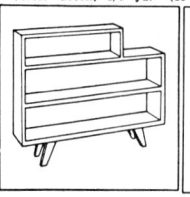

SWEDISH BOOKCASE £4/9/6
3' 6" long 2' 10" high. No. 23. Also available without top shelf £3/12/6. No. 22.

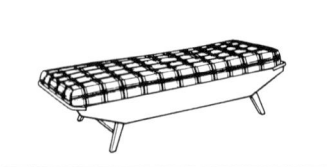

COMFORTABLE, MODERN DIVAN £5/17/6
Perfect for the contemporary living room and a valuable spare bed. 2' 6" wide. Takes a standard 6' mattress. No. 2. Also available 3' wide. £6/15/-. No. 3. 4' 6" wide £7/19/6. No. 4.

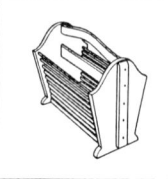

MAGAZINE HOLDER £2/17/6
Solves the newspaper and magazine storage problem in a jiffy. No. 28.

BEDSIDE TABLE £4/16/6
Fitted with drawer. Also makes a splendid telephone table. 27" high. 18" wide. No. 72.

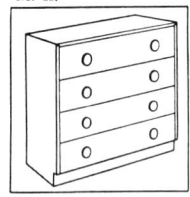

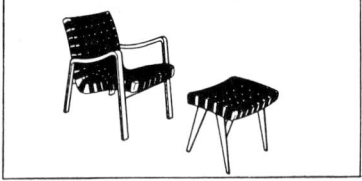

• *Left*: 'Timber-Pack' pre-cut furniture was produced in Melbourne from the late 1940s.
Australian Home Beautiful, June 1955

• *Below*: Webbed chair with footstool becomes a chaise longue — designer Douglas Snelling (1916–1985).

COLLECTION: PHILIP WARD-DICKSON

While Australians wanted to acquire modern furniture designs acclaimed in the wider world there was, thankfully, a growing confidence that we were capable of producing our own quality designs. Melbourne-based Frederick Ward (1900–1990) had gained a well-deserved reputation in the 1930s for simple functional furniture in Australian timbers. In 1947 he produced a series of designs for the *Australian Home Beautiful*'s 'Patterncraft' range. Readers were offered paper patterns and instructions for items such as a stool, easy chair, bookshelf, divan and magazine table.[3] By early 1948 the designs were available as 'Timber-Pack' kits which consisted of cut-out, sanded components of selected timber (generally kiln-dried hardwood), which simply required drilling and basic handfinishing after assembly.

By 1950, the Patterncraft/Timber-Pack range had increased to more than forty items and by 1955 the Timber-Pack catalogue offered over sixty home assembly packs. Included were a 'Swedish' dining table, webbing dining chairs, 'contemporary' lounge chair, 'Swedish' bookcase, four-drawer chest, bedside table and Fred Ward's 1947 design divan. The mail-order catalogue for 1958 offered over seventy packs and claimed savings of up to 50 per cent when compared to furniture sold by retailers.

An outstanding Australian designer in the 1950s was Grant Featherston (b. 1922). Working in Melbourne from 1947, he created commonsense, functional designs ideally suited to modern factory

• *Right*: Television gave new emphasis to the need for comfortable armchairs. The Fler SC58 boasted solid timbers, internal steel frame, 'Dunlopillo' seat, suspension springing and zip-off covers.

Australian Home Beautiful, November 1958

YOUR HOME
Deserves the Benefits only F L E R chairs can bestow.

The chair illustrated is the FLER SC58.
Patent No. 213246
F L E R BENEFITS:

IDEAL FOR T.V.

production. His 'Contour chair R152' of 1951 was comfortable, strong and relatively light. The seat and back were one continuous shape formed from two plywood sections (see page 11). Foam rubber provided the cushioning for the seat, while the back was padded with horsehair and wadding. The tapered legs were fitted into two diagonally-crossed rails which supported the shell. Discussing the chair in 1952, Featherston noted that while plywood chairs were not new certain details in their construction were original. Such details included the downward-sloping arms of the back which met the arms of the upward folding seat to form a joint between the seat and back.[4] His second design for mass-production was a wing chair with arms, again a boldly organic form, typical of mid-20th-century design.

The use of metal legs and framework in the immediate post-war years resulted in ingenuity of design and increasing sophistication. American George Nelson designed chairs for the Hermann Miller Company with legs of tapered tube. In the late 1950s Grant Featherston created a dining setting for Aristoc Industries of Glen Waverley, Victoria. The tapered legs were described as resembling a ballerina dancing on the points of her toes, which, along with the Eastern flavour of the crossed joints, led to the setting being named the 'Arabesque'. Two types of table were available, a round top and an ellipse shape. Both were surfaced in plastic laminate but natural wood was available on application. The chairs were upholstered with a foam cushion and covered with a choice of PVC cloth or woven material. Polished brass ferrules were fitted to the tapered legs to protect the floor surface.[5]

Furniture design and manufacture was a lively and competitive field in the period from 1945 to 1960. It was noted in 1956 that the people who were producing good modern furniture were the designers turned manufacturers rather than the ordinary manufacturers.[6] One of the well-known firms of that era, the Fler Company, was set up in Richmond, Victoria, in 1946. In 1949 they began producing a simple Swedish-style dining chair. It was created by Fred Ward in conjunction with Fritz ('Fred') Lowan and Ernest Rodeck, whose combined initials inspired the name 'FLER'. Lowen, the manufacturing end of the production, had spent summer holidays in Sweden; discussing the dining chairs he commented, 'They are typically Swedish. They represent the entire Swedish way of living — plain lines, no unnecessary ornaments, light natural woods. The Swedes are simple in their ways of living.'[7] In twelve parts, the chairs were of Pacific maple, a pale golden colour with undertones of mushroom pink which sometimes became a deep dull red. It was suggested that they would look best with a plain, uncovered table, preferably of the same wood.

The second Swedish-style Fler chair being planned in 1949 was an easy chair with loose cushions and upholstery.[8] A table to match the dining chairs soon followed and, by the early 1950s, Fler furniture was seen in the large retail stores in both Melbourne and Sydney. In 1956 the company released the 'People's chair', an all-steel construction with matt black finish and 'Texfoam' cushions with 'zipp-off' covers. Even the rubber padded armrests had patent zipp-off covers.[9] Apart from the standard two-arm chair, there were single-arm units which, when placed together, made up a settee. Another metal-framed easy chair of that period was the 'Flex-Back' by Melbourne artist and designer Raymond Wallis.[10]

With the arrival of television in 1956 the comfort of easy chairs and couches or settees was an even greater consideration. Fler advertised their chairs as ideal for watching television and by now their furniture was selling throughout Australasia. In 1953 they had become Fler Company & Staff Pty Ltd.

An important aspect of industrial design in the post-war era was the creation of appliances in harmony with modern interiors. Television sets and radiograms provided interesting scope for the designer when their cabinets were treated as items of furniture. The examples illustrated give some indication of the range of possibilities and high points of sumptuous design. The introduction to Australia of

179

• *Left*: Jungle Song, a twelve-colour print designed by Douglas Annand in 1947 for Silk and Textiles Pty Ltd of Sydney (see page 182).
Published in *Art and Design I*, 1949.

• *Below left:* Popular fabrics of the late 1950s: 'Opuntia', a flower print on textured cotton by Bevis, and 'Modern Note', brilliant colours on textured cotton by Grafton (England).
Australian Home Beautiful, April 1959

long-playing micro-groove in 1951 added a new dimension. Mantel radios were first given 'Bakelite' cabinets in the 1930s and by now were offered in an interesting range of modernistic designs.

• SOFT FURNISHINGS •

As interiors became standardised with few, if any, decorative architectural elements, colour schemes and soft furnishings played an increasingly important role in the achievement of individual expression. During the war it was a case of limited supplies and dwindling stocks. For curtains, hessian or burlap became a popular choice because it required no coupons. When peace came it took some years for shortages to ease. Early in 1947, *Home Beautiful*'s Esme Johnston wrote:

After the wartime drought in soft furnishings when we bore with our pre-war vintages in decor, and loose covers and curtains were on the dry cleaners' banned list, it is refreshing to note the welcome signs and portents in the shops -— fine and passable fabrics in good enough supply to indicate that better days have come at last.[11]

She also notes that the scarcity or total absence of imported fabrics had been 'a natural incentive to local designers and manufacturers to fill the empty shelves with Australian goods'. Melbourne's Frances Burke had been building a reputation for the design and production of hand-printed fabrics, and by the early 1940s was widely known. She had studied art and design at the Melbourne Technical

FURNITURE, FURNISHINGS AND FITTINGS

• Two boldly abstract fabrics by the Melbourne-based firm Tennyson. On the left is 'Furth' printed on a structure weave cotton and on the right 'Amon' also printed on structure weave cotton.

Australian Home Beautiful, April 1959

College, the National Gallery School and the George Bell School. With fellow-graduate Morris Holloway she founded Burway Prints in August 1937. It was the first registered textile screen-printery in Australia.[12] In 1942 Holloway left to establish Textile Converters and the original firm became Frances Burke Fabrics. In her search for an Australian style Frances Burke found inspiration in the collection of Aboriginal bark paintings at the National Museum of Victoria. The bold patterns, delicate stylisation and subtle earth colours were sensitively adapted to create designs which readily fitted contemporary ideals. A selection of her screen-printed fabrics were illustrated in 'Decorative Art', *The Studio Year Book for 1942*.[13] Modern in conception, the patterns shown were based on native flowers and formal elements. One, with a bold nautical theme, included yachts with anchor and wheel motifs.[14] A cotton fabric of a weight suitable for loose covers and curtains was usually chosen and in most designs the printing was monotone.

By the early post-war years, a number of Australian designers had entered the field. Esme Johnston noted in 1947 that the monotone print with its limitations had reached saturation point 'both in scope and public affection'. To meet the growing demand for greater colour and variety, screen prints were beginning to appear in three or four colours.

Made in Victoria and New South Wales, these prints are interesting and attractive. Well designed, they are mostly done in medium to large motifs, and show a classic influence, architectural, arboreal or heraldic.

Typical colour combinations were, chocolate, 'Pekin red' and off-white; 'phlox' pink, white and marine blue; 'brick red', parchment and delft blue; blue, raspberry and white or brown blue, flamingo pink and off-white. Three-tone prints might have two shades of green with off-white, two shades of blue with white or two shades of pink with parchment.[15]

Alexandra (Nan) Mackenzie and Anne Outlaw established Annan Fabrics in Sydney in 1941. Their bold multicoloured prints, typically based on Australian motifs such as native flowers and Aboriginal rock carvings, found a ready market. An exciting venture which began on a trial basis in 1946 and was repeated on a larger scale in 1947, called on the talents of a group of Australian painters to design textiles. The firm Silk and Textile Printers Ltd, founded in Sydney in 1939 by Orlando and Claudio Alcorso and Paul Sonnino, had decided to offer the Australian public a chance to enjoy the work of contemporary artists in the Modern Age Fabrics range.[16] Designs were contributed by Russell Drysdale (Free Forms), William Dobell, Margaret Preston, Donald Friend (Pearl Divers), J. Carrington Smith (Tasmanian Bush), James Gleeson (Totem), Jean Bellette (Myths and Legends), Francis Lymburner (Jugglers), Sheila Gray (Cross Section),

• *Right and opposite below*: Lounge suites varied from cumbersome moderne styles to various forms of 'contemporary'. The suite at right includes three chairs which join to form a settee. The suite opposite below carries over a style first seen in the inter-war period.

CATALOGUE: PATERSONS, MELBOURNE, 1957

Alice Danciger (Sea Fantasy), and about twenty other artists.[17]

Handwoven fabrics were also an important facet of local production. In Victoria, in 1940, Catherine Hardress and Edith (Mollie) Grove founded a business called Eclarte. They successfully produced high-quality handwoven furnishing and clothing fabrics for twenty-two years.

From November, 1958, Frances Burke began Australia-wide distribution of 'a few design favourites', printed on 48 inch (122 mm) cloth for her by a better-equipped manufacturer. With so much colour in modern interiors, she apparently felt that a single ground colour with the pattern in white was all that was needed for a printed soft furnishing.[18] It was known as 'Unit Colour Design'. 'The plain white of the pattern is in harmony with the almost universal white woodwork trim, and the single ground colour acts as a unit of a total colour scheme created by other factors in a room.' More than fifty designs were available in the traditional 36 inch (40.6 mm) width printed by the Burke printery and for a minimum of 15 yards (13.7 m), the customer was offered a choice of fifty-two colours.

Brighter colours and bolder patterns were the trend for furnishing fabrics in the immediate post-war years. American glazed chintzes with exuberant floral patterns and attractive colours contrasted with their British counterparts which tended to favour small traditional designs. They were particularly suited to bedrooms and sitting rooms and were washable and guaranteed fadeless with an everfast glaze.

Period-style prints based on designs from America's colonial era were ideal for cottage, colonial or Georgian schemes.

Curtains traditionally divide into two categories: the dense materials used to block out vision and to a greater or lesser degree light, and the semi-transparent materials used as glass or sash curtains. The main curtains varied depending on the type of interior and available funds. Fabrics used included chintz, chenille, cottage weave, folk weave, printed cotton, linen, poplin, cretonne, damask, repp, taffeta, satin, velvet and velour. For light curtains, often in combination with heavier types, the choices were, cotton net, brise net, fisher net, artificial silk net, madras, muslin, voile and Terylene.

Furniture fabrics included the substantial types listed for curtaining as well as tapestry, moquette, brocade, corduroy velvet, Genoa velvet, and the new plastic materials such as 'Vynex', 'Daynide' and 'Nylex'. 'Tapestry' had become a broad term encompassing a range of fabrics from high-quality traditional needlepoint tapestry, often seen as panels on expensive suites, to heavy-weight cotton or cotton mixed with silk or wool, with the pattern woven into the cloth.[19] For the classic 'Moderne' lounge suites (see opposite), the main upholstery would be Genoa velvet with a 'tapestry' fabric for the sides and back. Most of the average suites with wooden arms were covered with tapestry, with better-quality types being in uncut moquette. Plasticised cloth such as 'Vynex' was washable and therefore easily maintained. To create a softer looking surface, these were printed in various 'textural' patterns which suggested weaves. 'Houndstooth' was one such pattern released in the mid-1950s.

Tapestry weaves in the years immediately after the war were a means of creating some interest, while bright colour-fast dyes remained scarce. Typically they were 'two-tone' floral patterns with such colours as green, rust or brown on a background of deep cream or fawn. Furnishing velvets were similarly limited and typically in off-white, burgundy, rust, rose and blue-green. Antique or period-style suites might be upholstered in a pink Regency stripe,

• *Above*: Austrian-trained craftsman Schulim Krimper (1893–1971), arrived in Australia in 1939. Based in Melbourne, he produced fine handcrafted furniture throughout the 1940s and '50s.
An exhibition of twenty years work was held at the National Gallery of Victoria in 1959.
PHOTOGRAPH: MARK STRIZIC

• Chenille bedspreads were very popular in the post-war era.
CATALOGUE: STEELE & CO. LTD., MELBOURNE, 1957.
COLLECTION: JOHN AND PHYLLIS MURPHY

Fadeless chenille spreads

while ultra-modern furniture was usually in plain weaves.

From about 1949 things began to change. Australian and overseas manufacturers were warming up the competition and widening the range. Vivid colours and bold patterns were really celebrating the end of restrictions, including the need for coupons. British companies Sanderson and Grafton, in large full-colour advertisements, offered guaranteed fadeless furnishing prints which set a high standard in design and quality. Traditional patterns in printed linens, satins and chintzes were increasingly joined by 'contemporary' designs where abstract shapes and stylised motifs were produced in endless combinations. The 'nubbly' texture was a fashion favourite in both plain and patterned textiles. From the mid-1950s names such as Sundour, Kornblum, Hoad, David Whitehead, Tennyson, Wilson and Rodriguez were seen in association with popular fabrics. Sanderson also joined other English names such as Crown and Shand Kydd in a drive to revitalise popular acceptance of wallpapers. Bright new patterns along with elegant traditional designs each found a market.

One of the most popular fabrics in the 1950s must surely have been chenille. In thousands upon thousands of average households the chenille bedspread was a familiar part of daily life. Jeldi Manufacturing Pty Ltd began producing chenille in Australia in the early 1930s and became synonymous with the classic chenille bedspread. Their 1954 'Fanfare' bedspread was available in white, champagne, rose, blue, gold, green, beige and pastel shades of pink, green or blue. Other favourite weaves from the mid-1950s were 'Triple Ripple' and 'Princess' which was described as a 'knobbly' fabric. Printed linen, tapestry, folkweave, antique satin and rayon damask were also favoured for bedspreads.

• **FLOORCOVERINGS** •

The Australian demand for traditional, large patterned and floral carpets in Axminster was recognised by the British manufacturers as a national preference.[20] There were, however, a percentage of people who looked for subdued or contemporary patterns as well as those who wanted plain carpet of a suitable colour and perhaps an interesting texture. Wilton was typically a plain or two-tone carpet, often with a figured or relief

• Boldly patterned carpets remained popular for traditional or conventional interiors throughout the 1940s and 1950s.
COLLECTION: THE AUTHOR

Carpet makes a home more beautiful

pattern. Good-quality Wiltons and Super Wiltons were very expensive. Axminster used a thicker yarn with a deeper pile but was not so closely woven. Its colour combinations were its great advantage and one carpet could contain eighty different shades. Other types of carpet used were chenille axminster, tapestry and 'cord'. The latter was usually wool, woven in a loop pile. Nylon carpet appeared on the Australian market in the late 1950s.

An alternative choice in floorcoverings was the well-known wool-felt textile, 'Feltex', first seen as a plain material in the 1920s, with marbled pattern available from the 1930s. Patterned Feltex was widely available from 1950 and provided an economical substitute for carpet. In contemporary houses and holiday cottages, seagrass matting was another low-cost floorcovering. Rugs of various descriptions were seen in all kinds of houses. Sheepskin rugs made up to various sizes were available in 'deep burgundy and wine tonings', rust, blues and greens, pastel pink and natural. Indian woollen druggets were offered in plain oatmeal, off-white, grey, mottled green and 'reddish effects'.

As can be seen from the illustrations on page 173, the traditional linoleums as well as the newer 'lino tiles' were usually the bright colour elements in the post-war years. When the pattern was 'inlaid', that is, not just a surface print, they were exceptionally hard-wearing. Rubber and vinyl tiles were similarly practical and often boldly coloured or at least arranged in striking patterns (see page 191).

• LIGHTING •

If architects, designers and householders looking for simplicity and clean, functional design in lighting represented one end of the spectrum, with the desire for frills or featuristic effects at the other, the middle ground was taken up by an evergrowing range of popular light-fittings. Apart from the bewildering array seen in catalogues and advertisements, there were articles in magazines on how to make lampshades from fabric, parchment or plastic. The popular types of pendant fitting could be Moderne or 'Contemporary', the latter looking at times like models for spacecraft. In the 1950s, fluorescent lighting became familiar and was typically seen in kitchens and bathrooms. Apart from the early use of fluorescent indirect lighting in advanced house designs there was also a growing demand for 'downlights' fitted flush with the ceiling. Well-known firms in the lighting field were Kemthorne, Crown,

• This lighting of the 1940s carries over design characteristics of the inter-war years.
COLLECTION: THE AUTHOR

185

• This lighting from the mid-1950s is notably different from that on the previous page.
Australian Home Beautiful, December 1955

Aladdin, Rite Lite, General Electric and Duperite. Toward the end of the 1950s plastic shades, some as large ballooned out forms, began to find favour. Cone shades were still practical for wall brackets. High-quality fittings with white crystal cone shades were made by Orrefors, the famed Swedish manufacturers. Such refinement was in marked contrast to the popular table lamps where an exotic figure supported a startling black and yellow plastic shade. While many exterior lights were in a contemporary style, the 'Olde Worlde' lantern managed to find a place, even if 'Old English' was no longer a significant house style.

Australian domestic interiors of the 1940s and '50s were rarely triumphs of originality. Many, through the combination of increasing prosperity and the availability of goods and materials, achieved new standards in comfort and rational design. We also achieved high levels of pure kitsch and, while we might not have matched the extravagances seen in the United States, we were not far behind.

Chapter 10 Endnotes

1. Margaret Lord, *A Decorator's World, Living with Art and International Design,* Ure Smith, Sydney, 1969, p. 153.
2. Mary Jane Seymour, 'Australian Modern', *Australian Home Beautiful,* February 1950, p. 25.
3. 'You Can Make This Modern Furniture From Paper Patterns', *Australian Home Beautiful,* October 1947, p. 26.
4. Joan Leyser, 'Newest Australian Chair', *Australian Home Beautiful,* May 1952, p. 19.
5. Peter Hunt, '"Arabesque" Dining Setting', *Australian Home Beautiful,* August 1959, p. 27.
6. John Stuart Crow, *Australian Home Beautiful,* April 1956.
7. Isobel Kennedy, 'Simple but Suave', *Australian Home Beautiful,* June 1949, p. 37.
8. ibid.
9. 'Fler's People's Chair', *Australian Home Beautiful,* October 1956, p. 45.
10. ibid., p. 43.
11. Esme Johnstone, 'Renaissance in soft furnishings', *Australian Home Beautiful,* March 1947, p. 26.
12. John McPhee, *Australian Decorative Arts in the Australian National Gallery,* The Australian National Gallery, 1982.
13. *Decorative Art, The Studio Year Book,* 1942, vol. 36, The Studio Publications, London, p. 116.
14. Mary Jane Seymour, 'Let us Consider Fabrics', *Australian Home Beautiful,* April 1943, p. 5.
15. ibid., p. 31.
16. Museum of Applied Arts and Sciences, *Decorative Arts and Design from the Powerhouse Museum,* Powerhouse Publishing, Sydney, 1991, p. 126.
17. Professor Joseph Burke, 'Australian Artists Create New Textiles', *Australian Home Beautiful,* September, 1947, pp. 7-9.
18. 'Local Designer Adopts "Unit Colour" Theme', *Australian Home Beautiful,* November, 1958, p. 36.
19. Margaret Lord, *Interior Decoration, A Guide to Furnishing the Australian Home,* Ure Smith Pty Ltd, Sydney, 1944, p. 56.
20. 'All About Floors — Soft Floor Coverings: 1', *Australian Home Beautiful,* January 1956, p. 22.

CHAPTER ELEVEN
Renovations and Colour Schemes

To give houses of any era a measure of respect and to evaluate their quality and character one must gain some understanding of the intentions of their designers, builders and original owners. Appropriate colour schemes, along with thoughtful renovations and additions, can only add to our wider heritage and in most cases to the value of the house. As has been pointed out in earlier chapters, it is important not to presume that all 1950s houses were given gaudy colours or that the 1940s was entirely devoted to cream and ivory.

Restoring or renovating houses has become a huge industry and one of the popular activities for amateurs on weekends and holidays. There is a great deal of information available in publications and on radio and television, therefore the details in this chapter are a brief summary of the important considerations. To restore means to bring something back to an earlier or original condition, and to renovate basically means to make new again. These terms overlap, as do the activities involved.

Restoring the existing fabric of a building is often allied to the replacement of some elements which have decayed. Four or five decades can mean that some fundamental works are due, such as re-roofing or re-blocking. Naturally the situation varies considerably depending on the quality of construction and on subsequent maintenance. A well-kept brick house on solid foundations will probably require very little work on the basic fabric, whereas a neglected example of a poorly built house clad in timber or asbestos-cement could mean a great deal of work.

As most houses were designed to be viewed from the street and might well be an important component in a cohesive streetscape, the principles adopted for renovation usually include keeping the front, and as much of the sides as is seen, in original condition. Alterations and additions are best kept to areas where they will not detract from the character of the building. The term 'view shadow' is used in guidelines for additions and extensions and this means that anyone walking or driving along the street is not aware of changes to the structure.[1] This includes the roofline and the effect of works such as two-storey extensions. Houses designed on International Modern ideals were conceived 'in-the-round' and rejected 'facadism'. Extensions and alterations to such structures present a challenge which can only be based on individual evaluation.

Additions such as a family room or perhaps even a whole wing can be designed in three ways. The first is to exactly reproduce the details and forms of the original portions. The second is to complement them, using sympathetic materials, details and forms to capture the feeling, while honestly stating that this is new work. The third is a modern addition which imaginatively suggests a relationship, but in spirit and appearance has its own character. Conservation guidelines such as the Burra Charter (see Bibliography) suggest that the first option is undesirable in that it can lead to confusion between authentic, original and later sections of the house.

• Popular paint colours of the 1940s and '50s.

• AUSTRALIAN HOUSES OF THE FORTIES & FIFTIES

• OYSTER GREY	• LIGHT GREY-GREEN	• PALE BLUE	• AQUA	• LIGHT GREEN
• PALE LILAC	• DRESDEN BLUE	• PASTEL BLUE	• DUCK-EGG BLUE	• MIDDLE GREEN
• LILAC GREY	• LIGHT BLUE-GREY	• WEDGWOOD BLUE	• LIGHT TURQUOISE	• APPLE GREEN
• DOVE GREY	• BLUE-GREY	• COLONIAL BLUE	• JADE	• FOREST GREEN
• FRENCH GREY	• DARK GREY-GREEN	• MID BLUE	• PACIFIC BLUE	• OLIVE GREEN
• BLACK	• DARK BLUE-GREY	• ROYAL BLUE	• TURQUOISE	• MID BRUNSWICK GREEN

• These colours are an approximation only. Consult paint guides and contemporary publications for the exact colours of the period.

RENOVATIONS AND COLOUR SCHEMES

• PALE GREEN	• PALE CREAM	• TERRA COTTA	• LIGHT PINK	• TANGERINE
• CHARTREUSE	• IVORY	• CINNAMON	• BLOSSOM PINK	• VERMILLION
• PRIMROSE	• CREAM	• MUSHROOM PINK	• FLAMINGO	• CHERRY RED
• DAFFODIL	• BISCUIT	• DUSKY PINK	• CORAL PINK	• BURGUNDY
• CITRUS	• PALE STONE	• FUCHSIA PINK	• HIBISCUS	• INDIAN RED
• BRIGHT YELLOW	• BEIGE	• EGYPTIAN RED	• ROSE	• MISSION BROWN

> • Plain lines were typical of many contemporary fireplaces and surrounds.
> *Australian Home Beautiful*, April 1953

The second approach of seeking a harmonious relationship between the original portions and new work usually includes following the proportions, forms and materials. Proportions include ratios such as wall height to roof height, wall area to window area, the pitch of the roof and the shapes of the windows. Forms include the roof shape, and details such as curved corners in a 'waterfall' style house. Harmony is also achieved by choosing colours and textures in the new materials which match or at least blend with the originals. A brown brick addition to a 1950 cream brick house is unlikely to be successful in visual terms.

When restoring or renovating a house of any period it is important to look carefully at what survives of its original detail and overall character and to what degree you would want it to reflect its early state. Some people might be happy to have an original or carefully restored 1940s or '50s kitchen, but most will want to retain the spirit of those times while enjoying all the newer ideas in design and technology. The same can be said for the bathroom. Where the existing example is not satisfactory, the choice might be to create a larger well-appointed design which suggests the more luxurious schemes of the era under review.

Capturing the period of a house through decoration and furnishing is usually best achieved in the main living areas, the entrance hall or gallery and perhaps the master bedroom. The lounge and dining room, or living room with dining area, tend to have the notable elements such as ornamental plasterwork, mantelpiece and fireplace surround or perhaps exposed rafters and a timber panelled feature wall. Enthusiasts may remove later carpets and return to polished floors with rugs, or conversely, timber floors might be given a wall to wall carpet which echoes the type used in other houses during the same period. Many houses have all their original fittings and really only need appropriate paint colours. By studying descriptions and pictorial reference it will be possible to settle on a logical approach to the redecoration of a house in keeping with its fundamental character.

As long as houses from the 1940s and '50s are demolished for various reasons there will be a good supply of original materials and fittings available. There are also reproduction fittings or at least examples which will be in harmony with the period. Many companies are able to supply authentic plasterwork or details such as architrave and skirting board. Glass bricks are once again fashionable and can be obtained from specialist suppliers. There are renovating guides with lists of these firms throughout Australia. Building information centres in each state are also a valuable means to trace some requirements. Fibrous plaster is available from a few specialist suppliers, but unless there is a particular need standard plasterboard is satisfactory.

Old baths and handbasins can be found and it is possible to have the enamelled cast iron type restored, although it is best to be sure that the system used gives a high-quality, long-lasting surface. New sanitary-ware in styles which were current in the 1940s and '50s is available, as are plumbing fittings such as chrome-plated taps and shower sets. Firms such as Recollections, Brodware Industries and Olde English Tile Factory offer a range to suit houses built between 1930 and 1960. Sometimes these items are described as Art Deco' or 1930s style but these designs continued through a number of decades.

• COLOUR SCHEMES •

In her 1944 book on interior decoration, Margaret Lord writes:

In room decoration today, colour is one of the few means we have left of achieving individuality. Furniture and furnishings tend to become more and more standardised, so

• Striking colour schemes and bold patterns were increasingly favoured.
Australian Home Beautiful, April 1953

that if it were not for colour, all rooms would begin to look alike. With colour we can express personality, we can make our rooms warm or cold, friendly or gay, calm and restful or exciting, according to the colour we use.[2]

This was written at a time when conventional interior and exterior colour schemes were generally low-key. Only the avant garde architects and interior designers had taken to using bold colours in unusual combinations.

Throughout the 1940s and well into the 1950s interior colour schemes remained a temperate balance of one or two stronger colours with a larger area given over to ivories, off-whites, creams, greys, grey-blues, pale blues, soft pinks, mushrooms, buffs and soft greens. Without doubt, the most popular colour was blue — that is, blue ranging from the light sky blue of plumbago through azure to the deep blues including navy.

Turquoise was seen as a trim colour on 'contemporary' exteriors. Blue was typically seen in carpets and furnishings with walls of cream, grey, buff or beige and in brighter schemes with cheery yellows. Navy blue with pale lemon yellow was a striking combination. Walls of 'palest pale blue' were popular but somehow the creams and ivories were to maintain, in the post-war years, much of the favour they held in the late 1930s and early 1940s. The second most popular family of colours for carpets, curtains, rugs and upholstery were the sombre reds. These were identified as wine red, burgundy, rust red and pinky red. As stated in earlier chapters, bright cherry red was widely used in kitchens, at first with off-white, ivory or cream and later with other bright colours. Walls or furnishings in bedrooms and living rooms might be in oyster pink, phlox pink, dusky pink, soft rose, rose and dark rose.

In keeping with the interest in 'organic' architecture there were a myriad of shades suggesting natural earth colours. These included warm cream, buff, beige, light stone, cocoa brown, tobacco brown, cinnamon and biscuit. Greens were popular in carpets and furnishing fabrics, but again were generally subdued. They were more likely to be a lively shade of green when seen in bathrooms and kitchens. Pale green was seen on walls but mostly in kitchens, bathrooms and bedrooms. Bright yellows appeared early in fashionable interiors and one of the popular combinations was daffodil yellow and pale grey. Hand-blocked fabrics with a dominance of olive green or deep blue were often seen with primrose, daffodil or pale lemon walls, natural timber floors and white, off-white or cream Indian rugs.

Interior trimmings such as architraves and skirting boards, if not left natural or stained to a darker colour, were typically in white, off-white, ivory or cream. One bedroom is noted in 1949 as having woodwork and doors in moss green with 'delicate oyster walls' (a warm grey).[3]

Another contemporary-style house of the late 1940s is described as having a living area with grey walls and a maize yellow ceiling to pick up one of the many colours in the natural stone of the fireplace.[4]

By the mid-1950s the colour revolution was beginning to affect conventional interiors so that two, three or four bold colours might be used in one room. The popular combinations were now rich pinks with charcoal grey, yellow with orange, deep pink with blue-lilac, orange with blue-lilac, lime green with terracotta, turquoise with lemon, to list just a few. In

• AUSTRALIAN HOUSES OF THE FORTIES & FIFTIES

Protect your car...

1955, interior decorator Ruth Sloan suggested that a dining room might have Glade Green Feltex on the floor with terracotta walls and mustard yellow ceiling. For the curtains she chose cloud grey and for the chair coverings, a heavy textured material in bright nasturtium.

Startling combinations of up to five or six colours had gained wide acceptance by the late 1950s, although it must be remembered that both externally and internally such schemes were usually chosen for 'contemporary' or conventional houses. Georgian- or Colonial-style houses were unlikely to be given garish colours and organic architecture was typically subdued except perhaps for one or two strong colours. The 1958 illustration of a contemporary garage seen on this page perfectly illustrates the use of multiple colours. They are much the same as those used in kitchens when up to six different colours were combined on drawers and cupboard doors, not to mention the additional colours seen on the walls, ceiling, floors, and furnishings, along with the kitchenware and ornaments. This was the time when houses could have pink, blue or yellow under the eaves, a turquoise front door, vividly striped canvas sunblinds, exterior walls in dusty pink, blue-green, lemon, light green and a host of other hues.

• Contemporary garage late 1950s.
COLLECTION: THE AUTHOR

Chapter 11 Endnotes
[1] Bruce Rayworth, *Our Inter-War Houses, How to Recognize, Restore and Extend Houses of the 1920s and 1930s*, National Trust of Australia (Victoria), 1991, p. 35.
[2] Margaret Lord, *Interior Decoration, A Guide to Furnishing the Australian Home*, Ure Smith Pty Ltd, Sydney, 1944, p. 71.
[3] Esme Johnson, 'Moonacres on Oliver's Hill', *Australian Home Beautiful*, June 1949, p. 23.
[4] Nora Cooper, 'Outdoor Living Plus Indoor Comfort', *Australian Home Beautiful*, February 1950, p. 41.

• *Opposite page*: The Sussex Radiogram by Stromberg Carlson offered a five valve world range radio receiver and a fully automatic record player. Cost, 99 guineas.

Australian Home Beautiful, July 1954

CHAPTER TWELVE
Collecting the Memories

COLLECTING THE MEMORABILIA of a particular era can be a challenge. Some collectors cast their net widely, being quite happy to turn up all sorts of relics, while others narrow their search to a specific subject, such as studio pottery or mantel radios. Usually more recent times provide the best opportunities both for cost and availability. Some things, of course, were always rare and others were both sturdy and abundant and so can be expected to have survived in great numbers. Mass-produced chairs in chrome-plated steel, foam rubber and vinyl may vary in quality, but are still readily available. On the other hand, a finely crafted teak chair by Hans Wegner would be an uncommon discovery. The major galleries and museums have acquired outstanding examples of decorative arts and design, with well-informed private collectors early contributors to a growing awareness.

In any chosen field of interest it is important to learn as much as possible, so that decisions can be made based on sound knowledge. Beyond that, there is always the notion of going with gut feelings or a sense of possibilities. If you live in a house built in the 1940s or '50s, or simply have an interest in that era, there is a long list of collectables associated with domestic life. The field includes furniture, lighting, ceramics, glassware, plastics, metalware, tinware, fabrics, floorcoverings, mirrors, paintings, drawings, prints, photographs, sculpture, ornaments, toys, clocks, shadow boxes, pot-plant holders, garden ornaments, radios and radiograms, television sets, records, books, magazines and all sorts of fittings. Specialist shops and market stalls continue to be an important resource, but for those who enjoy the thrill of searching far and wide, garage sales and out of the way secondhand dealers are places where collectables of all kinds turn up, often at bargain prices.

Some collectables are readily defined as pure kitsch, others as examples of high-quality, functional or decorative design and many as simply reflecting an era. If your house has the distinctive character of one of the styles identified in this book it would be an interesting challenge to recapture the feeling of that period. Houses which were built to satisfy particular ideals in modern functionalism deserve to be furnished and decorated in a sympathetic manner. This need not mean slavish recreation of the original interiors, but simply capturing the spirit without sacrificing the comforts gained since that time. Where original furniture of the period is difficult to find, or even unprocurable, there are fortunately reproductions of some classic pieces. An example is the manufacture of original Grant Featherston designs by Gordon Mather Industries of Melbourne.

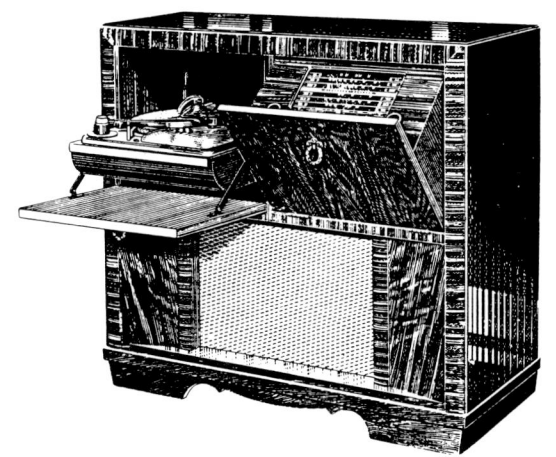

A conventional house will usually offer a range of possibilities, given that in their heyday they were furnished and decorated in a variety of styles from 'traditional' to 'contemporary' or indeed a mixture of whatever was available. Some collectors happily fill their houses with all sorts of memorabilia, including objects never seen

• *Left: I*nterior of a 1955 Melbourne house designed by John and Phyllis Murphy.
COURTESY: JOHN AND PHYLLIS MURPHY

• *Below*: The latest in contemporary styling, the Stromberg-Carlson 'Moderne' radiogram with three playing speeds and automatic record-changer.

Australian Home Beautiful, July 1954.

in an ordinary house of the 1940s and '50s. Most people will be satisfied in gathering such conventional pieces as a standard lamp, radiogram, coffee table and a selection of chairs. Kitchen canisters in plastic or enamelled tinplate are generally available and are both useful and decorative. 'Art Pottery' vases can be a perfect foil to the popular flowers of the era and when combined with a typical mirror the effect is enhanced.

Works of art are a wonderful way of establishing a mood. If original paintings, drawings and limited edition prints are beyond the budget, there are many pre-1960 popular prints to be found, and most are in their original frames. Family photographs have long been given pride of place, and these days copying services and sensitive framing can create old-style pictures in keeping with the decor.

Studying the descriptions and images in books, magazines and newspapers is the best way to learn about the things now seen as collectable. Looking at collections in both institutions and in period houses is also ideal. It is significant that the Historic Houses Trust of New South Wales acquired, in 1988, the Rose Seidler house and that it retains furniture by Charles Eames and Eero Saarinen, brought from New York by Harry Seidler in 1948.[1]

In time there will no doubt be numbers of museum houses of the period from 1940 to 1960. For historians and others there is still a rich resource of houses and interiors, but with each passing year a percentage are lost or drastically altered. Householders who continue to live in a basically unchanged residence built for them in the 1940s or '50s typically vary in age from sixty up into their eighties. Such places are filled with memories and provide a valuable continuity. When asked about each treasured possession or notable detail in the house, most of these older householders have plenty of stories to tell. Some people will even search in a drawer and turn up original receipts, or sketches and plans, ration coupons, catalogues — all memorable steps in achieving an Australian dream in that era of war and peace, of desperation, determination and abundant optimism.

The "MODERNE" 99 gns.
5 VALVE, WORLD RANGE
Designed with elegant simplicity to blend with modern or traditional furnishings. 3 speed, V.A. full automatic record changer. In blonde sycamore, natural maple, wallnut or rosewood. (Blonde sycamore 2 gns. extra.)

Chapter 12 Endnotes

[1] Kenneth Frampton & Philip Drew, *Harry Seidler: Four Decades of Architecture*, Thames & Hudson, London, 1992.

• BIBLIOGRAPHY •

Apperly, Richard, Irving, Robert & Reynolds, Peter. *A Pictorial Guide to Identifying Australian Architecture.* Angus & Robertson, North Ryde, NSW, 1989.

Archer, John. *Building a Nation.* Collins Australia, Sydney, 1987.

Australian Homemaker, vol. 1, no. 1, July 1954 — vol. 7, no. 2, August 1957.

Australian House and Garden. vol. 1, no. 1, December 1948 — vol. 25, no. 1, December 1960.

Australia's Yesterdays, A Look at Our Recent Past. Reader's Digest Services Pty Ltd, Sydney, 1974.

Banham, Reyner. *Los Angeles, The Architecture of Four Ecologies.* Penguin Books, Harmondsworth, Middlesex, 1973.

Barnett, F.O. & Burt, W.O. *Housing the Australian Nation.* Research Group of the Left Book Club of Victoria, Melbourne, 1942.

Barnett, F.O., Burt, W.O. & Heath, F. *We must go on, A study in planned reconstruction and housing.* The Book Depot, Melbourne, 1944.

Beiers, George, *Houses of Australia.* Ure Smith, Sydney, 1948.

Birrell, James. *Walter Burley Griffin.* University of Queensland Press, Brisbane, 1964.

Bodi, Leslie & Jeffries, Stephen.(eds.) *The German Connection, Sesquicentenary Essays on German–Victorian Crosscurrents 1835-1985.* Department of German, Monash University, Clayton, Victoria, 1985.

Boyd, Robin, *Australia's Home, Its Origins, Builders and Occupiers.* Melbourne University Press, Melbourne, 1952.

—— *Victorian Modern.* Architectural Students' Society of the Royal Victorian Institute of Architects. Melbourne, 1947.

Brogan, John R. *101 Australian Homes.* Building Publishing Company, Sydney, 1936.

Buildings of Queensland. Royal Australian Institute of Architects, Queensland Chapter, Jacaranda Press, Brisbane, 1959.

Bunning, Walter. *Homes in the Sun: The Past, Present and Future of Australian Housing.* W.J. Nesbit, Sydney, 1945.

Burra Charter. *(Charter for the Conservation of Places of Cultural Significance).* Australia ICOMOS. Published in the 'Conservation Plan' by James Semple Kerr, National Trust of Australia (NSW), Sydney, 1985.

Carroll, Brian. *A Very Good Business, One hundred years of James Hardie Industries Limited 1888-1988.* James Hardie Industries Limited, Sydney, 1987.

Clerehan, Neil (ed.). *Best Australian Houses: recent houses built by members of the Royal Australian Institute of Architects.* F. W. Cheshire, Melbourne, 1961.

Craddock, Trevor & Cavanough, Maurice. *125 Years — the Story of the State Savings Bank of Victoria, Melbourne, 1967.*

Cuffley, Peter. *Australian Houses of the '20s & '30s.* The Five Mile Press Pty Ltd, Melbourne, 1989.

Decoration and Glass. vol.1, no.1, May, 1935 — vol. 15, no.4, December 1949.

Decorative Art, The Studio Year Book. 1941-1942 (1943-1948 published as a single volume) 1949-50 (vol.39) — 1949-60 (vol.49).

Emanuel, Muriel (ed.). *Contemporary Architects.* Macmillan Press Ltd., London, 1980.

Frampton, Kenneth and Drew, Philip. *Harry Seidler: four decades of architecture.* Thames & Hudson, London, 1992.

Freeland, J. M. *Architecture in Australia: A History.* Penguin Books, Ringwood, Victoria, 1972.

—— *The Making of a Profession — A History of the Growth and Work of the Architectural Institutes in Australia.* Angus & Robertson in association with the Royal Australian Institute of Architects, Sydney, 1971.

Garden, Don. *Builders to the Nation, The A. V. Jennings Story.* Melbourne University Press, Melbourne, 1992.

Greenberg, Cara. *Mid-Century Modern, Furniture of the 1950s.* Harmony Books, New York, 1984.

Harris, Thistle Y. *Australian Plants for the Garden: A Handbook on the Cultivation of Australian Trees, Shrubs, Other Flowering Plants and Ferns.* Angus & Robertson, Sydney, 1953.

Howe, Renate. *New Houses for Old: Fifty Years of Public Housing in Victoria, 1938-1988.* Ministry of Housing and Construction, Melbourne, 1988.

Hudson, Nicholas & McEwan, Peter. *That's Our House, A History of Housing in Victoria.* The Ministry of Housing, Melbourne, 1986.

Johnson, Donald Leslie. *Australian Architecture 1901-51.* Sydney University Press, Sydney, 1980.

Koues, Helen. *The American Woman's New Encyclopedia of Home Decorating.* Garden City Publishing Company Inc., New York, 1951.

Knox, Alistair. *Alternative Housing — Building with the head, the heart and the hand.* Albatross Books, Sutherland, NSW, 1980.

—— *Living in the Environment.* Mullaya Publications, Melbourne, 1975.

Lake, Frances (ed.) *Daily Mail Ideal Home Book 1953-54.* Daily Mail, London.

Langer, Dr Karl. *Sub-Tropical Housing.* Faculty of Engineering, Queensland University, Brisbane 1944.

Latreille, Anne. *The Natural Garden, Ellis Stones: His Life and Work.* Viking O'Neil/Penguin Books, Ringwood, Victoria, 1990.

Lees, Stella & Senyard, June. *The 1950s...how Australia became a modern society, and everyone got a house and a car,* Hyland House, Melbourne, 1987.

Lewis, Edna Horton, *Furnishing on a Budget.* Georgian House, Melbourne, 1948.

Lewis, Miles. *Two Hundred Years of Concrete in Australia.* Concrete Institute of Australia, North Sydney, 1986.

Lord, Ernest E. and Willis, J. H. *Shrubs and Trees for Australian Gardens.* Lothian Publishing Company Pty Ltd, Melbourne, 1982.

Lord, Margaret, *A Decorator's World: Living with art and international design,* Ure Smith, Sydney & London, 1969.

—— *Interior Decoration, A Guide to Furnishing the Australian Home.* Ure Smith Pty Ltd, Sydney, 1944.

Luck, Peter, *Australian Icons, Things that make us what we are.* William Heinemann Australia, Melbourne, 1992.

McDonald, Kenneth, *The New Australian Home.* Published by Kenneth McDonald, Melbourne, 1954.

McPhee, John. *Australian Decorative Arts in the Australian National Gallery,* Australian National Gallery, Canberra, 1982.

Made in Australia — A sourcebook for all things Australian. William Heinemann Australia, Melbourne, 1986.

Marsden, Susan. *Business, Charity and Sentiment.* Wakefield Press, Netley, South Australia, 1986.

Middleton, G.F. *Earth Wall Construction,* Experimental Building Station Bulletin, no. 5, North Ryde, NSW, 1947.

Miller, Duncan. *Interior Decorating.* 'How To Do It' Series no. 13, The Studio Publications, London, 1937, 1944 & 1947.

Molony, John. *The Penguin Bicentennial History of Australia.* Viking, Ringwood, Victoria, 1987.

Molyneux, Ian. *Looking Around Perth: A Guide to the Architecture of Perth and Surrounding Towns.* Wescolour Press, Fremantle East, 1981.

Moore, Bryce. *From the Ground Up. Bristile, Whittakers and Metro Brick in Western Australian History.* University of Western Australia Press, Perth, 1987.

Moore, John D. *Home Again! Domestic Architecture for the Normal Australian.* Sydney, 1944.

Morgan, Ann Lee & Naylor, Colin. (eds.) *Contemporary Architects.* St James Press, London, 1987.

Museum of Applied Arts and Sciences, *Decorative Arts and Design from the Powerhouse Museum.* Powerhouse Publishing, Sydney, 1991.

O'Callaghan, Judith (ed.) *The Australian Dream: Design of the Fifties.* Powerhouse Publishing, Sydney, 1993.

Page, Marian. *Furniture Designed by Architects,* Whitney Library of Design, New York, 1980.

Page, Michael. *Sculptors in Space, South Australian Architects 1836–1986.* The Royal Australian Institute of Architects (South Australian Chapter), Adelaide, 1986.

Proudfoot, Helen. *Gardens in Bloom: Jocelyn Brown and Her Sydney Gardens of the 30s and 40s.* Kangaroo Press, Kenthurst, NSW, 1989.

Rayworth, Bruce. *Our Inter-War Houses, How to Recognize, Restore and Extend Houses of the 1920s and 1930s.* National Trust of Australia (Victoria) Melbourne, 1991.

Roe, F. Gordon. *English Cottage Furniture.* Phoenix House Ltd, London, 1949.

—— *Windsor Chairs.* Phoenix House Ltd, London, 1953.

St John Moore, Felicity. *Vassilieff and his Art.* Oxford University Press, Melbourne, 1982.

Sagazio, Celestina. (ed.), *The National Trust Research Manual, Investigating Buildings, Gardens and Cultural Landscapes.* Allen & Unwin, St Leonards, NSW, 1992.

Seventy Years of Wunderlich Industry, Wunderlich Limited Sydney, 1957.

Sharp, W. Watson. *Australian Methods of Building Construction.* Angus & Robertson, Sydney, 1946.

Shum, W.A. (ed.). *Australian Gardening of To-Day.* The *Sun News-Pictorial,* Melbourne, 1939.

Smith, Alex. *Complete Home Furniture Maker Illustrated.* Colorgravure Publications, Melbourne, C. 1950.

Tanner, Howard. (ed.) *Architects of Australia.* The Macmillan Company of Australia Pty Ltd, Sydney, 1981.

Taylor, Florence Mary. (ed.) *The Book of 150 Low-Cost Houses,* The Building Publishing Company, Sydney, 1945.

Taylor, Jennifer. *An Australian Identity: Houses for Sydney 1953–63.* University of Sydney Department of Architecture, Sydney, 1984.

The Australian Home Beautiful, vol. 20, no. 1, January 1941 — vol. 39, no. 12, December 1960.

The Australian Garden Lover, vol. 16, no. 10, January 1941 — vol. 36, no. 9, December 1960.

The Home. vol.1, no.1, February 1920 — vol. 23, no.9, September 1942.

The Home Gardener, vol. 25, no. 1, January 1941 — vol. 38, no. 6, June 1954.

The Sun Post-war Homes, Architects' Competition Designs. The Sun News-Pictorial, Melbourne, 1945.

Townsend, Helen. *Baby Boomers, Growing up in Australia in the 1940s, 50s and 60s.* Simon & Shuster Australia, Brookvale, NSW, 1988.

Tulloch, Dudley. *Details of Australian Building Construction.* Keating–Wood, Melbourne, 1933.

Unstead, R.J. & Henderson, W.F. *Homes in Australia.* A & C. Black Ltd, London, 1969.

Ure Smith, Sam & Morton Spencer, Gwen. (eds.) *Australian Treescapes: A Photographic Study.* Ure Smith Miniature Series, Sydney, 1950.

Ure Smith, Sydney and Burke, Prof. Joseph. (eds.) *Art and Design 1,* Ure Smith Pty Ltd., Sydney, 1949.

van Zyl, F. D. Wallace. (ed.). *Houses Around Adelaide.* South Australian Chapter, Royal Australian Institute of Architects, Adelaide, 1964.

Walling, Edna. *Cottage and Garden in Australia.* Geoffrey Cumberlege, Oxford University Press, Melbourne, 1947.

—— *Gardens in Australia, Their Design and Care.* Third edn. Oxford University Press, Melbourne, 1943.

—— *The Australian Roadside.* Oxford University Press, Melbourne, 1952.

Wallis, L. M. *The Painter's and Decorator's Guide.* Feature Syndicates Inc., Sydney, 1947.

Waugh, Andrew. *The Handyman's Complete Carpentry Guide.* The *Argus,* Melbourne, c. 1954.

Wolfe, Tom. *From Bauhaus to Our House.* Jonathan Cape Ltd., London, 1982.

CATALOGUES, ARTICLES AND UNPUBLISHED WORKS

*Designs for Homes under Credit Foncier Loan Conditions.*The State Savings Bank of Victoria, Melbourne, 1940.

Goad, Philip, 'Featherston Chairs: Microcosms of Melbourne Design 1947–1974. *Transition,* Department of Architecture, RMIT, no. 25, vol. 7, no. 1. Winter 1988.

—— *The Modern House in Melbourne, 1945–1975,* unpublished PhD thesis, Department of Architecture and Building, University of Melbourne, 1992.

—— 'Victorian Modern, Looking at the Twentieth Century'. *Trust News,* no. 9, June, 1992.

Home Designs, The Queensland Housing Commission, Brisbane, 1950.

Homes for Munition Workers within the Municipalities of Footscray, Braybrook, Essendon and Williamstown. The State Savings Bank of Victoria, Melbourne, 1941.

Lane, Terence. *Featherston Chairs.* Exhibition catalogue, National Gallery of Victoria, Melbourne, 1988.

Marioli, Frank. *The Work of John and Phyllis Murphy,* Unpublished assignment, Department of Architecture and Building, University of Melbourne, 1983.

Modern Ready-Cut Homes. G. E. Brown & Sons Pty Limited, Auburn, NSW, 1950.

Newell, Peter. *The House in Queensland. From First Settlement to 1985.* Unpublished Master's thesis, University of Queensland, Brisbane, 1988.

Nicholas, Nerida. 'Back to the Future'. *Australian Home Beautiful.* June 1991, pp. 66, 67 & 68.

Pickett, Charles. Modernism and Austerity: The 1950s House. Chapter 5, *The Australian Dream — Design of the Fifties.* Powerhouse Museum, Sydney, 1993.

Schoffel, Sarah. 'Women Architects and Victorian Modern: 1930–1960'. *Transition.* Department of Architecture RMIT, no. 26, vol. 7, no. 1, Winter, 1988.

Shepherd, Jane. Early Women Landscape Architects: Olive Mellor and Emily Gibson, *Transition,* Department of Architecture, RMIT, no. 25, vol. 7, no. 1, Winter 1988.

Standard Designs, Timber-Framed, Brick Veneer and Brick Construction. The State Savings Bank of Victoria, Melbourne, 1946.

Stones, Ellis. 'Boulders and Borders.' *The Australian Home Beautiful,* vol. 25, no. 7, July 1946, pp. 20, 21.

Stones, Ellis. 'Pools — Formal and Natural: Notes on the Use of Water in the Garden.' *The Australian Home Beautiful,* vol. 25, no. 9, September, 1946, pp. 10,11.

The Australian Dream — Design and the Home of the 1950s.

Exhibition catalogue. Powerhouse Museum, Sydney,1992.

20 Designs for Homes. Credit Foncier Department, The State Savings Bank of Victoria, Melbourne, 1957.

Walling, Edna. 'A Letter to Garden Lovers'. *The Australian Home Beautiful,* 1937–1950.

Welch Perrin's Buying Guide for the Primary Producer 1954–1955. Welch Perrin & Company Pty Ltd, Melbourne, 1954.

Whittle, Fiona. 'A 50s Fanatic' *The Period Home Renovator,* vol. 5, no. 1, 1990, pp. 36–40.

—— 'The Fabulous 50s'. *The Period Home Renovator,* vol. 5, no. 1, 1990, pp. 32—35.

INDEX

Aalto, Alvar, architect and designer, 176
Adelaide hills, 79
Adelaide, 69, 108, 133
adobe (mud-brick), 128, 130, 132
Age Small Homes Service, 40, 45, 105
Agricultural Bank of Tasmania, 63
Ahern house, Perth (WA), 108
Air raid shelters, 16
Air raids, 16
Albert Park (Vic), 101
Alexandra, Douglas, architect, 92, 100
Alphington (Vic), 100
Althofer, George, nurseryman, 145
America, 88, 101, 116, 123
American Arts and Crafts, 128, 166
American Home, 35
American House and Garden, 35
American influences, 31, 61, 120, 162, 168
    Colonial style, 40, 56, 61, 114, 120, 121, 168
Ancher house, Killara (NSW), 163
Ancher, Sydney, architect, 94, 95, 106, 110, 163
Anderson, Bruce, 44
Andrews, S.G., 132
Annan Fabrics (Sydney), 181
Annand, Douglas, artist, 180
appliances, household, 29
Architect (Western Australia), 36
Architect and Engineer, 36
Architects Journal, 36
Architectural Forum, 36
Architectural Record, 36
Architectural Review, 36, 37
Architecture (Aust), 36
Architecture in Australia, 36
Architecture (USA), 36
Aristoc Industries (Vic), 179
Armstrong, A.B., architect, 69,
Art and Design (Sydney), 165
Art Deco, 169
Art Moderne, 112, 154, 157, 169
Arts and Crafts Movement, 128, 137, 166, 176
asbestos cement,
    sheeting, 34, 62, 88,
    houses, 39, 76, 119
    roofing, 69, 121
Ashton, Edward R., architect, 117
Audette house, Castlecrag (NSW), 133
austerity designs, 76, 112, 114
Australian Aboriginal population, 21
Australian Cement Limited, 62
Australian colonial architecture, 36, 103
Australian Garden Lover, 141, 142
Australian Home Beautiful, 16, 26, 45, 52, 55, 57,
    62, 65, 78, 106, 116, 121, 128, 135, 144, 155,
    170, 173
Australian Home Builder, 143
Australian Homemaker, 35, 124
Australian House and Garden, 35, 132
Australian Labor Party, 23
Australian plants in gardens, 141, 143
Australian suburbs, 140, 141
Australian Women's Weekly Home Planning
    Centre, 43
A.V. Jennings Construction Company Pty Ltd, 55,
    56, 62, 68, 69

Baby Boomers, 23
Baldwinson & Booth, architects, 106

Baldwinson, Arthur, architect, 97, 106, 172
Balwyn (Vic), 26, 56, 88
'Banyan', Bendigo (Vic), 39
barbecue, 52, 53
Barlow, F.C. and Co (NSW), 85
Barlow, Marcus, architect, 56
Barnett, F. Oswald, 47
Bates, Smart & McCutcheon, architects, 58
bathrooms, 80, 85
Bauhaus, 92, 154
Baulkham Hills (NSW), 132
Baxter Cox & Associates (Melbourne), 69
Beaufort steel house, 67, 84
Beaumaris (Vic), 37, 64, 82, 100
Beauview Estate, 55, 56
bedrooms and nurseries, 162
Beiers, George, architect and author, 37
Belair (SA), 79
Bendigo (Vic), 14, 39
Benjamin house, Canberra (ACT), 90
Berger synthetic paint, 86
Bertoia, Harry, designer, 174
Best, Marion, interior designer, 43, 165, 170
Beulah Bush Nursing Hospital (Vic), 105
Bickleigh Vale subdivision, 121
Blackett & Foster, architects, 101
'blackouts', wartime, 16
Blake house, Castlemaine (Vic), 120
books and magazines, influence of, 35, 39, 51
books on architecture,
    Australian, 37
    imported, 39
Borland, Kevin, architect, 103, 105
Boyd house, South Yarra (Vic), 124, 165
Boyd, Robin, architect and author, 37, 11, 44, 46,
    67, 71, 74, 100, 101, 103, 106, 109
Breuer, Marcel, architect and designer, 39, 92, 108
brick,
    areas designated by councils, 61,
    dwellings, 61, 74, 76, 88, 119
    veneer, 61, 62, 119, 148
    types, 60 89
Brighton (Vic), 40, 159
Brisbane (Qld), 99, 109, 124
Brisbane River, 109
British Arts and Crafts Movement, 127, 128, 166
British Bourne polyurethane coating, 85
British Isles, 32
Brogan, John R., author, architect, 124
Brown, Jocelyn, 142, 147, 148
Brown, Joyce, designer, 43
Browne, Thomas A., 143
Brunt house, Kew (Vic), 86, 88
Buchan Laird & Buchan, architects, 100
Building Societies, 74, 75
building paper, 85
building,
    cost of, 74,
    materials, 73, 74, 80
    clubs, 79, 80
built-in furniture, 155
Bunning, Walter, architect and author, 37, 122
Burke, Frances, 44, 180, 181
Burke, T.M. estate agency, 56
'Burnie Board' hardboard, 84, 111
Burnley Horticultural College, 144
Burns house, Studley Park (Vic), 105
Burra Charter, 187
Burt, W.O., 47
Burwood (Vic), 26
bush gardens, 145

Bush, Haslock, Parkes, Shugg & Moon, architects,
    106
Busst house and studio, Eltham (Vic), 130, 131, 132
Butler, W.R. & E.R., architects, 100
'butterfly' roofs, 114

calcimine, 86
California Bungalow, 56, 114, 128, 132, 135
California, 37, 128
Californian architects, 94
Californian ranch style, 123, 124
Calwell, Arthur, 21
Canada, 99,
Canberra (ACT), 62, 69, 90
Cane-ite board, 82
Canterbury (Vic), 106
Cape Cod Cottage style, 57, 114
Castlecrag (NSW), 132, 135
Castlemaine (Vic), 120
cavity wall construction, 64
Cawood-Wharton prefabricated house, 69
ceiling heights, 73
cement sheeting, 82, 119
cement tiles, 20, 119
ceramic tiles, 85
Chancellor & Patrick, architects, 100, 102
Chancellor, David architect, 102, 103, 124
Cheesman, Jack, architect, 109
Chicago windows, 57, 119
Chicago, 114
Chifley, J.B., Prime Minister, 37
Chigwell (Tas), 113, 148, 151
chimneys, 120, 121
chip heaters, 25, 80
Church Point (NSW), 97
cindcrete bricks, 62
Claridge, Brian, architect, 109
Clerehan, Neil, architect and writer, 100, 154
climate, adapting to, 124
co-operative housing societies, 75,
Colonial Revival in America, 120, 121
Colonial style, 57, 61, 120, 121
Colonial style windows, 57
Colonial Sugar Refining Company, 82, 83
colour chart, 188, 189
Commonwealth Department of Works, 100
Commonwealth Experimental Building Station, 65,
    67, 130
Commonwealth Government, 67, 68
Commonwealth Housing Commission, 48, 162
Commonwealth price control, 73
Commonwealth-State Housing Agreement, 48, 68
concrete
    building blocks, 62, 119
    piers, 62,
    reinforced, 62, 124, 128
    pre-cast, 71
    formed *in situ*, 64, 71,
    houses, 71
contemporary', post-war, 122, 126, 173
cooking facilities, 25
Coombs, Dr. H.C., 39, 47
Cooper, Nora, 56, 67, 94
copper, washing, 25
Coral Sea Battle, 18,
cork flooring, 85
Corowa (NSW), 67
corrugated asbestos-cement roofing, 82, 121
corrugated iron, 37, 82
    roofs, 37, 82, 121
    traditional use, 37

cost of living, 74
cost of houses, 74
Cottage style, 121
Cottage style interiors, 166, 167
Cottesloe (WA), 139
courtyard garden, 147
courtyard styles, 116
Cowper, Murphy & Appleford, architects, 105
Crafers (SA), 135
Craftsman influence, 128
Crosby, Bing, 124
Cuffley, William, 18
curtains and curtain fabric, 183
Curtin, John, Prime Minister, 14

Dalkeith (WA), 106, 108
Dalton, John, architect, 109, 110, 111
Dandenong Ranges, 23, 26, 53
Darwin (NT), 14, 126
Daylesford (Vic), 50
Decoration and Glass, 36
Decorative Art, The Studio Year Book, 182
Denmark, 110
Department of Works (Commonwealth), 68
Depression, the Great, 14, 21, 32
Devonport (Tas), 106
Dickson, Robert, architect, 109
Dilston (Tas), 117
Dobell, William, studio and house, 97
Doley, Maurice, architect, 109, 137
Dorney, Esmond, architect, 59, 106
Douglas & Barnes, architects, 109
Downing, Dick, 132
Dripstone (NSW), 145
drive-in pictures, 31
Dromana (Vic), 102, 103
Dudok, Willem Marinus, architect, 94
Dulux 'Super-Satin' and 'Super Matt', 86
Dupain, Max, photographer, 165
Durasbestos asbestos cement, 82
Dykes, Edmund, interior designer, 165
Eames, Charles, designer, 174
Earl, James, architect, 100
Early American style, 40, 61, 168, 170
earth, building with, 67, 128, 130, 131
East Ivanhoe (Vic), 55
East Malvern (Vic), 57, 140
Eclarte handwoven fabrics, 182
Eggleston, Robert, architect, 132
electric appliances, 157
Ellenby, W. (SA), 79
Ellis, Russell, architect, 108, 109
Eltham, (Vic), 67, 126, 128
English Arts and Crafts, 128, 166
English Country Life, 35
English vernacular architecture, 35, 128
English, Frank, 130
environmental influence, 123, 127-137.
Essendon (Vic), 67
'Estapol' polyurethane coating, 85
Europe, 68, 94, 101
European functionalist architecture, 114
European hardboard, 83
European influence, 32, 92, 94, 106, 114
European Modernism, 92, 103, 106
Exhibition of American Housing, 39
Experimental Building Station, 65, 67
exterior colour schemes, 191, 192

Fallingwater, Bear Run, Pennsylvania, 133
Farrer, Reginald, 146
Featherston, Grant, 11, 44, 171, 175, 178, 194

Feltex, 165, 185
fences, 149
Ferntree Gully (Vic), 24
fibreboard, 82
fibro-cement, 82
'Fibrolite' asbestos-cement, 82
fibrous cement sheeting, 62, 82
fibrous plaster, 62
Fig Tree Pocket (Qld), 110, 111
fireplaces, 154, 160
First World War, 91, 92
Fisherman's Bend (Vic), 20
flat roofs, 88, 114, 122
    resistance to, 94
Fler chairs, 179
floor coverings, 85, 86
Floreat Park (WA), 114, 171
Florida, 57
Ford, Gordon, 126, 132
'Formica' plastic laminate, 86
forty-hour week, 73
Fowler system of prefabrication, 71
Fowler, Thomas Walker, 71
Frankston (Vic), 101, 102
Freeland, Professor J.M., 11
First World War, 91, 92
Fuller, Buckminster, architect, 108
functional architecture, 31, 73, 123, 124
functional design, 73, 123, 152, 161
furnishings, 180
furniture,
    American influence, 174
    designs, 174-179, 182, 183
    fabrics, 179, 182
    pre-cut kits, 176, 178

Galbraith, Jean, 142
garages, 51
garden design, 138, 142
gardening books and magazines, 141, 142, 143
gardens, 138-151
gates, 148, 149
Geelong (Vic), 100
geometrical designs, 124
Georgian and Colonial Georgian style, 57, 61, 120, 149, 168
Georgian furniture, 40, 168
Georgian influence, 57, 112, 120
Georgian Revival, 35, 56, 61, 112, 120, 149, 168
Georgian windows, 61, 121
German workers, 69
Germany, 14, 69, 92, 174
Givoni house, South Yarra (Vic), 92
glass bricks, 190
Glass, Peter, 128
Glazebrooks 'Spred Satin', 86
Glen Iris (Vic), 105, 106
Gordon (NSW), 94, 95
Gordon Institute of Technology, 100
Goulburn (NSW), 64
Grace Brothers, Sydney, 43
Great Britain, 14, 120
Greece, migration from, 21
Greene and Greene, architects, 128
Griffin, Walter Burley, 112, 114, 128, 132
Gropius, Walter, 39, 92, 94, 108, 110
Grounds, Romberg & Boyd, architects, 146
Grounds, Roy, architect, 37, 100, 101, 116, 124
Grove, Edith (Mollie), 182
Gunning house, Castlecrag (NSW), 135
'Gyprock' plaster sheet, 62

H-shape plan, 115
Harcourt, John, journalist, builder, 67, 130
Hardie, James and Co, 34, 38, 39, 46, 82
Hardress, Catherine, 182
Harris, Thistle Y., writer and naturalist, 145
Harvard School of Design, 92
Harvard University, 92, 99
Hawthorn (Vic), 106
Hayes & Scott, architects, 109
Healing, A.G. Limited, furniture, 174
Heath, Frank, 47, 58
Heathwood, Peter, architecture, 109, 110
Henty house, Frankston (Vic), 101, 102
Hickey house, Hawthorn (Vic), 106
Higgins, George, 64
'Hills hoist', 141
hire purchase, 29
Hiroshima and Nagasaki, 19
Hitch, John, architect, 109
Hobart (Tas), 106, 118
Holden car, 21, 22, 53
holiday houses, 38
Hollywood films, 9, 18, 101, 123
Holmesglen (Vic), 71
Home Gardener, The, 142
Home Plans Service Bureau, 43
home ownership, 75
Home, The, 35, 147
Horderns, Anthony, 43
Housing Commission of Victoria, 58, 71
housing costs, 73
housing shortage, 48, 73
Humphries, Barry, 31, 165
Hungarian refugees, 21

insulating materials, 84
'Insulwool' insulation, 84
interior colour schemes, 190-192
interior designers, 165
interiors, conventional, 165, 166
International aesthetic, 137
International Modern movement, 91
International style, 91, 110, 111, 118, 135, 161, 174, 172
Irwin, W.L., engineer, 103, 103
Italy, migration from, 21
Ivanhoe (Vic), 103, 123
Ivanhoe, East (Vic), 55

Jackson, Tony, 126
Jacobean style furniture, 152
Jacobsen, Arne, architect, 110
James Hardie and Co. Pty Ltd, 34, 46
Janeba, Fritz, architect, 132
Japan, 96
Japanese advance, 14
Jekyll, Gertrude, 145, 147, 148, 166
Jelinek, Alex, architect, 90
Jennings, A.V., Construction Company Pty Ltd, 55, 62, 68, 69
Johnson, Don, interior designer, 165
Johnson, J.W., architect, 114
Johnston, Esme, journalist, 180, 181
Jones, Raymond, architect, 106, 118
Jorgensen, Justus, 67, 128
Journal of the Royal Victorian Institute of Architects, 36
Judd, Horrie, 132
'Jutex' building paper, 85, 88

Kalsomine, 86
Kerosene lamps, 24

Kerosene refrigerator, 25
Kerosene stove, 25
Kew (Vic), 84, 86, 88, 102
Killara (NSW), 163
kitchen sinks, 85, 157
kitchens, 157, 172, 173
Knoll, Hans, furniture manufacturer, 174
Knox, Alistair, author, builder, designer, 67
Kotzman house, Ringwood East (Vic), 92
Koues, Helen, 40, 170
Krimper, Schulim, cabinetmaker, 90, 183
Kuringai Shire Council (NSW), 94
Kurrajong Heights (NSW), 98, 99

L-shaped plan, 115, 121
labour costs, 73
Ladies Home Journal (USA), 112
'Laminex' plastic laminate, 86
land speculation, 32
Lane Cove (NSW), 172
Langer, Dr Karl, architect, 99, 101, 109
Launceston (Tas), 80, 117
laundries, 158, 159
Le Corbusier, architect, 94, 96
Le Gallienne, Dorian, 132
Leach, Eric, architect, 108
Leith & Bartlett, architects, 100
Lembke, C., 122
Lewis, Edna Horton, author, 40, 161
Leyser house, Kew (Vic), 102
lighting, 185, 186
Lindsay, Daryl, artist and gallery director, 154
linoleum, 85, 86
living and dining areas, 160, 161
loans, housing, repayment of, 74, 75
'Loch Sloigh', Croydon (Vic), 58
log cabins, 121, 124
Lord, Ernest E., horticultural writer, 145
Lord, Margaret, interior designer, 40, 43, 152, 153, 163
Losch house, Wahroonga (NSW), 124
Low, Stuart, interior designer, 165
Lowan, Fritz (Fred), 179
Lower Plenty (Vic), 130
Loxton (SA), 80
Lund, Neville, architect, 109
Lutyens, Edwin, architect, 97
Lysaght steel sheet, 36

Macfarlane house, Croydon (Vic), 58
MacKenzie, Alexandra (Nan), 181
MacKnight, Archibald C., architect, 67, 128
MacKnight, Charles A., Architect, 67, 128
magazines, influence of, 35, 78, 120, 123
Mahony, Marion, architect, 128
Maldon (Vic), 132
Malta, migration from, 21
Malthoid, 88
Malvern (Vic), 57
Manne, Henry, on functional furniture, 174
mantels and fireplace surrounds, 154, 160
Marryatville (SA), 137
Marseilles tiles, 20, 120
Masonite Tempered 'Presdwood', 85
Masonite, 82, 83
materials, cost of, 73
Mather house, Glen Iris (Vic), 105, 106
Mathsson, Bruno, designer, 176
Mayfield, Laurie, 126
McDonald, Kenneth, architect, 39, 132
McGrath, Raymond, architect, 37
McIntosh, Stuart, architect, 126

McIntyre, Dione, architect, 11, 102, 103, 105
McIntyre, Peter, architect, 84, 88, 102, 103, 105, 123, 124
McKinna Brothers, contractors, 103
McKinna, David, 103
Mediterranean influence, 57
Melbourne Centenary Home Exhibition, (1934), 39
'Melbourne School', 124
Melbourne Technical College, 105, 130, 180
Melbourne, 17, 26, 37, 39, 55, 58, 64, 67, 97, 101, 102, 124, 130, 176, 179
Mellor, Olive, 140, 143, 144
Mendelson Erich, architect, 96
Mentone (Vic), 100, 122, 123
Menzies, Robert, Prime Minister, 14
Mewton, Geoffrey H., architect, 101
Middle Harbour (Sydney), 133
Middleton & Talbot, architects, 100
Middleton, George F, 130
Mies van der Rohe, Ludwig, architect, 94, 110
migration, post-war, 20, 48
milk deliveries, 25
Mingbool (SA), 25, 69
Ministry of Post-War Reconstruction, 47
Mitchell, George, architect, 100
Mockridge Stahle and Mitchell, architects, 100.
Mockridge, John, architect, 100,
Modern Home Building Advisory Bureau, 39
modern design, 153
modern Functionalist architecture, 108, 109, 124
Monash, John, 64.
Mondrian, Piet, artist, 146
Montmorency (Vic), 132
Montsalvat, Eltham (Vic), 128, 130
Moore, John D, architect and author, 37
Mooroolbark (Vic), 121
Mornington Peninsula, 100, 101
Morris William, 128, 176
Mortlock, Bryce, architect, 153
Mosman Park (WA), 108
Mount Lawley (WA), 26
Mt Gambier, 62, 66, 69
Mt Gambier stone, 62, 66, 119
mud-brick (adobe), 122, 127-132
Muller house, Whale Beach (NSW), 133
Muller, Peter, architect, 133, 134, 135
Murphy, John and Phyllis, architects, 40, 100, 101, 105, 106
Myer Emporium, 43, 45
Myer Home Plans Service Bureau, 43, 45
Myer-Ansett house, 67

Namatjira, Albert, artist, 29
National Gallery of Victoria, 154
National Gallery School, Melbourne, 180
National Security Regulations, 55
National Trust of Australia, 13
native gardens, 137, 144
native plant nurseries, 145
Negus, Raymond E, 145
Nelson, George, architect and designer, 175, 179
Neutra, Richard J., architect, 94
New Canaan, Connecticut (USA), 135
New England style, 57
New South Wales, 31, 37, 64, 76, 95, 120, 122, 124, 141
New York, 93, 99
New York State, 61
Newell, Peter, architect, 109
Niemeyer, Oscar, architect, 99
Nindethana Nursery (NSW), 145

Noguchi, Isamu, sculptor and designer, 175
North Adelaide (SA), 109
North Ryde (NSW), 65
Northbridge (NSW), 13, 154
Northern Territory, 126

Old English style, 35, 56, 57, 114, 120
Olinda (Vic), 122
Olympic Games, Melbourne (1956), 29
Olympic Swimming Stadium, Melbourne, (1956), 102
'open plan' designs, 76
Operation Snail', 69
Outlaw, Anne, 181
Overend, Best, architect, 132
owner-built houses, 76, 78, 79

paint colours, 188, 189
paints, new developments, 86
Palm Beach (NSW), 43, 134
Palmer, George (SA), 79
Palmer, Vance, author, 37
paths and driveways, 148
Patrick, Rex, architect, 102, 103
'Patterncraft' pre-cut furniture, 176
Pearl Harbor, 14
pergolas, 147
Perrot, Leslie M., architect, 64
Perth (WA), 28, 29, 80, 108, 114, 171
Petheridge & Bell, architects, 100
pise de terre construction, 122, 128, 130, 132
plastic laminates, introduction of, 86
plywoods, 83
Polomka, Brian, architect, 109
polyurethane coatings, 85
Port Phillip Bay, 19, 102, 103
Port Pirie (SA), 80
Post-War Austerity housing, 114, 121
Post-War Brisbane Regional style, 109, 124, 126
Post-War Melbourne Regional style, 124
post-war reconstruction, 48
Poyntzfield, Gordon (NSW), 94, 95
Prairie House, 112
prefabricated houses, 68
Punchbowl (NSW), 67
Pymble (NSW), 106

Queensland Housing Commission, 49, 51, 126
Queensland Plywood Board, 110
Queensland, 82, 109, 126
Queensland, housing in, 75, 126

radios, 35
Railton housing scheme, Tasmania, 121
Ranch style, 121, 123, 124
rationing, wartime and post-war, 16, 21, 105
refrigerator, 25
Regional styles, 124
regionalism, 97, 103, 109
rehabilitation schemes, 20
renovations and alterations, 187-190
restrictions, post-war, 74, 105
Retraining Scheme, Commonwealth Government, 20
Richardson house, Palm Beach (NSW), 134
Richardson house, Toorak (Vic), 106, 146
Richardson, Mervyn Victor, 141
Richmond (Vic), 58
Rickard, Bruce, architect, 135
Riley Newsum prefabricated house, 62, 69
Ringwood East (Vic), 92
Rio de Janeiro, 99
Risom, Jens, designer, 174

River House, Peter McIntyre, 105
Robinson, William, 145
Rochester (Vic), 64
Rock Around the Clock, 29
rock gardens, 145, 146
Rodeck, Ernest, 179
Romberg, Frederick, architect, 91, 96, 97, 101
Romcke Pty Ltd (plywoods), 68
roofing materials, 88
rooflines, 112, 113, 124
Rose family house, Turramurra (NSW), 106
Rose Seidler house, Turramurra/Wahroonga, 97 176
Rose system of concrete casting, 64, 65
roses,
      popular choices, 150, 151
      standards, 151
rotary clothes hoist, 140
'Rotoscythe' lawn mower, 141
Royal Australian Institute of Architects, 40, 43, 122
rubber flooring, 85
Rutherglen (Vic), 128
Rutledge house, St Lucia (Qld), 111
Ryan, Catherine, 18
Ryan, John, Flight Sergeant, RAF, 17, 19

Saarinen, Eero, architect and designer, 174
Salvisberg, Otto Rudolf, architect, 96
Sandringham (Vic), 71
Sandy Bay (Tas), 106
Saphin house, Brighton (Vic), 40, 159
Scandinavian furniture, 176
Second World War, 9, 32, 49, 74, 91, 94, 152
'Sectionit' prefabrication system, 67
Seidler, Harry, architect, 13, 92, 97, 106, 108, 113, 114, 154, 176
Seymour, Mary Jane, 155
Shannon house, Wahroonga (NSW), 106
Shaw, Don, interior designer, 165
Sherrard, L. Hume, architect, 33, 35, 60, 64, 65, 116
Shire of Eltham (Vic), 130
Shugg & Moon, architects, 106
Silk and Textile Printers Ltd, 181
'Sisalkraft' building paper, 85
skillion roofs, 114
Skipper, Matcham, 130
Skipper, Sonia, 126, 130
sleepouts, 58
slum reclamation, 48
Small Homes Service (NSW), 43, 44, 45, 77, 80, 81, 124
Small Homes Service (Vic), 40, 43, 45
Smith, Blair, 77, 78, 79
Snelleman house, Ivanhoe (Vic), 103, 123
Snelling, Douglas, 44. 174. 178
Snowy Mountains Hydro-Electric Authority, 21, 68
Snowy Mountains Scheme, 21, 97
Sol Green Housing Scheme, 57
Sorrento (Vic), 100, 101
South Australia, 20, 25, 29, 48, 60, 62, 69, 80, 108, 109, 137
South Australian Home Builders Club, 79
South Australian Housing Trust, 48, 51, 58, 60, 68, 77
South Australian School of Mines and Industries, 133
South Yarra (Vic), 124, 165
Spanish Mission style, 58
Spears, James F., architect, 37, 76, 77, 100
Spears, Mrs. Jim, 76
Spowers, Godfrey, architect, 100
Springfield (SA), 108, 109

St Ives (NSW), 106
St Lucia (Qld), 109, 111
Stahle, Ross, architect, 100
State Advances Corporation, Queensland, 126
State Housing Commission of Western Australia, 51, 116, 139
State Savings Bank of Victoria, 29, 33, 37, 48, 49
Steele and Co. Ltd., 163
Stephenson & Turner, architect, 37
Stewart, Gerald, 106
Stirling West (SA), 121
Stones, Ellis, landscaper and designer, 145, 146
stonework, 145, 146, 147
'Stonygrad', the Vassilieff house, Warrandyte (Vic), 135
Structuralist influence, 124
Studio, The, 17
styles, description of, 112-126
suburban blocks, 123, 140
suburban sprawl, 26, 32
Sullivan, Louis, architect, 114
Sulman Medal, 94, 99
Summerhayes, Geoffrey, architect, 108, 109
sunrooms, 162, 163
Surfers Paradise (Qld), 37
Sussman house, Kurrajong Heights (NSW), 98, 99
'Swedish Modern' furniture, 152
Swedish style furniture, 17, 176, 178, 179
Swinburne Technical College, 105
Sydney (NSW), 16, 36, 44, 97, 106, 124, 130, 132, 147, 168, 172, 179
synthetic alkyd enamels, 88

T-shape plan, 56, 116
tapestry bricks, 60
Tasmania, 27, 48, 63, 80, 120, 121, 148, 151
Tasmanian Housing Commission, 63
Tasmanian Housing Department, 121
Taylor, Florence M. (editor), 40.
television
      arrival, 29
      influence of, 9, 29, 31, 162, 173
Tennyson fabrics, 181
terrazzo, 86
The Studio, 17
tiles,
      cement, 20, 119
      terracotta, 20, 119, 120
timber, use for interior and exterior surfaces, 84, 106, 108, 121
'Timbrock' hardboard, 83
Toorak (Vic), 106, 116, 146
Townsing house, Cottesloe (WA), 139
Townsing house, Mount Lawley (WA), 26
Toyne, Gilbert, 140, 141
train services, suburban electric, 31
triple-fronted brick veneer, 61, 119
Triton Constructions (Aust) Pty Ltd, 21
Tropical or Subtropical style, 126
Tudor style, 114
Turramurra (NSW), 97, 106

U-shaped plan, 115
United Kingdom, 20
United States of America, 62, 94, 101, 108, 120, 123, 124, 128, 135, 162, 168
University of Adelaide, 133
University of Manitoba, 99
University of Melbourne, 100, 101, 103, 105
University of Pennsylvania, 133
University of Queensland, 110
Upwey (Vic), 97

Vandyke Brothers (NSW), 67
Vassilieff, Danila, artist, 135
Veneer and Plywood Pty. Ltd, 68
Ventura, Upwey (Vic), 91, 96, 97
verandahs and porches, 73, 105, 106, 109, 123
'Victa Rotomo', lawnmower, 141
'Victorboard' plaster sheet, 62
Victoria, 31, 48, 60, 62, 64, 76, 101, 109, 121, 135, 140
Victorian Housing Commission, 58, 71
Victorian Railways, housing, 69
'Victorian Type' house, 37, 71, 100, 109
Vienna, Austria, 99
vinyl floor tiles, 86

Wahroonga (NSW), 13, 97, 106, 124
Waks house, Northbridge (NSW), 154
Walcott house, Whale Beach (NSW), 133, 134
Walkley, Gavin, architect and academic, 109
wall surfaces, 84, 85, 88, 89, 160
Walling, Edna, 13, 40, 121, 137, 141, 142, 144, 145, 147, 148, 166
walls, fences and gates, 149
War Housing Program, 55, 65
War Service Homes, 49, 75
War Service Homes Act, 75
War Service Homes Commission, 126
War Service Housing Loans, 20, 49
Ward, Donald C., 39
Ward, Elinor, 170
Ward, Frederick, 176, 178, 179
Warrandyte (Vic), 77, 132, 135
'Warrandyte Style', 132
washing machines, 159, 160
Waterfall Austerity designs, 119
Waterfall style, 10, 118
weatherboards, 61, 62, 88, 119, 121, 123, 126
weddings in wartime, 18
Wegner, Hans, designer, 176, 179
Wender & Duerholt (Germany), 69
Wesley Hill (Vic), 10, 51
Western Australia, 80, 116, 139, 151, 166
Western Australian State Housing Commision, 116, 139
Westwood, Bryan, 37
White, Mary, interior designer, 165
Whittle, Fiona, 11
Wilkinson, Professor Leslie, architect, 57
Wilson, William Hardy, architect, 120
Winbush, Harry, architect, 120
Windows, 88, 133, 135, 172
Windwood, G.A., 71
Women architects, 103
Women's Land Army, Australian, 18
Women's Weekly home planning centre, 43
Woodville Gardens (SA), 20
Woodville West (SA), 60
Workers Homes Act, 75
Wright, Frank Lloyd, architect, 94, 108, 112, 128, 133, 135, 170
Wunderlich Limited, 39, 45, 76, 82, 89
Wurster Bernadi & Emmons, 94

Yarra River, 132
Yuncken Freeman Brothers Griffiths & Simpson, architects, 69, 82, 105

Zegelin house, Nanneella (Vic), 64, 65
Zegelin K.F., 65